Migration, Temporality, and Capitalism

Pauline Gardiner Barber • Winnie Lem
Editors

Migration, Temporality, and Capitalism

Entangled Mobilities across Global Spaces

Editors
Pauline Gardiner Barber
Dalhousie University
Halifax, NS, Canada

Winnie Lem
Champlain College
Trent University
Toronto, ON, Canada

ISBN 978-3-030-10267-8   ISBN 978-3-319-72781-3   (eBook)
https://doi.org/10.1007/978-3-319-72781-3

This Palgrave Macmillan imprint is published by the registered company Springer International Publishing AG part of Springer Nature.
The registered company address is: Gewerbestrasse 11, 6330 Cham, Switzerland

CONTENTS

Notes on Contributors

Naor Ben-Yehoyada is Assistant Professor of Anthropology at Columbia University. He specializes in maritime, political and historical anthropology, specifically the maritime aspect of Israeli-Palestinian history and post-WWII region formation processes between Sicily and Tunisia.

Catherine Bryan has a PhD in Social Anthropology and teaches at the Dalhousie School of Social Work. Her areas of research interest include social reproduction, migration and political economy. Her work has appeared in Anthropologica, the *Journal for Migration and Ethnic Studies*, and the *Journal of Immigrant and Refugee Studies*.

Ayşe Çağlar has been University Professor at the Department of Social and Cultural Anthropology at the University of Vienna since 2011. Before that she was a professor at the Department of Sociology and Social Anthropology at the Central European University, Budapest (2003–2010) and a Minerva Fellow at the Max Planck Institute for the Study of Ethnic and Religious Diversity, Göttingen. She took her PhD in Anthropology at McGill University in Montreal and Certificate of Habilitation both in anthropology and sociology at the Free University Berlin in 2004. Among her fields of interest are: globalization, trans-nationalization and nationalism.

Pauline Gardiner Barber is a Professor of Social Anthropology at Dalhousie University. Her research on Philippine global migration appears in various collections she has co-edited, most recently with Routledge and Berghahn, and in journals such as *Journal for Migration and Ethnic Studies, Dialectical Anthropology,* and *Focaal*.

Winnie Lem is an anthropologist and Professor of International Development Studies at Trent University, with a cross appointment in Women's Studies. She is currently co-editor in chief of Dialectical Anthropology. Her publications include: *2012 Migration in the 21st Century: Political Economy and Ethnography* (edited with Pauline Gardiner Barber) New York: Routledge; 2012; *Confronting Capital: Anthropology, Critique, Praxis* (edited with Belinda Leach and Pauline Gardiner Barber) New York: Routledge; 1999; *Cultivating Dissent: Work, Identity and Praxis in Rural Languedoc*, Albany. State University of New York Press.

Karen Fog Olwig is Professor at the Department of Anthropology, University of Copenhagen. She has worked on the role of the family and kinship in migration and the relationship between geographic, social and economic mobility within a Caribbean context. Her current research examines the impact of biometrics on family reunification among refugees in Denmark.

Turid Fånes Sætermo is a Postdoctoral Researcher at the Department of Neuromedicine and Movement Science at the Norwegian University of Science and Technology. She has a PhD in Social Anthropology. Her research focuses on migration, transnationalism, belonging, narratives, migration policies, work-life, marginalized youth and work inclusion.

Anja Simonsen is an anthropologist currently on a post-doctoral position at the University of Copenhagen. She conducted fieldwork in Somaliland, Turkey, Greece and Italy on Somali migrants and refugees, centering her research on migration, social invisibility, mobility, hope, uncertainty, Somalis and biometric technologies. She is part of the project Biometric Border Worlds, which explores the interrelationship between the making and the experience of biometric technologies within the context of migration.

Anne-Christine Trémon is Senior Lecturer in Anthropology at the Université de Lausanne. She obtained her PhD at the Ecole des Hautes Etudes en Sciences Sociales (EHESS) in 2005 and since then she has been a postdoctoral fellow at the Institute of ethnology, Academia Sinica in Taiwan, a Lecturer at the Ecole des Hautes Etudes en Sciences Sociales (EHESS) and the Ecole Normale Supérieure (ENS) in Paris, and a EURIAS Fellow at the Netherlands Institute for Advanced Study in 2012–2013. Her research examines Chinese globalization and the Chinese diaspora in a global anthropological and historical perspective. She has studied the colonial history and contemporary identifications of the Chinese community in French Polynesia, and, more recently, the diasporic relations and social and economic transformations in a former emigrant village of the Shenzhen special economic zone in China.

CHAPTER 1

Migration, Temporality and Capitalism: A Brief Introduction

Pauline Gardiner Barber and Winnie Lem

MIGRATION AND CAPITALISM: SETTING THE SCENE

What have been called the 'timescapes of modernity' (Adam 1998) are synonymous with migration and the changing forms of capital.[1] Timescapes are often encapsulated in terms of ages. The period from the late twentieth to the early twenty-first century, so it has been suggested, is the 'age of migration', in which the scale and scope of the global mobility of people across borders has been and continues to be unprecedented (Castles et al. 2014). Yet, following Wolf (1982), clearly other ages were also substantively shaped by migrations that enabled the dynamics of accumulation. Capitalism and its transformations are distinguished by a dominant set of

---

[1] We would like to acknowledge the editorial assistance of Shiva Nourpanah, herself a migration scholar. With good humour and intelligence, she has steered this project to publication. Thank you, Shiva.

P. G. Barber (✉)
Department of Sociology and Social Anthropology,
Dalhousie University, Halifax, NS, Canada

W. Lem
International Development Studies, Trent University,
Peterborough, ON, Canada

© The Author(s) 2018
P. G. Barber, W. Lem (eds.), *Migration, Temporality, and Capitalism*, https://doi.org/10.1007/978-3-319-72781-3_1

1

social relations associated with accumulation and surplus appropriation. From the sixteenth to the mid-nineteenth century, the ages of mercantile capitalism prevailed within regimes of colonialism and imperialism in which the key dynamics of accumulation entailed buying cheap and selling dear. Mercantile capitalism and its economies based on the traffic of people—basically, forced migrants commodified as slave-labor—were key in the setting up of the preconditions for the emergence of industrial capitalism (Williams 1944). Mercantile capitalism was superseded by the age of industrial capitalism, in which the appropriation of surplus through the relationship between wage labor and capital enabled the reproduction of national economies from the mid-nineteenth to mid-twentieth centuries. Industrial capitalism in this period was sustained in the war-torn economies of Europe through the mobilization of migrant labor from localities on the margins of Europe, its colonies and Asia.

In the late twentieth century, we see the emergence of what has been described as 'post-industrialism'. In this era, under the aegis of neoliberal forms of global transformations, a key dynamic of accumulation centers on finance and the appropriation of surpluses through interest and speculation (Ho 2009). Here, we question how the temporal designation of the age of migration reveals (and conceals) capitalism's continuing quest for access to global labor along with capital markets. This volume highlights the significance of migration in capitalism's long durée as we draw upon Marx's observation in *Capital* concerning the formation and reformation of surplus populations under capitalism as "one of the most energetic agencies for its reproduction" (Marx 1977: 785). Throughout history, the forces of change within capitalism have rendered populations as mobile and immobile, insiders and outsiders, citizens and denizens, and necessary and disposable, in different places and over time. These same forces have also simultaneously repurposed and eliminated localities as sites for capital accumulation.

Capitalism's Concern with Time and Mobile Workers

We are proposing that the history of global capitalism is the manipulation of time and space as capital seeks ever greater efficiencies through the bending of time to accumulation imperatives. Along with temporal adjustments associated with new reckonings of time under industrialization and so-called modernization came the disruptions, sometimes violently accomplished, of encouraging people into mobility, both as internal and international migrants. Writing about industrial capitalism and time discipline in Western

Europe, E.P. Thompson (1967) noted that the arrival of clock time in the fourteenth century coincided with the imposition of "Puritan discipline and bourgeois exactitude" (p. 46) so central to European industrialization. As peasants were (and are to this day) compelled to partake in the new social relations of wage work with employers, a long struggle ensued over the discrepant temporalities of agricultural versus factory time: from the task-oriented rhythms of rural labor routines to the timed labor power which employers purchase through the wage relation. Such struggles over time and the routines and rhythms of daily life continue to pervade the workplaces of today; such struggles can become more acute in circumstances where migrant workers are employed to address labor gaps as they interact with employers' demands, the scrutiny of local workers, and the legal policy frameworks that define the legitimacy of their status. Migrants without status can also serve as a potential labor pool for employers who may draw upon them as a kind of labor surplus: disposable but available to replace—and thus discipline— those who hold the available jobs.

Historically, as ever more efficient industrial technologies held out the promise of greater efficiencies for labor control, and colonization and technologies for both movement and communications opened new territories for the exploitation of resources and people, we see the capitalist's obsession with controlling labor time's productivity taken to new heights. For example, at the turn of the twentieth century, industry applied Frederick Winslow Taylor's theories of scientific management, which involved rigid time management in the disciplining and deskilling of workers (Braverman 1974). Digital technologies have further enabled the efficiencies of capital's productivity through the flexibilization of production regimes entailing the redistribution of production into chains across time and space. While the new regimes of mobility (Glick Schiller and Salazar 2013) can involve various forms of mobile capital for accumulation, including the inducing of migrants to invest and even speculate in property and infrastructure projects in places they left behind (see Pido 2017), here we primarily explore the conditions and temporalities of capitalist enterprises, labor markets, state regimes, family relations, and the biographies of migrants. We also emphasize how capitalist enterprises rely upon the labor of immobile populations, people who function as relative surplus populations, of Marx's "industrial reserve army" (Marx 1977: 783); those who are bought in on an 'as needed basis' and then let go, as disposable surplus populations in instances where capital moves to labor and then withdraws (Kasmir and Carbonella 2014). Or again, where mobile populations cross borders in anticipation of labor contracts that offer no stable employment or the prospect of obtaining the official documentation necessary to settle in the destination country. In the latter case, mobile people can also be considered as disposable labor surplus, stuck in time and precariously situated within a national space. Commencing from these kinds of scenarios in which people engage with capital, our primary concern is with the temporal entanglements of mobile populations with global capitalism, and primarily with those groups who undertake international migrations inspired by the hope of a better, more settled future.

DISCREPANT TEMPORALITIES

Our volume thus focuses its attention on the world of capitalist change and highlights how migration has been shaped by forms of capital accumulation in distinct eras. We examine the disjunctures of time wrought in the lives of migrants as they confront the shifting dynamics of accumulation. To do this, we offer the optic of discrepant temporalities to highlight the inconsistencies and disjunctive time scales in the lives of migrants as they contend with change within regimes of labor, security, family and citizenship under different phases of capitalist transformation in the past as well as the present. Toward this end, we propose that our concept of discrepant temporalities best conveys the variations and disjunctures between time scales that frame migrant lives relative to the temporal priorities of neoliberal state agendas. Our ethnographic interventions focus on such discrepancies within distinct regimes of labor, security, family, and citizenship as such fixes are periodically advanced to enlarge the scope of capitalist accumulation and as remedies for crises of capitalism. As chapter authors show, temporal discrepancies occurred within distinctive political and economic regimes in the past, as legacies of colonialism; see Trémon (Chap. 5) and Olwig (Chap. 3). Such discrepancies have become ever more acute under neoliberalism as its pro-market ideologies privilege temporal and spatial fixes as a modus operandi for capitalism; illustrated here in Simonsen (Chap. 6), Bryan (Chap. 7), Sætermo (Chap. 8), and Barber (Chap. 9). In confronting the present then, we focus on the current era in which socio-economies of localities across the globe are shaped by the principles and practices of neoliberalism. As an ideologically inspired and effective economic doctrine, neoliberalization, with its doctrine of free markets, has prodded with differing policy mechanisms in different contexts, the unfettering of certain state obligations toward the welfare of citizens while removing various forms of hard won labor protections (Kasmir and Carbonella 2008). Such policies have resulted in the intensification of wealth disparities between countries differently positioned in global power hierarchies.

As our ethnographic cases reveal, time is animated, plied with differential meanings and values (material, social, and symbolic) for different classes in different spaces. Time is never neutral. It is an intensely political phenomenon, just as it is a social phenomenon, culturally prescribed and subjectively experienced. Seen from the perspective of individuals, including the migrants whose mobilities are detailed in the ethnographic studies that follow, time's passing has uniquely personal consequences that add ethnographic substance to our analysis of the political and economic conditions for the production and reproduction of migrating populations. State policies and practices relating to the mobilities of capital and people across borders are typically motivated by notions of time, whether in policy deliberations or in discourses about the role migration plays in national histories and identity. Migrants, and those who depend upon them, have to contend subjectively and materially with making sense of, and often paying a price for (literally), the many challenges associated with their movement, not the least of which stem from various temporal disjunctions associated with the entangled mobilities set in motion under global capitalism.

The essays collected here explore the relationship between the processes of migration and the temporal conditions of capitalist transformation, some of which attend to long-scale temporalities of imperial relations, for example, in China (Lem, Chap. 10, and Trémon, Chap. 5) and Britain (Olwig, Chap. 4). They also probe the temporalities associated with specific forms of migration for work and professional training and possibly the aquisition of permanent residency and eventual citizenship, such as was realized by migrant nurses in Britain (Olwig, Chap. 4). Related is the case of those who migrate for social reproductive labor, such as the migrants who work in hotels in Canada (Bryan, Chap. 7). A further thread explored by a number of authors—especially Simonsen (Chap. 6), Ben-Yehoyada (Chap. 4), Sætermo (Chap. 8) and Barber (Chap. 9)—concerns the temporalities manipulated by specific state regimes to control the mobilities of different designations of migrants, some of whom live in the protracted uncertainty of not knowing whether states will accept them as potential citizens under immigration regimes. Given our collective purpose is to inquire into the complexities and contradictions that prevail in the relationships between migration, time and capitalism, we focus on the significance of various scales of time in shaping people's spatial mobilities.

Indeed, capitalism has a long and fractious relationship with temporality, observed as much in the central dynamic which previously reshaped the economic system into industrial capitalism, as in the current era, when finance capitalism has a larger profile. Under industrial capitalism, as Marx (1977) observed, what an employer purchases when hiring a worker is the creative capacity to labor, usually in the form of time structured into the wage bargain through the working day. Hence, the labor process has always been a site of struggle over the commodification of time. It is in this sense that, as Benjamin Franklin (1748) observed so long ago, time is money. In a world where the significance of finance capital as a driver of growth and accumulation is increasing, the dynamics of the credit and debt system, combined with the proliferation of financial instruments through which profits can be made, are premised on notions of delay in anticipation of future profits (Appadurai 2016; Holmes 2014). Working from such premises about the dynamics of contemporary capitalism—and mindful of how global capitalism has expanded its reach through the movement of capital and people—each of the chapters in this volume can be read as an interrogation of the ways in which migrants in different locations confront and are confronted by the dynamics of accumulation within different time periods.

We also illustrate here how the primacy of time embodied in practices to enhance accumulation enables the reproduction of differentiated forms of inequality. The production of commodities and people whose labor is commodified and rendered mobile (and immobile) includes practices that enhance speed, turnover and the maximization of efficiencies and efficacies of security. Social differentiation and economic polarizations result. While such practices and their social effects are stark and expansive in the contemporary world of capitalism (Piketty 2014), the time scale of such global inequalities extends from the era of incipient capitalism and colonialism to the present (Wolf 1982). The social polarities of contemporary migration, then, replicate the historical forces and projects present at the dawn of industrial capitalism, but they gain additional potency through present-day juxtapositions of human mobility.

Migration and the Imbrications of Time with Space

Overall, the volume demonstrates that the relationship between temporal and power discrepancies poses important challenges for migration scholars. Our contention is that such discrepancies are particularly acute under neoliberalism because its pro-market ideologies privilege temporal and spatial fixes as a modus operandi for capitalism. Our notion of 'temporal-spatial fix' uses as a point of departure the work of David Harvey (1989), who proposes the idea of spatial fix as one of the solutions to the challenges of surplus accumulation present in capitalist economies. As Harvey notes, neoliberalization and the rise to dominance of a market "ethic" entails "creative destruction" of prior ways of living and attachments. While Harvey privileges capitalism's remediation through geo-spatial expansion (Harvey 2003), here we expand upon his original notion by tracking the imbrications of time with space.

Several aspects of neoliberalism's temporal-spatial fixes are critical to our investigation of migration's temporal disjunctions. As market transactions intensify and geographically expand through the compression of time and space, so too the contours of migration are reworked and reflected in the shifting priorities of policy. Temporal-spatial fixes can be discerned in national and supranational policies that govern migration, and in the alternating dynamic of the opening and closing of borders to migrants. As Barber's ongoing research reveals, a recent shift favoring temporary migration over permanent, for example, has occurred in so-called 'countries of immigration', which include Australia, New Zealand and Canada (see Chap. 9). In these contexts, temporal-spatial fixing results in discrepancies of time as temporary labor migration is calibrated to labor market fluctuations that are themselves products of the manipulation of the mobilities of various forms of capital. In this fixing, many temporary labor migrants are rendered as surplus populations through neoliberal austerity and adjustment policies that prevail both in their home countries and in their countries of relocation. The paradoxes of this dynamic become more evident as competition for capital-bearing migrants intensifies, even as record numbers of displaced persons are being officially designated as refugees who begin their journeys through violence and dispossession (Kasmir and Carbonella 2014).

The temporal agendas of capitalism, therefore, have long been instrumental in conditioning migration pathways. For migrants themselves such agendas have been key in informing decisions about relocation that focus on questions of whether, where, when, how, and how often. The apparatuses of migration (see Feldman 2011) have also promoted the mobilities of certain forms of migration over others: for example, the circular migrations of contract workers in Southeast Asia, the 'guest workers' in many parts of Europe, temporary foreign workers in Canada, or the precariously situated, permanently undocumented Latino population in the United States.

Another strand of migration's changing contours under the temporal agendas and spatial fixes of capitalism is the feminization of migration, in which the increasing informalization and precariousness of local livelihood opportunities presses women into migration (Piper 2011). The feminization of migration has accompanied the rise of export processing in light industries as the new international division of labor has dispersed the production of commodities across the globe. Also, the emergence of service and financial complexes as key spheres of accumulation in sustaining the reproduction of capital has created the demand for feminized and mobile labor (Sassen 1999). Assuming the role of breadwinners, women migrants strive to sustain the reproduction of their families as they labor for the reproduction of capitalism itself. Here we see "creative destruction" in the disruption of the temporal rhythms of family life as members are geographically dispersed (Barber 2013; Barber and Bryan 2012; Lem 2015).

Migration and Time as a Research Agenda

An exclusive emphasis upon migration and time is a relatively new arena in migration scholarship. While temporal reckoning has long fascinated anthropologists, few studies have sought to confront the centrality of how capitalism manipulates time in the production of global inequalities, both historically and in the contemporary world. In this volume, we explore the ways in which the agendas of capitalism have long been instrumental in conditioning migration. Our work here therefore enters into current discussions of temporality as a feature of migrant experience to offer a theoretically robust and ethnographically informed investigation of migration and temporality set within an overall framework defined by the political economy of capitalism.

Our consideration of the relationship between migration and time intervenes in the voluminous cross-disciplinary migration literature of the past two decades. As some scholars have noted, few studies exist that problematize this relationship. This is the case despite a call made over a decade ago for greater attention to time in the study of migration (Cwerner 2001). On the one hand, some scholars have observed migration constitutes "a process as much concerned with time as it is with space" (Roberts 1995: 42; Pine 2014). On the other hand, as Melanie Griffiths (2014) suggests, despite long-standing recognition that variations exist between people's experiences of time, and that time is central to the framing of social life and bureaucratic systems, migration scholars have tended to neglect the temporal dimensions of mobility. Moreover, as Alfred Gell (1992) has noted, studies of temporality focus mainly on identifying the ways in which time is experienced, and hermeneutical philosophies of personal experiences of time have been used to analyze the temporal dimensions of social life. Where issues of temporality have been broached in the migration literature, they have been framed for the most part by a phenomenological approach: the experience of time's passing. Migrants whose journeys incorporate periods of immobility, stasis and even isolation, tend to predominate as, for example, in the studies of migrants detained within camps. Temporal issues that emerge from detainment draw largely from Giorgio Agamben's (2005) "states of exception". For migrants who are confined to camps, waiting defines their experience and time itself appears suspended. Griffiths (2014), for example, captures camp experiences of time using terms such as "sticky", "suspended", "frenzied" and "ruptured". Moreover, moving somewhat beyond a focus on the hermeneutics of migration time and toward an economics of camps, Rueben Andersson (2014) emphasizes how these 'spaces of exception' are not at all economically exceptional. Rather, they are tied to the economies of capitalism as places that prepare laborers in waiting. For Andersson, camps generate considerable profits for private contractors involved in an industry of "camp-making".

We build upon and extend such observations to propose first, that the distortions of migrants' temporalities that arise within economies of capitalism also define migration outside the regimes of camps. For example, as Barber argues here (in Chap. 9), discrepant temporalities are embodied in the "just in time" immigration system structured through the transnational entanglements of neoliberalism in the Philippines and Canada. In that system, the temporal rhythms associated with the bureaucratic processing of migration documents aids in the political subordination of migrants who become "suspended" in migration time. Distortions of temporality also exist, for example, in the temporal cycles of reproduction of family life for women migrants. Lem (2015) has noted this for women migrants from China who work in the service economy in Paris, having become a surplus mobile population because of the imperatives of economic restructuring in China's pro-market reforms. Second, as the contributors demonstrate, we propose a conceptualization of the relationship between time and migration that moves beyond discussions of time expressed only in terms of experiential temporalities (see Çağlar Chap. 2).

We note the complexity of this relationship as one that is intrinsically linked to structures of capitalist change.

The authors assembled here reflect upon the social consequences for migrants of market-driven manipulations of time-space fixes that shape the trajectories of movement and the life plans of migrants. The notion of the 'discrepant temporalities of migration' foregrounds the ruptures between when and how migration is imagined collectively and individually, and then 'managed' by states colluding with powerful elites to assert programs directed toward those marked as suspect strangers. Discrepant temporalities also suggest how migrants, people forced into migration, and asylum seekers may all assess their transnational options, plan their journeys and project new lives along timelines that are often out of sync with the temporal priorities of agents and institutions who exert power over the spatial locations of mobile people. Our concern is to explore the extent to which such plans are realized in conjunction with and despite polices and plans that reflect the vagaries of the market orientations of neoliberalism.

These chapters may thus be read as mapping out of a research agenda of the variations in the relationship between migration and time. We argue for a conceptualization that is sensitive to the materializations of discrepant temporalities between different agents—the powerful and the powerless—within the different regimes that affect the lives of migrants. We ask how temporal discrepancies shape the landscapes of migrant agency. How are migrants' plans realized in conjunction with and despite the alternating dynamic of the opening and closing of borders? How do migration apparatuses, in Feldman's sense (2011), privilege certain migrants while discouraging others through practices that disrupt the trajectories of many mobile people, particularly the displaced and dispossessed? Our work questions how we think through the significance of the manipulations of chronological time in migration regimes. In their negotiations with the different agents in migration regimes, how do migrants contend with and contest the ordering of time in their social relations of work and complicated understandings of transnational belonging? How do the different participants in migration regimes, the relatively powerful and the powerless, reckon with the ordering of time in relation to work, family, kin, networks, sociability, authority, and history?

In pursing these research questions, we demonstrate that time is a pre-eminent, defining feature of migration as migrants project their lives forward into an unknowable future. Our task becomes more pressing because the contours of uncertainly and that which cannot be known are amplified for the spatially displaced. Spatial displacement, therefore, also means temporal displacement as the future for migrants predicated on the past defines what arguably might be called the "conditions of impossibility".

This volume and the key themes addressed herein make a theoretical case for a research agenda on migration's discrepant temporalities by adopting the lens of critical political economy. The authors explore the ways in which the primacies of time under capitalism operate in relation to the spatial mobility of people to enable the reproduction of inequalities in political and economic regimes in the past and the present. We suggest that while notions of time-space compression have pervaded many areas of globalization scholarship, little attention has been accorded the social consequences for migrants when market driven manipulations of time-space fixes intervene in the trajectories of movement and life plans of migrants.

In making this case, Ayşe Çağlar, in Chap. 2, argues that although an increasing number of migration scholars have started to address the spatial frameworks informing migration scholarship (including their limitations) and to focus on the location of migrants in space, the temporal narratives of migration scholarship have been rather neglected. When they are addressed, she continues, the focus is usually on the differential ways migrants experience time. Her chapter concentrates on the temporal frames informing different conceptualizations of migration scholarship and their impediments, rather than approaching time from a phenomenological perspective. In this way she shifts the focus from an analysis of how different (discrepant) temporalities shape the landscapes of migrant agency to an analysis of the power geometry of "now" (of the contemporary), which reconfigures the social, economic and political forces (including of migration and migrant practices) in relation to the processes of value creation at a particular historical conjuncture. Its central argument is that different approaches to migration (integration, multiculturalism, postmigrancy) entail distinct temporal (and spatial) frameworks (chronotopes), which situate migrants in time in distinctive ways in their analysis. Although these temporal frames are rarely addressed in migration scholarship, they constrain the way we conceptualize migrant dynamics, agencies and sociabilities. She argues that studies based in these chronotopes introduce culturalizing and racializing logics in various forms and hinder the analysis of migrant emplacement and agency in relation to the temporality of value regimes. By scrutinizing the valorization processes of (post)migrant cultural production in Vienna, she situates the post-migrant perspective in scholarship and its strategic success in Vienna within the broader dynamics of urban restructuring at a particular conjuncture. Unraveling the spatial and temporal frameworks of migration scholarship and their impediments, she urges migration researchers to bring the study of "migrants" and "non-migrants" into a common analytical lens. In this way, she argues, we could approach "migrants" and "non-migrants" in their contemporaneity vis-à-vis the constellation of the forces of capital and the urban restructuring of "now".

In Chap. 3, Karen Fog Olwig emphasizes that migration is usually described as a process taking place through time as well as space. She notes that while there has been increasing interest in migrants' movements and relations in space, including the simultaneity of migrants' social engagement in the sending and receiving societies, the temporal framework of these processes has been subject to less scrutiny. This chapter argues that time, like space, does not entail a linear and gradual progression of change, but unfolds unevenly in different, coexisting temporal modalities. Her work draws on Ernst Bloch's observation that "[n]ot all people exist in the same Now" (1977 [1932]: 22) because societies are characterized by non-synchronism, or non-contemporaneity, in the form of coexisting phenomena that can be associated with different historical periods. She notes that this means migrants operate within a bumpy timescape that can be linked to different historical eras, historical moments and phases of life. This chapter then explores how the timescape of the post-WWII period shaped the migratory experiences of the West Indians who traveled to Britain for training in the nursing profession. Olwig suggests that this timescape involved the conjuncture of the post-war epoch of British reconstruction, the Victorian time warp of the British hospital system, and the late-colonial era of British devolvement in the Caribbean. While Bloch developed the notion of non-synchronism to understand how certain segments of society may attempt to claim, or maintain, a certain social position by clinging to the past, the argument in this chapter is that the young Caribbean migrants, situated in the transitional period from youth to adulthood, used this complex timescape as a springboard for physical, social and personal mobility. Her chapter is based on life story interviews with West Indian women who trained as nurses at British hospitals in the period from the 1950s to the 1970s.

In Chap. 4, Naor Ben-Yehoyada compares two scenes of migration—over sea and over land—to reveal how the crux of the current situation resides not in migration as a problem but in the dynamic relationship of migration and its interdiction. This relationship includes related changes in migration flows, in interception policies, and in the frames that politicians, officials, journalists and activists use to understand the situation. The chapter makes several related claims. First, the changes involved a shift not only in number of people but also in kind. Second, the question regarded not only the qualities or characteristics of the persons themselves—migrants or refugees, but also and crucially the relationship between them and their oft-reluctant hosts. Third, this question therefore permitted a set of relationships of different temporal scopes and their corresponding geopolitical casting orders and potential responsibilities. The chapter then follows the differences in the framing of migrants' projects between the two routes, which were articulated in 2015. The maritime scene has cast migrants in danger of drowning as the emblems of abstract humanity and has foregrounded the obligation of universal hospitality, which requires neither context nor history—'the sea of (abandoned) brotherhood'. On the contrary, the landed 'Western Balkan' routes into and across European member states, have cast migrants as refugees of war, demanding and meriting (depending on point of view) refuge, aid and hospitality—'the fields of care'; these routes invoked both a context and a history. The image of the route itself stretched beyond landfall in Europe and to migrants' paths throughout EU territory. As a result, the obligation that these scenes posed to Europeans and their institutions changed as well: from humanitarian benevolence to retributive justice and historical accountability.

Anne Christine Trémon, the author of Chap. 5, focuses on how over the long twentieth century Chinese migrants and their descendants in colonial Tahiti (today's French Polynesia) mobilized kin transnationally, to accumulate capital. Families were shaped by successive changes and reversals in legal-political and economic events and conjunctures. Using a multi-generational perspective, she examines their transnational practices of 'flexible kinship': strategies of flexible (re)location and gender-selective legal recognition of family members in response to fluctuations both in legal and political immigration regimes and in economic opportunities. Transnational practices are not necessarily translocal. In making this distinction, the concept of 'flexible kinship' moves beyond the preoccupation within transnational studies with movement or dispersal in space. The shift highlights the importance of addressing practices that involve not just a spatial extension of networks, but also practices that cross legal boundaries within the host locality itself. These legal manoeuvres are temporal in that they seek to evade constraints and also to accumulate a variety of resources—different kinds of capital—through the exploitation of differentials in regimes of citizenship and mutating economic contexts. The practices of flexible kinship can be analyzed at the juncture and disjuncture of two temporalities: the migrants' own, that is, their perspectives, life trajectories and family dynamics across generations; and the global temporality of capitalism and hegemonic relations in the world-system, which influences regimes of citizenship and policies toward migrants and their descendants. Trémon shows how the discrepancies between temporalities and the migrants' resulting strategic adjustments delineate three periods in a history of distancing from and rupture with the Chinese homeland. She further argues that successive changes and reversals in conjunctures have shaped a habitus that maximizes economic and legal security for families and individuals, especially women. Today, flexible kinship practices by descendants of Chinese migrants are less oriented to the country of origin than to other destinations. The concept of discrepant temporalities is therefore also a useful guide to the progressive shift and reorientation from a migratory to a diasporic transnationalism.

In Chap. 6, Anja Simonsen draws on her fieldwork in Somaliland, Turkey and Greece to explore the tension between time and uncertainty as young Somali migrants make the risky journey toward Europe. Refusing to categorize the migrants as refugees, and therefore more deserving than the migrant, her chapter shows how many young Somalis find themselves in a state of uncertainty and do not know what their future steps will be in terms of where or when to move. For Somali migrants, or young Somalis wanting to migrate, this experience of uncertainty is closely linked to the notion of *wakhti lumis* ('losing time', present tense) or *wakhti lumay* ('lost time', past tense), which refers to an inability to make sense of the time spent in the past and the present. She discusses how it was when they had nothing but time—when time was in the lowest acceleration—that they referred to time as lost. Put differently, they lost time by having too much of it. 'Losing time' involved a certain kind of meaningless waiting, with little if any control of what was coming ahead and a feeling of making no progress in life. Individuals made constant attempts to minimize the experiences of 'lost time', yet the success of their efforts was conditional on events and relations to people beyond their control. Their lives, in other words, were characterized by 'social contingency', understood as individuals' particular dependency on circumstances that were largely unknown. This chapter illuminates the way that attempts by the young Somali migrants to minimize 'lost time' in Somaliland as well as

en route in a situation where their travel, usually without any legal documents, often meant being 'stuck in motion' while waiting in, for example,
Turkey or Greece. By examining the everyday life of young, undocumented Somali migrants who found themselves in a constant context
of uncertainty in their travels to obtain immigration status, the author
shows how experiences of 'lost time' leads to the development of certain
kinds of strategies, including attempts at onward migration.

In Chap. 7, Catherine Bryan focuses also focuses on the waiting of
migrants as they seek to complete their migration projects in Canada's
province of Manitoba, a process which is conceptualized as the reproduction of precarious labor in liminal spaces. Bryan's rural small town
fieldsite seems, at first glance, unlikely, given that migrants in Canada
have tended to gravitate toward urban centres. However, in Manitoba,
provincial immigration policies have allowed for several generations of
Filipinos to settle in both urban and rural regions, most recently, as Bryan
describes, by holding out the promise of transfer to permanent resident
status through provisions laid out under the provincial nominee program.
Bryan undertakes careful review of the ways in which immigration policy
mediates in the relationship between labor and capital in Manitoba. By
focusing on Philippine migrants who work in the service economy, having arrived as temporary foreign workers seeking permanent residence,
she problematizes the simultaneity of the cyclical and sequential processes that are embedded in capitalism's insatiable desire for unfettered
access to labor and the unintended consequences of that access over time.
However, the main focus of Bryan's chapter is to explore the temporal
conditions surrounding the arrival and eventual settlement of this group
of Philippine workers. With rich ethnographic detail the chapter shows
how Filipinos living and working in Canada negotiate the temporalities of waiting which she juxtaposes with how family members in the
Philippines simultaneously address the uncertainties of waiting. In both
sites we see the ways in which communication technologies facilitate the
navigation of time and space in daily life routines. Such daily routines
of social reproduction are then linked to how the employer, a hotel in
Manitoba's central west, obtains additional benefit, or value, from the
migrant workers as they perform social reproduction labor in that setting.
The transnational ethnographic detail in Bryan's study exposes the double configuration of waiting: waiting and working, both comforted and
distracted by the technologically mediated presence of kin left behind in
the Philippines.

In Chap. 8, Turid Sætermo also examines how migration trajectories are imagined and configured at the juncture and disjuncture of political-historical moments. The migration pathways examined in this chapter were set in motion during the period when middle-class skilled émigrés began leaving Venezuela during the 2000s, as political and economic turmoil intensified during the Chavez presidential era. This period coincides with the neoliberalization of the Canadian immigration system, also described in the chapters by Bryan (Chap. 7) and Barber (Chap. 9). Sætermo's migrants, who had completed their emigration to Montreal when she encountered them, speak of their migration aspirations less in terms of material wants and more in terms of their projections for a better life in Canada. They are at pains to demonstrate how they constitute the 'right' fit with Canada's neoliberal template for the selection of the high-skilled immigrant. However, in their temporal projects both forward and backward looking, these skilled migrants feel the need to justify their departures in terms of a more hopeful future in Canada. At the same time, they also position themselves in Venezuelan society through reference to their class identities and skills. Sætermo provides a close reading of the discrepant temporalities experienced by migrants as they describe their experiences with Canada's neoliberal immigration policy dictates during the pre-migration and post-migration periods. Again, the concept of liminality seems to well describe the transnational waiting period, but various other time-based metaphors also crop up as migrants describe and retroactively (post-migration) reflect upon the ambivalence and disjunctive temporal frames experienced in the pre-migration period.

Following on from the previous two chapters and building on their analysis, Pauline Gardiner Barber, in Chap. 9, also considers the transnational entanglements of neoliberal migration policies by considering the consequences of Canada's restructuring of policies of immigration and the economy, this time for Manila-based Filipino migrants-in-waiting and for Canadian workers in various labor markets. The chapter first reviews how both countries came to rely on labor export; to global labor markets, some of them feminized, in the case of the Philippines, and, for Canada, as the Philippines became its top source country for permanent and temporary migrants. Using Marx's ideas about surplus populations and the idea of structured contingencies from Kalb (2012), she argues the entangled neoliberal policy priorities and discourses falsely privilege immediacy and "just in time" flexibility in labor markets. To demonstrate how a temporal perspective enhances our analysis of the social and political consequences of neoliberalism, the chapter juxtaposes the "untimely coincidences"

(Neveling 2014) associated with the politics of waiting in Manila for service workers hoping to enter Canada as temporary foreign workers. The hope is they will become later identified as skilled workers and therefore, eligible for permanent residence. The chapter's examples of labor recruitment, waiting and pre-departure training in Manila occur at the very site where Filipinos assembled as "people power" to confront the dictatorial President Marcos in 1986. The multiple meanings of that site and the manipulation of Canadian workers to compete with Filipino workers in certain labor markets, provide an example of how class politics are set in motion through global migrations.

Winnie Lem lays out in Chap. 10 how we might imagine a political economy of temporality in relation to migration. In line with Olwig and Caglar, she notes that many analysts discuss migration as a phenomenon that occurs across a spatial scale as people traverse different locations. Her chapter then proceeds to explore how migration may be situated within a temporal scale by reflecting on the ways in which different dimensions of temporality are aligned with the processes of accumulation, profit generation, and exploitation that underpin the reproduction of capitalism. More specifically, Lem first addresses the question of how transformations of these processes over time have configured distinctive forms of human mobility over space. With this analysis Lem questions how the relationship between space and time prevails as a dialectic. She then highlights the implications of this dialectic in the lives of migrant women by focusing on the daily cycle of two forms of capitalist reproduction: the reproduction of capitalism's distinctive regimes of accumulation, and the social reproduction of people though the pursuit of livelihoods within migration. Lem draws on the example of the mobilization of physical and affective labor that is embodied in the examples of women from the northeastern provinces of China who have been displaced by the vagaries of changing regimes of accumulation and have relocated transnationally to Paris, where the finance and service complexes are significant in informing the dynamics in the reproduction of capital.

In this volume, our ethnographic examples reveal the ruptures between when and how migration is imagined collectively and individually, and then managed by states that collude with powerful elites to assert programs directed toward those 'others' often discursively marked as "strangers at our gates". The chapters connect these processes to people's displacement and emplacement as migrants, asylum seekers and refugees, as well as to their formation as suspect neighbors, non-citizens, and disposable workers.

REFERENCES

Adam, Barbara. 1998. *Timescapes of Modernity: The Environment and Invisible Hazards.* London: Routledge.

Agamben, Giorgio. 2005. *States of Exception.* Chicago: University of Chicago Press.

Andersson, Rueben. 2014. Time and the Migrant Other: European Border Controls and the Temporal Economics of Illegality. *American Anthropologist* 116 (4): 795–809.

Appadurai, Arjun. 2016. *Banking on Words: The Failure of Language in the Age of Derivative Finance.* Chicago and London: Chicago University Press.

Barber, Pauline Gardiner. 2013. "Grateful" Subjects: Class and Capital at the Border in Philippine – Canada Migration. *Dialectical Anthropology* 37 (3–4): 383–400.

Barber, Pauline Gardiner, and Catherine Bryan. 2012. Value Plus Plus: Housewifization and History in Philippine Care Migration. In *Migration in the 21st Century: Political Economy and Ethnography,* ed. Pauline Gardiner Barber and Winnie Lem, 215–235. New York: Routledge.

Bloch, Ernst. 1977 [1932]. Nonsynchronism and the Obligation to Its Dialectics. *New German Critique* 11 (Spring): 22–38. Translated by Mark Ritter from "Erbschaft dieser Zeit".

Braverman, Harry. 1974. *Labor and Monopoly Capital: The Degradation of Work in the Twentieth Century.* New York and London: Monthly Review Press.

Castles, Stephen, Hein de Haas, and Mark J. Miller. 2014. *The Age of Migration: International Population Movements in the Modern World.* London: Guildford Press.

Cwerner, Saulo B. 2001. The Times of Migration. *Journal of Ethnic and Migration Studies* 27 (1): 7–36.

Feldman, Gregory. 2011. *The Migration Apparatus: Security Labor and Policymaking in the European Union.* Stanford: Stanford University Press.

Franklin, Benjamin. 1748. *Printed in George Fisher, The American Instructor: Or Young Man's Best Companion. … The Ninth Edition Revised and Corrected,* 375–377. Philadelphia: Printed by B. Franklin and D. Hall, at the New-Printing-Office, in Market-Street.

Gell, Alfred. 1992. *The Anthropology of Time: Cultural Constructions of Temporal Maps and Images.* Oxford: Berg.

Glick Schiller, Nina, and Noel Salazar. 2013. Regimes of Mobility Across the Globe. *Journal of Ethnic and Migration Studies* 39 (2): 183–200.

Griffiths, Melanie. 2014. Out of Time: The Temporal Uncertainties of Refused Asylum Seekers and Immigration Detainees. *Journal of Ethnic and Migration Studies* 40 (12): 1991–2009.

Harvey, David. 1989. *The Conditions of Postmodernity: An Enquiry into the Origins of Cultural Change*. Oxford: Blackwell.

———. 2003. *The New Imperialism*. Oxford: Oxford University Press.

Ho, Karen. 2009. *Liquidated: An Ethnography of Wall Street*. Durham, NC: Duke University Press.

Holmes, Douglas. 2014. *Economy of Words: Communicative Imperatives in Central Banks*. Chicago and London: Chicago University Press.

Kalb, Don. 2012. Thinking About Neoliberalism as if the Crisis Was Actually Happening. *Social Anthropology/Anthropologie Sociale* 20 (3): 318–330.

Kasmir, Sharryn, and August Carbonella. 2008. Dispossession and the Anthropology of Labor. *Critique of Anthropology* 28 (1): 5–25.

———. 2014. *Blood and Fire: Toward an Anthropology of Labor*. New York and Oxford: Berghahn Books.

Lem, Winnie. 2015. *Discrepant Temporalities and Migration Scholarship*. Presenting in Panel on Migration's Discrepant Temporalities. American Anthropology Association Meetings, Denver, November.

Marx, Karl. 1977. *Capital: A Critique of Political Economy*. Vol. 1. New York: Vintage Books.

Neveling, Patrick. 2014. Structural Contingencies and Untimely Coincidences in the Making of Neoliberal India: The Kandla Free Trade Zone, 1965–91. *Contributions to Indian Sociology* 48 (1): 17–43.

Pido, Eric. 2017. *Migrant Returns: Manila, Development, and Transnational Connectivity*. Durham and London: Duke University Press.

Piketty, Thomas. 2014. *Capital in the Twenty-First Century*. Boston: Harvard University Press.

Pine, Frances. 2014. Migration as Hope: Space, Time and Imagining the Future. *Current Anthropology* 55 (59): S95–S104.

Piper, Nicola. 2011. Towards a Gendered Political Economy of Migration. In *Migration in the Global Political Economy*, ed. Nicola Phillips, 61–82. Boulder: Lynne Rienner Publishers.

Roberts, Brian. 1995. Socially Expected Durations and the Economic Adjustment of Immigrants. In *The Economic Sociology of Immigration: Essays on Networks, Ethnicity, and Entrepeneurship*, ed. A. Fortes, 42–86. New York: Russell Sage Foundation.

Sassen, Saskia. 1999. *Guests and Aliens*. New York: The New Press.

Thompson, Edward P. 1967. Time, Work-Discipline, and Industrial Capitalism. *Past and Present* 38: 56–97.

Williams, Eric. 1944. *Capitalism and Slavery*. Richmond: University of North Carolina Press.

Wolf, Eric. 1982. *Europe and the People Without History*. Berkeley: University of California Press.

CHAPTER 2

Chronotopes of Migration Scholarship: Challenges of Contemporaneity and Historical Conjuncture

Ayşe Çağlar

Prologue

Since the second half of the 2000s decade, an increasing number of artists and cultural producers in Germany, Austria and lately in Switzerland have been expressing their discontent with the ways migrants were situated within mainstream cultural policies and institutions. They argue that migrant-origin artists and cultural producers have lacked access to the central cultural institutions in these societies and that they have been marginalized in a particular way within the field of arts and culture. They coined the term 'post-migrant' to capture the experiences and subjectivities of those people whose lives bear the traces of migration but who have not necessarily experienced migration. According to one of its prominant advocates, the term 'post-migrant' is a battle cry that aims to seek new possibilities for migrant narratives and participation beyond the current dominant ethnic and religious frameworks in the society (Langhoff 2011).

A. Çağlar (✉)
Department of Social and Cultural Anthropology,
University of Vienna, Vienna, Austria

© The Author(s) 2018
P. G. Barber, W. Lem (eds.), *Migration, Temporality, and Capitalism*, https://doi.org/10.1007/978-3-319-72781-3_2

It is a call for an intervention, especially in the arts and particularly in the-atre to challenge the hegemonic logic and institutions of cultural production in their societies.[1] By challenging the marginal positioning of migrants in arts and cultural production, migrant-origin artists aimed to shift the axis of centrality and marginality in this field and introduce a new landscape of value vis-à-vis the location of migrants and migration in society by countering the dominant and normative categories of migration industries and knowledge practices.

Two pillars of arguments about the post-migrant condition in Vienna were articulated: (a) migrants' representational deficiency in the field of cultural production and Viennese cultural life. The prominent cultural institutions and cultural policies and funding institutions in Vienna failed to reflect the demographic reality of the society (EDUCULT 2012) in a city where almost half its population is of migrant origin (Akbaba et al. 2009; EDUCULT 2012; Sievers 2014).[2] In contrast to the city's self-image as a diverse and open city (Akbaba et al. 2009: 2), traditional cultural institutions in cultural policies and funding remained more or less closed to migrants (Sievers 2014); (b) marginalization of migrant artists through frameworks informed by concepts like intercultural bridging and/or integration. While migrant artists were marginalized as artists—and their cultural production marginalized within contemporary artistic and cultural work—the individuals acquired recognition and access to resources through social policies and funding mechanisms based on their alleged integration function rather than artistic concerns and their artistic qualities. Those migrant artists who argued for a post-migrant intervention called for challenging the culturalized logic of this kind of marginalization, which not only disregards the multiple dynamics of agencies and sociabilities and the diverse source of artistic and cultural productions of those identified as 'migrants' but also the centrality of migration in the society. They highlighted the contemporaneity of their work with 'non-migrant' artists' work. They confronted the dominant tropes of multicultural perspectives, which confine the sources of migrant action and biographies to cultural/ethnic communitarian origins. Though still

[1] See, for example, Langhoff (2011), Bazinger (2012), Wahl (2013), Akbaba et al. (2009), and Garage X (2014).

[2] In 2016, "50 percent of the Viennese [had] a migration background, i.e., they were born abroad or [had] at least one parent who was born abroad. 27 percent [were] non-Austrian passport holders and 34 percent were born abroad" (City of Vienna 2017).

holding to migrants' differences which they claim to be the product of complex trajectories, memories, multiple, simultaneous cross-border belongingness, and frames of action of post-migrants, the advocates of the post-migrant perspective aim to shift the focus from identity and differences to relations in which one 'acts' as if all were equal, i.e., to a focus on practices of sociability (Simmel 1949; Glick Schiller and Çağlar 2013).[3] Rather than highlighting interactions about differences, post-migrant intervention aimed to highlight those relations based on a sense of being human and on mutual affect, respect and pleasure arising from shared domains of commonality.

In 2011, Shermin Langhoff, one of the main proponents of post-migrant intervention in theater in Germany, was appointed co-director of the prestigious *Wiener Festwochen* (Vienna Festival).[4] This event marked the start of post-migrant intervention resonance in the landscape of arts and culture in Vienna. Although migrants' share in allocated funds in arts and culture is generally still very low (Akbaba et al. 2009; Bratic 2011; Sievers 2014), the visibility of migrant-origin artists has increased in cultural life in Vienna over the last decade (Sievers 2014: 35). Several new off-theatre groups with an explicit post-migrant agenda and manifesto acquired not only more visibility but also increasingly more funds in comparison to the 1990s and 2000s. Post-migrant intervention secured more visibility within *Wiener Festwochen*, reaching a prominent place in the most recent festival in 2017. In the context of increasing right-wing populism with a clear anti-immigrant political stance in Europe, including in Austria, this limited though increasingly successful post-migrant intervention in the institutions of cultural production in Vienna in the 2010s poses a puzzle.

In this chapter, I focus on these revaluation processes of migrant cultural productions within the broader dynamics of value regimes acted out in Vienna. First, I concentrate on how temporality is discussed in migration studies. Then, I focus on the temporal framings informing the main approaches in migration scholarship. Drawing from Mikhail Bakhtin's work on different ways in which practices are understood in connection to space and time (Bakhtin 1981), I look at the chronotopes of migration

---

[3] For the concept of sociability and its importance for migration studies, see Simmel (1949: 257) and Glick Schiller and Çağlar (2013).

[4] However, before taking up the co-directorship of the 2014 *Wiener Festwochen*, Langhoff resigned from this position (in 2013) to become the director of one of the central state cultural institutions in Berlin, namely, Maxim Gorki Theater. See Çağlar (2016).

scholarship. I explore how these chronotopes, in varying ways, inscribe the sources of 'migrant' dynamics into particular spaces and times, which in turn impede the study of migrants and those identified as non-migrants sharing the same 'Now' as their contemporaries. I argue that in order to be able to address and explore the shared temporalities of migrants and non-migrants and their domains of commonality, we need to bring migrants and non-migrants into a common analytical lens. This in turn requires an analytical vocabulary for addressing migrant settlement processes beyond methodological nationalism (Glick Schiller et al. 2003), and its ethnic lens (Glick Schiller et al. 2006). I explore the beginning of this vocabulary in the concepts of dispossession, displacement and emplacement (Glick Schiller and Çağlar 2015; Çağlar and Glick Schiller 2018). Furthermore, I argue, it is important that studies on migration and time engage with the concept of historical conjuncture (Clarke 2014; Glick Schiller and Çağlar 2015; Çağlar 2018; Çağlar and Glick Schiller 2018; Kalb 2011). In the last part of the chapter, I situate the temporality of the revaluation process of the post-migrant intervention in Vienna, referred to in the Prologue, within the city's regional and global repositioning struggle taking place at a particular historical conjuncture.[5]

Introduction

Temporality is an important but insufficiently discussed topic in migration studies. Although there has been an increasing interest in the importance of space in the analysis of migratory movements, migrants' practices and migrant settlement processes (Westin 1998; Malmberg 1997; Glick Schiller and Çağlar 2009; Çağlar 2006, 2016; Pine 2014), time, which is an integral element of the construction of space (Massey 1992) has been rather neglected in migration scholarship. There have been several studies on the temporal aspects of migration focusing on how migrants experience time (Cwerner 2001), how time matters from the perspective of the state in regulating, controlling and governing migrants through visas and a plethora of permits (Hammar 1994), and how migrants' time is appropriated within the "temporal economics of illegality" and the labor market (Andersson 2014).

---

[5] Parts of the arguments and the empirical material of this chapter are based on my article "Still 'migrants' after all those years: foundational mobilities, temporal frames and emplacement of migrants" (Çağlar 2016).

Studies that focus on the importance of time in migrants' life-course and pace of life explore how migrants experience time as rhythms, cycles and ruptures (Griffiths et al. 2013; Andersson 2014). 'Temporal habits', expectations, perceptions and symbols of time (Elchardus et al. 1987) take centre stage in these studies. In most cases, there is a strong focus on the hermeneutics and semiotics of time (Zerubavel 1987) and an attempt to theorize the different temporal frames of migrants' experience and its consequences. The relationship between migration, time and culture establish the main axis of these studies, highlighting the multiple and often discordant temporalities of migrants and migration (Cwerner 2001).

There are also studies that explore time as a central variable in laws and policies that regulate border controls and migrants' visas and consequently their status of legality/illegality, which in turn shapes their practices, expectation and settlement processes (Hammar 1994). In recent years, an increasing number of studies have focused on the temporalities of refugees, asylum seekers and irregular migrants. The relationship between waiting, mobility and time establishes the focus of these studies (Ibanez-Tirado 2017). Other studies discuss how various institutional actors produce and reproduce temporariness within the complex judicial processes of refugee displacement and settlement (Ramsay 2017). The major emphasis in this increasing number of studies on refugees is on time and 'refugeeness', namely on the relationship between temporariness and belonging, with a particular focus on refugees' contested sense of temporalities. Similarly, studies on different modalities of time, i.e., on mythic time, time of origins and shared pasts that are crucial in the construction of nations as "imagined communities" (Anderson 1983), address the relationship between migration, citizenship and temporality (Baubock 1998). These studies highlight the relationship between time, migration, belonging and inclusion.

In the context of an increasing number of studies on "times of migrants and migration", some migration researchers who also study the temporal dimensions of migration caution us against essentializing migrants' particular experiences of time by separating them as a category. They argue that time, like space, should be seen as a constitutive element of every social practice and not only of migrants' social life, and that a multiplicity of times is the case for everyone in society. "[T]here is no sui generis temporal experience [of migrants] that is not (and cannot be) shared by other people, the 'non-migrants'" (Cwerner 2001: 15). However these critical voices developed neither into studies scrutinizing shared temporalities of migrants and 'non-migrants' nor into an analysis of the temporal assumptions underlying the frameworks that migration scholars utilize in their analyses of migrants' practices and settlement processes.

Chronotopes of Migration Scholarship: Veiling the Shared Temporalities

In migration scholarship, different approaches to migrant settlement processes such as integration, multiculturalist, transnational and post-migrant all situate migrants in *time* in distinctive ways and operate with different kinds of temporal regimes in conceptualizing migrant dynamics, subjectivities and sociabilities. Drawing from Bakhtin's concept of chronotopes (Bakhtin 1981), I focus on the chronotopes of migration scholarship, i.e., how migrants and their practices are conceptualized in connection to space and time in migration scholarship in varying ways. As matrices, chronotopes refer to a set of connections between time and space by which "movement in space can be figured as movement in time and vice versa" (Lomnitz 2012). All approaches to migration are informed by spatial and temporal frameworks which situate the dynamics of migrant practices and relations in space and time. The *spatial* frameworks, particularly the spatial impediments of migration scholarship, have received more attention, especially in relation to methodological nationalism (see Glick Schiller and Çağlar 2009; Glick Schiller et al. 2006; Amelia et al. 2012; Çağlar 2013). For this reason, despite the mutually constitutive nature of spatial and temporal frameworks, I concentrate in this chapter on the temporal impediments of migration scholarship. Here I focus on those perspectives that view migrants through the lens of integration and post-migrancy. The multiculturalist and transnational frameworks in migration scholarship share many of the spatial and temporal impediments of these models.

Framing migrants through an integration perspective means situating migrants in space and time in a particular way, namely in a linear and a sequential process. Migrants are expected to 'uproot' themselves from the spaces of their 'home countries' (and of the 'culture' which is projected to the 'ancestral home') and integrate themselves into the countries of settlement *in time*. A temporal predicament is assumed in the models of integration that operate with concepts of assimilation, integration and/or acculturation. The theories and policies based on these concepts are informed by temporal norms. They operate with a normative understanding of time, especially in terms of 'the future'. The present of migrants is viewed and evaluated from the point of view of this temporal predicament, which refers to an ideal state of full integration. This is the basis of the teleology involved in integration models (Favell 1998; Schinkel 2017). As integration refers to *a process of perpetual becoming*, the deficiency of the migrant (in terms of achieving integration) and the means to overcome this deficiency play an important role in the integrationist approaches to migrant settlement and in the policies based on them. The integrating migrant can never fully embrace the ideal 'host' society. S/he is in *a perpetual state of integrating*. Such a view is clearly based on a temporal logic informed by a temporal norm. The present becomes a transition (an evolution) into a hypothetical and ideal future, and the past and the present of the migrant are evaluated from the perspective of this ideal.

The post-migrant perspective, which emerged as an intervention and a challenge to an integrationist understanding of migrancy and society (Yıldız 2010; Foroutan et al. 2014; Yıldız and Hill 2014; Tsianos and Karakayali 2014) is also based on a particular spatio-temporal narrative. The prefix 'post' clearly indicates a category of temporal location. In the post-migrant perspective, too, the present is evaluated from a temporal grid, but this time instead of being evaluated from the point of an ideal future, it is evaluated *through the grid of an inscribed past* (Çağlar 2016). However, it is not just any kind of a past-fixated trajectory within which we find the legacy of the past in the present; it is about the *immutable traces* of a particular past experience, namely the experience of migrancy anchored in an initial cross-border *spatial* mobility *or* its memory in the present. The 'post-migrant' designation prioritizes the role of a particular past (the trespassing of the border of an ancestral home) in framing the subjectivities, lives and actions of those designated as post-migrants (Çağlar 2016). Although the proponents of the post-migrant perspective challenge it, there is a *temporal prepositioning* present in the perspectives operating with the concept of post-migrant (see Espahangizi 2016; Tsianos and Karakayali 2014; Mecheril 2014). This temporal frame also links the post-migrant to predefined spaces, which function as the grid of the post-migrant's current subjectivities and sociabilities. In that sense, the chronotope of post-migration perspectives resembles what many students of post-socialism have criticized in relation to scholarship on the societal dynamics of "post-socialist" societies (Chari and Verdery 2009). These chronotopes perpetuate a language of transition.

While in integrationist models, the transition is *towards* a normative future, in post-migrant frameworks of migration scholarship, the transition is *from* an (implicitly) inscribed past. In both perspectives, the temporality of the Now, i.e., the contemporary, is situated either in relation to a normative future or to an immutable past or its memory. Rather than situating the dynamics and relations of migrants within the contingency of time and place shaped by the power geometry of the Now, these models situate the temporal experiences of migrants in relation to a predefined past. There is a past-fixated filtering of the sources of migrants' present practices and sociabilities. Its temporal logic moves the analysis of migrants' agency and *current* practices away from the broader context of the dynamics shaping the Now.

Ironically, the prioritization of a particular past projects a constrained trajectory, i.e., a path dependence, to migrant dynamics and hinders the analysis of migrants' subjectivities and practices in relation to a changing configuration of social forces. This temporal prepositioning of migrants' relations, memories and sociabilities that the concept of post-migrant entails puts *a priori closure* to the complex, multiple and changing ways people who are designated as migrants (post or not) are positioned *in time*. Accordingly, particular kinds of histories (pasts) and social processes connected to them are highlighted in exploring their current dynamics, practices and sociabilities. They are considered to shape the Now of migrants' discrepant temporalities.

In contrast to the *deficiency* model of the integration perspective, the post-migrant framework portrays migrants with an *excess* resulting from their particular past. Thus, the chronotopes of both the integration and post-migrant perspectives introduce an *a priori* divide in inscribing those who are designated as 'with' a migrancy background and those 'without' into different domains of sociability and temporal predicaments. Both perspectives operate with what Lomnitz calls a "split chronotope" (2012: 353). Migrant practices and sociabilities are approached on the one hand as if they were *con*temporaneous with the 'non-migrants'/'natives' of the societies where they settle and on the other hand as if they were in a perpetual transition either from an inscribed and path-dependent past or towards a normative future. Such a division *denies* migrants the same analytical lens through which the activities and relations of those regarded as the 'native'/'non-migrant' inhabitants of a locality are studied.

To anchor migrants' frames of reference in other times is to operate with the assumption that migrants do not exist in the same Now of non-migrants. These temporal frameworks hinder us from analyzing migrant lives and sociabilities within the shared temporalities of the other residents of the places where they settle. These chronotopes veil the shared temporalities of migrant practices, relations and sociabilities, which are shaped by the configuration of social forces at a particular conjuncture. The consequence of situating migrants' frames of action and of reference into elsewhere and to *other times* different from 'native'/'non-migrant' frames of action is in Fabian's words (1983) "a denial of coevalness", i.e., of contemporaneity of migrants with non-migrants. This obscures their domains of commonality, resulting from their subjection to common forces, though with unequal access to power and resources. The ethnic lens deployed by many migration scholars obstructs seeing and studying the commonalities between migrant and non-migrant populations by concealing the *diversity* of migrants' relationships to their place of settlement and to other localities around the world (Glick Schiller et al. 2006: 613). This lens is based on—and it reproduces—a denial of shared temporality (Çağlar 2013). Consequently, the conceptual divide between 'migrants' and 'non-migrants', anchored in methodological nationalism and the related ethnic lens, subjects migrants to a particularist and very often culturalist lens, whereas, 'natives'/'non-migrants' are studied in relation to acknowledged the historical dynamics of social forces and political economy (Çağlar 2013, 2016).

As a result, migrant practices and their dynamics are approached through "typological time" (Fabian 1983) as if they were categorically different from the practices and dynamics of non-migrants (Çağlar 2013, 2016). Perspectives based on a denial of coevalness prevent us from seeing the experiences, norms and values migrants and natives share—the domains of commonality between migrants and 'non-migrants' resulting from their shared temporality, i.e., their simultaneous embeddedness in social, economic and political processes, networks, movements and institutions that exist both within and across state borders at a particular space and time in a given historical conjuncture.[6]

To overcome the discontents of the aforementioned chronotopes of migration scholarship, we need to take the shared temporalities—shaped

---

[6] In criticizing researchers focusing on the times of migration and migrants' temporal predicaments, Cwerner rightly argues that scholars have often treated migrants either in relative isolation and, to some extent, outside time and history, or within a largely assumed scale of evolutionary time (2001: 30). According to him, this is particularly misleading in an increasingly interconnected globalized world. Unfortunately, as a remedy against this tendency, he urges migration scholars to engage with the (ethnic) interconnectedness of migrants within the changing cultural and political geographies of the world (2001: 31–33).

by the configuration of social forces at a particular time and place—as our entry point to the analysis of migration. Rather than assigning migrants and non-migrants to different temporalities and *to different fields of power* from the beginning, it is important that in our analysis, we situate migrants as contemporaries of all other urban residents. Such a radical contemporaneousness will allow us to see migrants and non-migrants through a common analytical lens so we can study how all residents of a place (migrant or not) build their lives within the configuration of social forces given at an historical conjuncture.

EMPLACEMENT: A BUILDING BLOCK OF A NEW VOCABULARY

One of the first steps of going beyond the impediments of the chronotopes in migration scholarship is to develop a framework that does not subject the analysis of emergent migrant sociabilities and their dynamics either to the overarching power of a kind of 'immutable' selected past or to a foundational spatial mobility that puts the priority on the nation state and an ethnic lens. Instead, we need a framework to capture the social structuring of sociabilities, migrant subjectivities and daily life in migrants' places of settlement within the power contingencies of a particular place and time without denying the contemporaneousness of those designated as 'migrants' with the 'natives'/'non-migrants' (Çağlar and Glick Schiller 2018). This urges us to develop a new analytical vocabulary. As we show in our work, making concepts of displacement, dispossession and emplacement central to the analysis of migrants and city-making processes might be useful (Çağlar and Glick Schiller 2018) for conceptualizing migrants and non-migrants as sharing the same time/space, although with unequal access to resources and power.

This conceptual network enables us to trace the connections between the ways in which all the residents of a place (migrant or not) respond to the ongoing processes of capital restructuring and repositioning of the places where they strive to build their lives. It is important to note that to speak of urban and capital restructuring is simultaneously to explore dispossession and displacement: the processes of dispossession and displacement are entangled with the accumulation of capital and the restructuring processes of cities (Çağlar and Glick Schiller 2018). In today's world, dispossession is central to the generation of wealth, which produces various forms of spatial and social displacement (Harvey 2004; Çağlar and Glick Schiller 2018; Miraftab 2014). These displacements and dispossessions are an integral part of restructuring processes, which reassemble, disassemble and re-represent social and political space, institutions of governance and social forces (Çağlar 2014; Çağlar and Glick Schiller 2011, 2018; Glick Schiller and Çağlar 2015). The concept of emplacement enables us to capture the instantiation of the set of dynamics in space and time within the configuration of interlocking forces of a particular historical conjuncture. Highlighting these processes of dispossession, displacement and emplacement that all city residents are subject to allows us to go beyond the split chronotopes of migration scholarship I have referred to, which operate with an a priori divide between migrants and 'non-migrants'/'natives'.

A common analytical lens is important to highlight the common forces migrants are subject to together with all residents of the considered place in the Now. Like all residents of that particular place, migrants are also emplaced in varying ways in relation to the constraints and the opportunities of their places of settlement. Emplacement, which is a processual concept, enables us to situate all residents of a city within transformations of space over time by linking space, place and power (Smith 2002; Massey 2005; Harvey 2006). It refers to "the relationship between the continuing restructuring of place within multiscalar networks of power, and a person's efforts, within the barriers and opportunities that contingencies of local place-making offer, to build a life within networks of local, national, supranational, and global interconnections" (Çağlar and Glick Schiller 2018: 28). This concept enables us to study migrant subjectivities, relations and sociabilities, in relation to restructuring efforts and the resulting revaluation and devaluation processes in the places of settlement.

> By situating migrants as contemporaries of all other urban residents, and by analyzing their practices as coeval, it becomes clear that all city inhabitants (migrant or not) build their lives within processes of displacement and emplacement that are enabled and shaped by the power geometry at that historical conjuncture. (Çağlar and Glick Schiller 2018)

TEMPORALITY OF VALUE REGIMES, MIGRANTS AND DIVERSITY POLICIES

Now deploying this analytical vocabulary I come back to the relative 'potency' of post-migrant intervention referred to in the Prologue. In explicating the relative success of post-migrant intervention and the recent heightened visibility and presence of migrants in arts and cultural institutions and funding schemes, it seems that situating the valorization of post-migrant cultural production within broader processes of value creation might be more useful. Migrants in arts and cultural production became an asset in Vienna at a particular historical conjuncture, and this valorization is related to broader processes of value creation, diversification and capital accumulation. As studies on regimes of value show, revaluation is connected to global movement of capital accumulation and its temporalities (Narotzky 2017). Thus, to understand the temporality of the value regime we are dealing with, we need to situate this revaluation process within the power geometry (Massey 2012) of an historical conjuncture. Continuous production of difference is crucial for the complex process of capital realization, and especially within the processes of urban restructuring, production of difference is particularly important as the competitive value of a place is created through difference (Glick Schiller and Çağlar 2009; Narotzky 2017).

To explore the emplacement of the post-migrant intervention in Vienna, a conjunctural analysis, which will direct our analytical attention to the multiplicity of forces and possible lines of emergence from particular "intertwinings of relations of power and contradictions" (Clarke 2014: 115) might be useful. This will enable us, above all, to examine the multiscalar, globally extending relationships of Vienna to processes of accumulating wealth and power as realized at a particular historical moment conjuncture. We could then situate the processes of revaluation and devaluation (including migrant cultural production) within the changing configuration of the historical conjuncture.

As I argued elsewhere, this change in visibility of post-migrant intervention in public debates on arts and culture in Vienna (clearly manifested, for example, in the choice of artistic director and the orientation of Vienna Festival in 2012, or in programs such as "Pimp My Integration") and the increasing access of migrant artists to cultural institutions (especially to theaters with avant-garde ambitions) were closely entangled with the urban repositioning struggle of Vienna taking place in the 2000s (Çağlar 2016). The broader context of this valorization process was the city's efforts to reorganize its institutions, governance and resources and assets to reposition itself more favorably within multiscalar fields of power to keep its competitive worth, and thus to accumulate capital and regenerate wealth (Glick Schiller and Çağlar 2009, 2013).

There were two important dynamics behind the emplacement of post-migrant intervention within the cultural landscape of Vienna in the 2000s. One was the particular dynamics of the tourist industry, which is one of the major sources of income for the city; the other was the city's shift to diversity policies (City of Vienna 2012; URBACT 2011). In the 2000s, one of the main challenges confronting Vienna's competitive positioning in the tourist industry was its aging tourist profile. In the context of rising competition posed by cities such as Budapest, Prague, Berlin and Warsaw, which succeeded in attracting a younger group of tourists, this profile had to be diversified. Especially in the field of arts and culture, which plays an important role within the city's tourist industry, the development of avant-garde arts and experimental off-theaters became important so the city could retain its competitive value. Post-migrant intervention found a fertile ground and funding in off-theaters, especially within the pressures to shift to diversity policies.

Migrants became an asset in arts and cultural landscape in Vienna especially within the diversity policies adopted in the 2000s, which could also be seen as projects of revaluation (of difference). The multiple and transnational ('transcultural') connections and subjectivities of migrants, which established the basis of their *de*valorization in the 1980s and 1990s, became increasingly valuable within diversity policies. It is important we situate these diversity policies in Vienna temporally, i.e., in relation to the urban restructuring and repositioning struggle of the city within a particular historical conjuncture.

Since the early 2000s, diversity increasingly became part of Vienna's self-representation (Çağlar 2016). There has been a shift to diversity policies where diversity increasingly became not only a means of governance but a resource for the economic competitiveness and the socioeconomic performance of the city (Hadj-Abdou 2014). Following a number of expert reports and recommendations about Vienna in the early 2000s, migrants came to be revalued as part of the assets for the branding of the city as open, diverse and cosmopolitan (Hadj-Abdou 2014: 1900). In the assessment of the city's competitive positioning, in addition to the city's capacity to attract global flows of capital, global headquarters, global firms and global talent, the city's performance in terms of its connectivity, cultural assets, immigrants and visitors was also taken into consideration. However, Vienna was positioned unevenly in these fields, especially in terms of coping with the challenges its diverse population posed and in terms of facilitating the inclusion of its migrants. These shadowed the city's competitiveness (McDearman et al. 2013: 1–3; Çağlar 2016). These assessments were followed by documents suggesting a shift to a policy that would valorize diversity. The documents clearly connected diversity policies, branding together the city as diverse and cosmopolitan and its efforts to regenerate wealth. Thus, migrants were revalued and became assets to be valorized by capital within this context (Çağlar 2016).

It is noteworthy that one of the main institutions in Vienna, the Association of Business for Integration (*Verein Wirtschaft für Integration*), which was established in 2009 in close association with Raiffeisen Bank, provides venues for and contributes to the debates on diversity, on Vienna being a world-open city, and on the inclusion of migrants and the reevaluation of their capabilities. In fact, "the director of this association as well as the supervisory president of the *Wiener Festwochen* ... have been among the participants of several events organized as part of the post-migrant intervention in the city" (Çağlar 2016: 12). Valorization of diversity and of post-migrant cultural productions is deeply entangled with business.

IN CONCLUSION: NONSYNCHRONISM

Bloch (1977 [1932]) uses the notion of 'non-synchronism' to argue that "[n]ot all people live in the same Now" (1977: 22), thus not all contradictions and subjectivities of the Now could be captured through an analysis of the contemporary political economic structure. Furthermore, he sees torpidity in non-synchronism, i.e., in the surmounted remnants of older economic being and consciousness that are not part of the Now (1977: 29). Bloch's notion of non-synchronism proved crucial in addressing temporal discrepancies that shape subjectivities and agency (Barber and Lem's introduction to this volume) and in arguing against the "all-embracing centrality of capital" (Franquesa 2016: 70).

It is possible to approach the chronotopes of migration scholarship I explored earlier in this chapter through the lens of non-synchronism. Indeed, non-synchronism is central to the chronotopes of both integration and post-migrant frameworks. Like the non-synchronism of peasants in the city, who according to Bloch, stand on a bad footing with Today (1977: 27), within the chronotopes of integration perspectives, migrants lag behind in the Now due to the remnants of their lives and 'habits' anchored in the spaces and times of their 'homeland', 'culture' and 'tradition'. Similarly, the immutable traces and power of a migration experience and/or its memory and the resulting multiple simultaneous belongingness and frames of action that mark the post-migrant chronotope could also be read in reference to the power Bloch sees in non-synchroneousness. While migrants' alleged non-synchroneousness is a problem for the integrationist model, the idea of non-synchronism acquires a positive and transformative power in the post-migrant framework.

By situating migrants' frames of action and reference into other spaces and to other times, the lens of non-synchronism in migration studies might lead scholars to deny contemporaneity, i.e., coevalness to migrants with the non-migrants in their analysis, which I critically addressed in this chapter. However, this would be a very narrow reading of Bloch, as if he simply refers to the simultaneity of multiple and discrepant temporalities in the Now without addressing the dialectic between the synchronous and non-synchronous contradictions shaping subjectivities and political lives. According to him, the power of "not all people existing in the same Now" is not simply the power of simultaneity of multiple temporalities. He says, "... [h]aving everything that is past, in infinite polyphony as it were, without a dominant voice, is mere historicism" (1977: 37). I argue that the power geometry of the Now at a particular historical conjuncture shapes the nature and power of this dominant voice. Thus, the valorization/devalorization of non-synchronous (and discrepant temporalities, for that matter) is reconfigured in relation to these dominant voices.

Those who approach relations of capital as multiple unequal *social relations* constituted within social fields of power repeatedly underlined legitimizing narratives of racialized, culturalized and gendered differences, i.e., the "coloniality of power", as being fundamental to appropriations and the processes of dispossession underlying capital accumulation (Butler 2009; Quijano 2000; Piketty 2014; Kalb and Tak 2005; Clarke 2014; Hart 2001). They rightly urge us to analyze both processes in relationship to each other. However, once these constructed differences take the form of a positive valuation—as it is the case in 'diversity' and post-migrant narratives—these valorizations are often approached as if they were detached from the processes of capital accumulation. As a result of efforts to favorably position Vienna regionally and globally to attract spatially mobile capital, migrancy, migrant cultural productions and their transnational reach as well as 'discrepant temporalities' acquired value as part of Vienna's locational assets.

Building on the scholarship that links processes of production of differences to structures of dispossession and accumulation of capital (Harvey 2004, 2006; Smith 2002; Narotzky 2017; Narotzky and Smith 2006; Kalb 2011; Çağlar 2006; Çağlar and Glick Schiller 2011, 2015, 2018), this chapter situates the relative success of post-migrant intervention in Vienna in relation to the strategies of differentiation that are central for the generation of wealth in Vienna within the neoliberal global context of 'competitive states'. I explore the emplacement of the post-migrant intervention in the city in connection to these processes of valorization/ devalorization processes taking place at a particular conjuncture.

I have shown temporality as crucial in analyzing regimes of value including the revalorization and devalorization[7] of migrants and how it is important to conceptualize time also in relation to changing historical conjunctures. Migrants and post-migrant intervention in the art and cultural fields acquired value and relative power to reach out to transnational and supranational actors within the power geometry given by a historical conjuncture. With the changing configurations of intersecting multiscalar networks of power, landscapes of value in city-making processes also change. Post-migrant cultural productions became an asset to be valorized by capital within the realignment of conjunctural forces. The mix and potency of the strategies of differentiation and valorizations in Vienna was very much shaped by the power geometries of a particular historical conjuncture. With the changing conjuncture in Europe, where since 2015 refugees have acquired a central position globally and regionally, 'refugees' and 'refugeeness' rather than 'migrants' and 'migrancy' started to acquire prominence in cultural institutions of Vienna. They increasingly became an asset even for established cultural institutions such as *Burg Theater* or *Volkstheater* in reaching out to supranational institutions (such as United Nations) and their funding. As illustrated in plays such as *Schutzbefohlene* or performances such as *Gimme Shelter* in *Burg Theater* or in *Die Reise* in *Volkstheater*, refugees started to find their way to the central cultural institutions in Vienna, which ironically to a large extent still remain more or less closed to 'post-migrant' artists.

REFERENCES

Akbaba, Ülkü, Ljubomir Bratic, Sarah Galehr, Andreas Görg, and Gabrielle Pfeiffer. 2009. Kunst, Kultur Und Theater Für Alle! [Art, Culture and Theater for All!]. http://www.iodo.at/kulturstudie090606.pdf.

Amelia, Anna, Devrimsel D. Nergiz, Thomas Faist, and Nina Glick Schiller, eds. 2012. *Beyond Methodological Nationalism Research Methodologies for Cross-Border Studies*. London: Routledge.

Anderson, Benedict. 1983. *Imagined Communities*. London: Verso.

[7] The processes of valuation and devaluation I have referred to are often closely entangled with the valorization and devalorization of groups and/or the places and practices that are associated with them. In our case, valorization of migrants (as well as post-migrants) was very much part of processes of value creation and the generation of wealth.

Andersson, Ruben. 2014. Time and the Migrant Other: European Border Controls and the Temporal Economics of Illegality. *American Anthropologist* 116 (4): 795–809.

Bakhtin, Mikhail. 1981. Form of Time and Chronotope in the Novel. In *The Dialogic Imagination: Four Essays*, ed. Mikhael Holquist, 84–258. Austin: University of Texas Press.

Baubock, Rainer. 1998. Sharing History and Future? Time Horizons of Democratic Membership in an Age of Migration. *Constellations* 4 (3): 320–345.

Bazinger, von Irene. 2012. "Gespräch mit Shermin Langhoff Wozu postmigrantisches Theater?." *Frankfurter Allgemeine Feuilleton*. http://www.faz.net/aktuell/feuilleton/buehne-und-konzert/gespraech-mit-shermin-langhoff-wozu-postmigrantisches-theater-11605050.html. Accessed 9 September 2014.

Bloch, Ernst. 1977 [1932]. Nonsynchronism and the Obligation to Its Dialectics. *New German Critique* 11: 22–38.

Bratic, L. 2011. Die Wahrheit der Kulturpolitik. *Kulturrisse* 2. http://kulturrisse.at/ausgaben/urbane-raeume-zwischen=verhandlung=und=verwandlung/kulturpolitiken/die-wahrheit-der-kulturpolitik. Accessed September 9, 2013.

Butler, J. 2009. *Frames of War: When Is Life Grievable?* London: Verso.

Çağlar, Ayşe. 2006. Hometown Associations, the Rescaling of State Spatiality and Migrant Grassroots Transnationalism. *Global Networks* 6 (1): 1–22.

———. 2013. Locating Migrant Hometown Ties in Time and Space. Locality as a Blind Spot of Migration Scholarship. *Historische Anthropologie* 21 (1): 26–42.

———. 2014. *Nations Unbound and Beyond: The Global Perspective and the Spatio-Temporal Frameworks*. Workshop presented at the Perspectives on Nation Unbound: The Transnational Migration Paradigm in the Current Conjuncture, Amsterdam, October 27.

———. 2016. "Still 'migrants' after all those years: foundational mobilities, temporal frames and emplacement of migrants." *Journal of Ethnic and Migration Studies* 42 (6): 952–969.

———. 2018. "Minorities, War and Historical Conjuncture: A Multiscalar Approach to City Making in a Disempowered City:" in A. Gingrich ed. *Anthropology in Transition Austrian RAI Series*, Sean Kingston Publishing.

Çağlar, A., and N. Glick Schiller. 2011. Introduction: Migrants and Cities. In *Locating Migration: Rescaling Cities and Migrants*, ed. Nina Glick Schiller and Ayşe Çağlar, 1–22. Ithaca: Cornell University Press.

———. 2015. A Multiscalar Perspective on Cities and Migration. *Sociologica Italian Journal of Sociology* 2: 1–9.

———. 2018. *Migrants and City Making. Multiscalar Perspectives on Dispossession*. Durham and London: Duke University Press.

Chari, Sharad, and Katherine Verdery. 2009. Thinking Between the Posts: Postcolonialism, Postsocialism, and Ethnography After the Cold War. *Comparative Studies in Society and History* 51 (1): 6–34.

City of Vienna. 2012. Monitoring Integration Diversity Reports Vienna 2009–2011. https://www.wien.gv.at/menschen/integration/grundlagen/monitoring/index.html.

———. 2017. Facts and Figures – Vianese Population According to Migration Background. https://www.wien.gv.at/english/social/integration/basic-work/facts-figures.html. Accessed October 26, 2017.

Clarke, J. 2014. Conjunctures, Crises, and Cultures: Valuing Stuart Hall. *Focaal: Journal of Global and Historical Anthropology* 70: 113–122.

Cwerner, Saulo B. 2001. The Times of Migration. *Journal of Ethnic and Migration Studies* 27 (1): 7–36.

EDUCULT. 2012. Pimp My Integration. http://educult.at/forschung/prozessbegleitung-zur-projektreihe-postmigrantische-positionen/.

Elchardus, Mark, I. Glorieux, and M. Scheys. 1987. Temps, Culture et Coexistence. *Studi Emigrazione* 24 (86): 138–154.

Espahangizi, Von Kijan. 2016. Das #Postmigrantische Ist Kein Kind Der Akademie. http://geschichtedergegenwart.ch/das-postmigrantische-kein-kind-der-akademie/.

Fabian, Johannes. 1983. *Time and the Other: How Anthropology Makes Its Object.* New York: Columbia University Press.

Favell, Adrian. 1998. The Europeanisation of Immigration Politics. *European Integration Online Papers (EIoP)* 2 (10). http://eiop.or.at/eiop/texte/1998-010a.htm.

Foroutan, Naika, Canan Coskun, Schwarze Benjamin, Beigang Steffen, Arnold Sina, and Kalkum Dorina. 2014. *Hamburg postmigrantisch: Einstellungen der Hamburger Bevölkerung zu Musliminnen und Muslimen.* Berlin: Berliner Institut für empirische Integrations- und Migrations- forschung. Online. www.bim.hu-berlin.de/media/BIM_Hamburg%20postmigrantisch%202014.pdf. Accessed September 15, 2017.

Franquesa, Jaume. 2016. "Dignity and indignation: bridging morality and political economy in contemporary Spain." *Dialectical Anthropology* 40(2): 69–86.

Garage X: Asli Kislal Detail. http://www.garage-x.at/portal/index.php?option=com_flexicontent&view=items&cid=44:garage-kuenstler-detail&id=773:asli-kislal-detail. Accessed 7 October 2014.

Glick Schiller, Nina, and Andreas Wimmer. 2003. Methodological Nationalism, the Social Sciences, and the Study of Migration: An Essay in Historical Epistemology. *International Migration Review* 37 (3): 576–610.

Glick Schiller, Nina, and Ayşe Çağlar. 2009. Towards a Comparative Theory of Locality in Migration Studies: Migrant Incorporation and City Scale. *Journal of Ethnic and Migration Studies* 35 (2): 177–202.

———. 2013. Locating Migrant Pathways of Economic Emplacement: Thinking Beyond the Ethnic Lens. *Ethnicities* 13 (4): 494–514.

———. 2015. Displacement, Emplacement and Migrant Newcomers: Rethinking Urban Sociabilities Within Multiscalar Power. *Identities* 23 (1): 1–16.

Glick Schiller, Nina, Ayşe Çağlar, and Thaddeus C. Guldbrandsen. 2006. Beyond the Ethnic Lens: Locality, Globality, and Born-Again Incorporation. *American Ethnologist* 33 (4): 612–633.

Griffiths, Melanie, Ali Rogers, and Bridget Anderson. 2013. *Migration, Time and Temporalities: Review and Prospect.* Oxford: COMPAS Research Resources Paper.

Hadj-Abdou, Leila. 2014. Immigrant Integration and the Economic Competetivenes Agenda: A Comparison of Dublin and Vienna. *Journal of Ethnic and Migration Studies* 40 (12): 1875–1894.

Hammar, Tomas. 1994. Legal Time of Residence and the Status of Immigrants. In *From Aliens to Citizens: Redefining the Status of Immigrants in Europe*, ed. Rainer Bauboeck, 187–197. Aldershot: Avebury.

Hart, K. 2001. Money in an Unequal World. *Anthropological Theory* 1 (3): 307–330.

Harvey, D. 2004. The 'New' Imperialism: Accumulation Through Dispossession. *Socialist Register* 40: 63–87.

———. 2006. *Spaces of Global Capitalism: Towards a Theory of Uneven Geographical Development*. London: Verso.

Ibanez-Tirado, Diana. 2017. 'We Sit and Wait': Migration, Mobility and Temporality in Guliston, Southern Tajikistan. *Current Sociology*. http://sro.sussex.ac.uk/70080/1/accepted%20version%20we%20sit%20and%20wait%20sep%202017.pdf.

Kalb, D. 2011. Introduction. In *Headlines of Nation, Subtexts of Class: Working-Class Populism and the Return of the Repressed in Neoliberal Europe*, ed. D. Kalb and G. Halmai, 1–36. Oxford: Berghahn.

Kalb, D., and H. Tak. 2005. Introduction: Critical Junctions—Recapturing Anthropology and History. In *Critical Junctions: Anthropology and History Beyond the Cultural Turn*, ed. D. Kalb and H. Tak, 1–28. Oxford: Berghahn.

Langhoff, Shermin. 2011. Die Herkunft spielt keine Rolle – 'Postmigrantisches' Theater im Ballhaus Naunynstraße: Interview mit Shermin Langhoff. *Bundeszentrale fuer politische Bildung.* http://www.bpb.de/gesellschaft/bildung/kulturelle-bildung/60135/interview-mit-shermin-langhoff?p=all. Accessed March 12, 2015.

Lomnitz, Claudia. 2012. Time and Dependency in Latin America Today. *South Atlantic Quarterly* 111 (2): 347–357.

Malmberg, Gunnar. 1997. Time and Space in International Migration. In *International Migration, Immobility, and Development: Multidisciplinary Perspectives*, ed. Tomas Hammar, Grete Brochmann, Kristof Tamas, and Thomas Faist, 21–49. Oxford: Berg.

Massey, Doreen. 1992. Politics and Space/Time. *New Left Review* I (196): 65–84.

———. 2005. *For Space*. London: Sage.

Massey, D. 2012. Power-Geometry and a Progressive Sense of Place. In *Mapping the Futures: Local Cultures, Global Change*, ed. J. Bird, B. Curtis, T. Putnam, and L. Tickner, 60–70. London: Routledge.

McDearman, B., G. Clark, and J. Parilla. 2013. *The 10 Traits of Globally Fluent Metro Areas*. Global Cities Initiative. A Joint Project of Brookings and J. P. Morgan Chase. http://www.brookings.edu/~/media/Multimedia/Interactives/2013/tentraits/Vienna.pdf. Accessed September 15, 2014.

Mecheril, Paul. 2014. Was Ist Das X Im Postmigrantischen? *Sub/Urban* 2 (3): 107–112.

Miraftab, Faranak. 2014. Displacement: Framing the Global Relationally. In *Framing the Global: Entry Points for the Search*, ed. Hilary Kahn, 37–50. Bloomington: Indiana University Press.

Narotzky, Susana. 2017. Making Difference: Concluding Comments on Work and Livelihoods. In *Work and Livelihoods – History, Ethnography and Models in Times of Crisis*, ed. Susana Narotzky and Victoria Goddard, 205–217. New York: Routledge.

Narotzky, S., and G. Smith. 2006. *Immediate Struggles: People, Power and Place in Rural Spain*. Berkeley: University of California Press.

Piketty, T. 2014. *Capital in the Twenty-First Century*. Translated by A. Goldhammer. Cambridge, MA: Harvard University Press.

Pine, Frances. 2014. Migration as Hope: Space, Time, and Imagining the Future. *Current Anthropology* 44 (Supplement 9): 95–104.

Quijano, A. 2000. Coloniality of Power and Eurocentrism in Latin America. *International Sociology* 15 (2): 215–232.

Ramsay, Georgina. 2017. Incommensurable Futures and Displaced Lives: Sovereignty as Control Over Time. *Public Culture* 29 (3): 515–538.

Schinkel, Willem. 2017. *Imagined Societies: A Critique of Immigrant Integration in Western Europe*. Cambridge: Cambridge University Press.

Sievers, Wiebke. 2014. A Contested Terrain: Immigrants and Their Descendants in Viennese Culture. *Identities: Global Studies in Culture and Power* 21 (1): 26–41.

Simmel, Georg. 1949. The Sociology of Sociability. *American Journal of Sociology* 55 (3): 254–261.

Smith, Neil. 2002. New Globalism, New Urbanism. *Antipode* 34 (3): 427–450.

Tsianos, Vassilis, and Jıliane Karakayali. 2014. Rassismus Und Repräsentationspolitik in Der Postmigrantischen Gesellschaft. *ApuZ* 64 (13–14): 33–39.

URBACT. 2011. Zoom on Vienna. *URBACT*. http://urbact.eu/fr/results/zoom-on/?zoomid=10.

Wahl, Christine. 2013. "Theaterpionierin Langhoff: Ich habe mich selbst gelabelt." *Der Spiegel Online*. http://www.spiegel.de/kultur/gesellschaft/shermin-langhoff-uebernimmt-maxim-gorki-theater-in-berlin-a-933453.html. Accessed 5 October 2014.

Westin, Charles. 1998. Temporal and Spatial Aspects of Multiculturality: Reflections on the Meaning of Time and Space in Relation to the Blurred Boundaries of Multicultural Societies. In *Lurred Boundaries: Migration, Ethnicity, Citizenship*, ed. Rainer Bauboeck and John Rundell, 53–84. Aldershot: Ashgate Publishers.

Yıldız, Erol. 2010. Die Öffnung Der Orte Zur Welt Und Postmigrantische Lebensentwürfe. *SWS Rundschau* 3: 318–339.

Yıldız, Erol, and Marc Hill. 2014. *Nach der Migration Postmigrantische Perspektiven jenseits der Parallelgesellschaft*. Bielefeld: Transkript Verlag.

Zerubavel, Eviatar. 1987. The Language of Time: Towards a Semiotics of Temporality. *The Sociological Quarterly* 28 (3): 343–356.

CHAPTER 3

The Timescape of Post-WWII Caribbean Migration to Britain: Historical Heterogeneity as Challenge and Opportunity

Karen Fog Olwig

THE TIMESCAPE OF MIGRATION

I've got a picture of when I was leaving. My mum ... the nice suit my mum made me, a nice check suit with, like, a waistcoat. And I'm waving back, looking and smiling and going off. My mum said I went ... quite well. She cried. [...] I was excited, and I was sad too, because I want to do it, but then I was sad—I'm leaving my mum and my sister, really, and, you know, worrying about how things would be when I wasn't there. And it was a big step. I'd never been anywhere ... never slept at a relative before. It was my dad who found out that this recruitment was happening, and he sent off the papers. He also helped pay for my travel expenses. He just wanted the best for me. I really didn't have much to do with it.

I came 1968, September. Somebody met me, put me on a train from London, all the way up here—all these miles away. A sea of white faces, which I was never used to. Got here, and I had to get a taxi myself. It was on York Road. It's not a hospital any more. The door was locked, so I just knocked on it, and somebody came and let me into the Nurses' Home [residence].

K. F. Olwig (✉)
Department of Anthropology, University of Copenhagen, Copenhagen, Denmark

© The Author(s) 2018
P. G. Barber, W. Lem (eds.), *Migration, Temporality, and Capitalism*, https://doi.org/10.1007/978-3-319-72781-3_3

43

> These days, women are doing everything that men do, don't they. I think, back then it wasn't like that. I think nursing was the only way, really, for women to leave wherever you were to come out and forge a different life somewhere else. [...] But I didn't just use it for that reason, I actually wanted to be a nurse, yes.

Julia,[1] quoted above from a 2011 interview, was one of the thousands of young Caribbean women who travelled to Britain in the post-WWII period in order to train in nursing.[2] Most of them were recruited by British hospitals, where there was a great need for nurses following the establishment of the National Health Service, in 1949. This recruitment peaked in 1970. The following year the Immigration Act, restricting the entry of trainees in nursing from the Commonwealth, was passed, but it was not until the 1980s, when foreign nurses' work permits began to be revoked, that the British recruitment came to a halt (Baxter 1988: 14, 16). As Julia's narrative suggests, moving to Britain to become a nurse was not a simple matter of young West Indian women deciding to take advantage of training opportunities in Britain. The family, often including relatives abroad, played a key role in this migration by helping with the application and preparations for the trip and, in many cases, assisting financially. Parents often actively promoted nursing as an attractive occupation for their daughters. But the young women clearly also had their own motives for doing nursing in Britain. It presented not only a good profession, but a way, perhaps the only way according to Julia, for them to leave home and stake out a life of their own in another place. West Indian nursing in Britain thus represented a conjuncture of several different concerns: the British need for care workers at the hospitals, the West Indian parents' ambition to secure a good future for their daughters and the young women's desire to develop their own life away from home.

Migration is usually described as a process that occurs through time as well as space. While there has been increasing interest in migrants' movements and relations in space, including their simultaneous engagement in the sending and receiving societies, the temporal framework of these processes has been

[1] I have changed the name of all the interviewed nurses in order to protect their anonymity.

[2] This study of Caribbean nurses in Britain received economic support from Aksel Tovborg Jensens Legat, the University of Copenhagen and the Carlsberg Foundation. An earlier, shorter paper was presented at an international seminar on "Migration and Temporality", organized by the Migration Research Group at the University of Copenhagen, in June 2015.

subject to less scrutiny. There has often been an assumption, however, that migration involves a move from tradition to modernity. In contemporary migration research, for example, young people's imaginaries of the exciting modern life to be enjoyed in the Western world are viewed as important drivers of migration (Adams 2009: 803; Salazar 2011; Bredeloup 2013: 172; Groes-Green 2014).[3] Migration destinations, however, do not comprise uniform timescapes of modernity, even if they are imagined in this way; rather, they can be seen to display considerable temporal heterogeneity. This is captured in Ernst Bloch's notion of non-synchonism (1977 [1932]: 22): "Not all people exist in the same Now. They do so only externally, by virtue of the fact that they may all be seen today. But that does not mean that they are living at the same time with others." Bloch was particularly interested in people or classes that cling to the ways of a bygone past in order to preserve their historically grounded, often privileged, social status, and refuse to identify with their contemporary society, where this position is challenged. Bernard Giesen (2004: 28) goes further and suggests that the "coexistence of phenomena that we relate to different historical periods" should not necessarily be regarded as evidence of 'non-contemporaneity'. This understanding reflects "the modernist insistence on the purity of style, that does not allow for mixing past and present", as well as "the modern idea of a radical opposition between past and future, the present being a turning point between a past that will [not] and should never return and a future that is seen as the field of creativity, surprise, invention and innovation" (2004: 29). In contrast to this understanding, he contends, "the coexistence of historically heterogeneous phenomena" should be regarded as "the normal situation" (2004: 29). Further along these lines, Hanns-Georg Brose proposes that the coexistence of "historically heterogeneous phenomena" may be completely unproblematic. This is because such phenomena often exist within particular "subsystems and organizations" that are associated with different kinds of lived time, such as working time or leisure time that takes place in different physical and social settings (2004: 16). The coexistence of historically heterogeneous phenomena, as I will show, may depend on immigrant workers from less socioeconomically privileged hinterlands who are willing to accept (at least temporarily) a low status position in an unequal 'traditional' subsystem because of the access it affords them to the more 'modern' subsystems. A case in point is the migration of the prospective West Indian nurses to Britain.

---

[3] This migration may just be directed at nearby urban areas that have the "attributes of western modernity" (Bredeloup 2013: 172).

While British society was undergoing a period of rapid social and economic change after the Second World War, it had a number of subsystems that were identified as traditional, or old-fashioned, and tied to a class or category of people intent on maintaining their privileged status. As shall be seen, nursing, organized as a profession for middle-class women during the latter part of the nineteenth century, comprised such a subsystem. In the course of the twentieth century, as a new range of career paths became available to women, nursing, with its close links to Victorian moral codes and class relations tied to gendered hierarchical structures, experienced increasing difficulty attracting young British women. The hospitals, however, found fertile grounds for recruiting nurses in the late- or post-colonial societies of the (former) British Empire. Not only had these places undergone a period of general economic decline, but the administrative, educational and healthcare institutions introduced there by the British in the Victorian era continued to constitute powerful societal structures. Furthermore, the social norms and cultural values associated with these institutions, centering on gendered codes of proper conduct, remained highly influential. In the West Indies, employment in the (post)colonial institutions, and adherence to their value system, thereby formed an important foundation of the emerging middle class (Olwig 1993), with nursing and teaching as key occupations for women. Opportunities in these professions were limited, however, with few training opportunities. The possibility to train in nursing at British hospitals therefore presented a welcome possibility to receive qualifications in a well-known, highly esteemed profession that conferred respect upon the family. At the same time, it also offered the young women the promise of being able to build a life of their own in a modern society away from home.

This chapter will examine the intentions, ambitions, desires and feelings associated with this convergence of interests and show how it was an integral part of the complex timescape within which this migration took place. The analysis is based on ethnographic life story interviews with 80 women who left the Caribbean in the post-war period in order to train as nurses at British hospitals.[4]

[4] The women came from a broad range of Caribbean societies (Anguilla, Barbados, Dominica, Grenada, Guyana, Jamaica, St. Kitts-Nevis, St. Lucia, St. Vincent and Trinidad-Tobago) and began training during the 1940s (1), the 1950s (10), the 1960s (54), and the 1970s (16). Fieldwork took place in Britain (intermittently 2009–2016), Barbados (January 2013), Trinidad-Tobago (January and October 2013), Guyana (October 2013) and St. Kitts-Nevis (February 2015).

An Occupation Suitable for Women

When Julia was let through the door to the hospital where she was going to train, she entered a world of its own, demarcated from the rest of society by not only thick walls but also an occupational structure that was very much a relic of nineteenth century British Victorian society and its particular gender and class system. Until the middle of the nineteenth century, care for the sick and elderly was primarily the responsibility of the family, and in particular to women, who were expected to devote themselves to the home. In the upper classes, private (female) nurses were hired to care for the seriously ill, whereas the poor were placed either in charity hospitals operating with the help of 'charitable contributions', or in 'the workhouse', institutions for the poor where the seriously ill were more or less left to die (Abel-Smith 1977 [1960]: 2–8). Most of the care work was performed by women from the servant class, but women from the upper levels of society were recruited for higher positions in the hospitals. They were usually "'distressed gentlewomen,' ladies from the middle class who, for some reason, needed to earn their own living and sought to capitalize on their customary skills of domestic management in matron posts" (Dingwall et al. 1988: 69). While many of the hospital nurses were competent, the profession in general had a bad reputation, nurses being accused of being heavy drinkers who received alcoholic drinks as "part of the system of rewards" in order to help them "face the confusion and stench of the hospital wards" (Abel-Smith 1977 [1960]: 13, 241; Baly 2002 [1973]: 124).

The latter part of the nineteenth century saw major efforts at reorganizing nursing, most famously by Florence Nightingale, who developed a new system of hospital care headed by a female matron and focusing on thorough practices of hygiene, dedicated yet restrained care for the patients, and a strict regime of discipline. The importance of proper conduct was emphasized at the training school for nurses established by Nightingale, where women were selected on the basis of their personal qualities rather than their educational qualifications (Abel-Smith 1977 [1960]: 22). The nurses wore uniforms that "provided an absolute boundary between the body of the nurse and that of her patients and male doctors, whilst at the same time exemplifying her womanliness" (Brooks and Rafferty 2007: 48) and they lived in special "homes", intended to offer "a cultural and educational background for young women who had left an educated middle-class home, and to raise the sights of those who had not" (Baly 2002 [1973]: 126). Furthermore, and just as significantly, the homes operated with strict curfews for the night, thus shielding the women from the temptations and dangers of the surrounding society.

With long and demanding work schedules, close supervision and "its own body of traditions which were drawn from the army, from the religious orders, and possibly also from the new girls' public schools" (Abel-Smith 1977 [1960]: 244), nurses' lives have been described as characterized by "cloistered separateness" (Carpenter 1977: 165). It was, however, through this formal, highly regulated system that nursing was turned into "a suitable and respectable career for women" (Abel-Smith 1977 [1960]: 29). This successful transformation of the occupation has been attributed to its appeal to a relatively large group of unmarried upper- and middle-class British women who had few prospects of getting married and were therefore "condemned by social sanctions to idleness in the home" (Baly 2002 [1973]: 124; Abel-Smith 1977 [1960]: 17). Nursing, with its devotion to the care of others and upholding of proper manners, fit the Victorian image of respectable women as concerned with "good works" while maintaining a high standard of "delicacy" (Baly 2002 [1973]: 124). As an occupation for women, it did not compete "with the superior sex in the learned professions" (Abel-Smith 1977 [1960]: 17) and therefore offered an ideal "outlet for the social conscience and frustrated energies of the Victorian spinster" (Baly 2002 [1973]: 124). It was not considered appropriate for married women to be nurses, however, and those who married therefore had to give up the profession.

By the 1950s, when West Indian women began to be recruited by the British hospitals, British nursing still operated to a great extent according to the principles set down during the Victorian era. In a 1983 study of nurses in leading positions at British hospitals (Hardy 1983), the women described their life as student nurses during the 1940s and 1950s as "disciplined," "monastic" and "secluded". They were expected to have a "marriage-like commitment to the institution" and discouraged from engaging in outside activities on their own. They were lectured on the "student menace" and admonished not to go out with the (male) students. Only three had married (1983: 159, 146). As noted by Abel-Smith (1977 [1960]: 245), "While young women were being emancipated in their own homes, nurses continued to be treated with Victorian authority."

A High-Status (Post-)Colonial Profession

The West Indian women who signed up for training in Britain were quite familiar with British nursing. It was introduced to the colonies with the establishment in 1896 of the Colonial Nursing Association (later the Overseas Nursing Association), which stationed trained nurses endowed with "cheerfulness and tact" in different parts of the empire in order to provide care for the bedridden and "counteract negative attributes of the colonial environment by recreating the more civilised standards of medical care available at home" (Howell et al. 2011: 1158–1159). Overseas nursing was patterned on the British system to the extent that the residential quarters for nurses built in 1928 in Barbados were named the Florence Nightingale Nurses Home, and a brick from Nightingale's home in London was placed in the wall of the staff nurses' living room (Hunte 2009: 42). An important aim of instituting 'proper' standards of nursing was to replace the local midwives and nurses, who were believed to offer "well-meaning but damaging ministrations" (Howell et al. 2011: 1161). These women, who had been highly regarded in the local communities as care providers and midwives, drawing on African-Caribbean traditions of herbal medicines (Olwig 2015), were gradually phased out as formal hospital training became the requirement for those who wished to practice as nurses and midwives. By the 1950s, when emigration to British hospitals began, the training programs at the West Indian hospitals were nevertheless still regarded as inferior to those in Britain, and British nurses continued to dominate West Indian nursing in the sense of occupying leading positions well into the 1950s (Hunte 2009: 82).

The Caribbean nurses described the hospitals of the West Indian society in which they grew up as being characterized by a "stiff upper lip" atmosphere and the presence of stern matrons—a far cry from the "cheerful" and caring system envisioned by the Overseas Nursing Association. They emphasized that a trained nurse was looked up to in West Indian societies as "somebody that mattered in the community" and as a person who had displayed "an ambition to become something; not like going selling in a shop or selling in a store or that sort of a thing." Nurses in the West Indies were well aware of their special position in society and sought to uphold an image of respectability by carrying themselves in a dignified way. One nurse who began her training in the West Indies thus recalled that it was considered very important they maintained "a certain demeanor" and did not "frolic" when they wore the uniform.

The position of respect enjoyed—and cultivated—by the nurses must be seen in the light of their close association with the institutional system that became the backbone of the West Indian societies after abolishment of slavery. Closely tied to the Enlightenment, the mission of these institutions was to "improve" the condition of the black population through education and the propagating of Christian morals that could lift the population out of its "ignorance" and "backwardness" and turn it into a free population of the modern world (Olwig 1993, 2010). In a critical discussion of the notion of the Enlightenment, Stuart Hall notes that while it "represented itself as 'universal'", its "universality inevitably became harnessed back to the West. 'We' were the enlightened ones, whose civilizational duty and burden was to enlighten everybody else—the unenlightened, the noncosmopolitan'" (Hall and Werbner 2008: 349). The project of enlightening the British West Indies was not harnessed to a generalized West, however. It was closely tied to the cultural values and social norms of the British Victorian era of the late nineteenth century, when the institutional structure of the post-emancipation West Indian societies was established. A proper education thus meant knowledge of British history, geography and literature, whereas genuine moral values and civilized behavior were assessed in terms of the ability to conduct oneself according to British tenets of respectability. For women central aspects of this respectability included speaking "proper" English, devotion to the spiritual and physical care of the family and the home as well as modesty and physical restraint in relations to persons of the opposite sex (Wilson 1973; Olwig 1993). This culture of respectability differed from the ways of the African-Caribbean lower class, who spoke Creole English, whose women played an active role beyond the home and the church, and whose families were based on networks of relatives many of whom were born outside marriage. Nevertheless, Victorian respectability became a key mark of middle-class status in the late-colonial West Indian societies. Families desiring to be recognized as part of the middle class thus reared their children to aspire to a good British education, while making great efforts to protect them from the harmful influence of the local culture.

The culture of respectability played an important role in the families of the West Indian nurses in Britain, who mostly had grown up in the late-colonial West Indian societies. Dorothy recalled how her father, a businessman, had sent her to the best schools, insisted that she dress "nicely"—by, for example, prohibiting her from wearing dresses he found too short—and brought her up to speak and behave in accordance with British middle-class norms. She grew up with her father and stepmother, being the child of an extramarital relationship, and her father refused to let her see her biological mother, who lived in a poor neighborhood and had little education, fearing she would have a bad influence on his daughter. As Dorothy explained, he used to say, "If you speak to people blacker than yourself, they tend to bring you down." She was not allowed to leave the house on her own, but could sit on the veranda, and if she was permitted to attend a church function or a party, such as a birthday celebration in the family, her father brought her and picked her up. Many nurses described a similarly strict and closely supervised upbringing where they were not allowed to "mix" with those perceived to be of the lower classes, often equated with people who had darker skin color. Jane, for example, recalled that because she and her sisters could move only in particular social circles and were not allowed to play with neighboring children, they were called "black white ladies", an ambiguous term that acknowledged their cultural whiteness, while pointing to their black physical appearance:

> [H]e taught me those things, you know, how to pronounce my words, and how to write, and he showed me how to join my letters ... how you must eat at the table [...], how to hold a knife and fork. We always sat at the table.

In West Indian middle-class culture, the highest mark of achievement for women was becoming a teacher, a nurse or a civil servant, occupations that signaled good education, excellent manners and high morals. There were, however, few positions and, in the case of nursing, limited training opportunities. Good connections were therefore often necessary for a young woman to be considered for an opening. In this situation of local social and economic constraint, migration through the British recruitment of nurses offered an ideal solution. Training at a British hospital, which was regarded as superior to that offered at the local West Indian hospitals, would enable the young women to acquire a profession that would increase, or consolidate, the family's status in the local community. While it meant travel far from home, the parents believed the young women would be safe at the British hospitals because they would be staying in nurses' homes under the watchful care—and supervision—of senior nurses. At the same time nursing offered a way of leaving home. Indeed, many nurses explained that for them the possibility of getting away from the parents' strict upbringing and traveling abroad on their own was a main attraction of doing nursing in Britain. As Selma explained, "I felt that there was a bigger world out there. That I would want an opportunity to make decisions for myself." At a time when nursing had been rejected by many young British women as an overly disciplined, hopelessly old-fashioned occupation (Dingwall et al. 1988: 99, 119–120), it was embraced by Caribbean women as both a high-status profession and an avenue to exciting new experiences away from a tradition-bound home.

NURSING TIME: THE NURSES' PROFESSIONAL LIFE

The training hospitals that the West Indian women encountered were embedded in a Victorian "subsystem" located in "different and separated settings" and with its own kind of "lived time" (cf. Brose 2004: 16). Most of the West Indian women were trained in smaller hospitals outside the major cities where it was particularly difficult to attract young British women for nursing. These training environments, associated with the quiet countryside, were also favored by the West Indian parents, who worried that life in the modern cities might have an adverse influence on impressionable young West Indian women. Jasmin, for example, had to abandon her plan to train at a major London hospital: "My mother did not think it was a good idea for me to be in London, because it was a big, dangerous city, and she preferred for me to be in a smaller place."

The West Indian nurses described being enrolled in a hierarchical nursing regime organized around training and practical work involving long working hours, discipline and willingness to perform hard physical work. They were required to live under the watchful eye of a senior nurse in the nurses' home, where they were not allowed to receive male visitors in their rooms and were subject to a curfew, usually at 10 p.m., when the doors were locked. They often spoke of the senior nurses as "old spinsters", or even as "something out of Jane Austen", women who had dedicated their entire life to the wards and felt "threatened by the young vital nurses" who entered the hospital. They therefore became "bitter" and "uptight" and tried to keep the young nurses in their place by assigning them the most unpleasant tasks, like washing bedpans and in general giving them a hard time. Some of the matrons apparently also exploited the West Indian women's vulnerable position as immigrants, and one West Indian nurse remembered being warned, when she was introduced to the matron: "If I disobey in whatever way, did not comply with the rules and whatever, I would be posted back home." It was also a common practice of the British hospitals to channel West Indians, and other immigrants, into the shorter program of practical nursing or the more limited programs of mental and fever nursing rather than offering them the comprehensive program for registered nurses that would have given them more career opportunities. Of the 80 nurses I interviewed, only 33 were initially enrolled in the longer program for registered nurses. In this way, the senior nurses attempted to keep the West Indians in the lower echelons of the nursing hierarchy, where the physically and emotionally strenuous care tasks were performed, the so-called 'dirty work' that became associated with immigrants (Olwig 2017).

At the same time as the West Indian nurses experienced the British training hospitals as old-fashioned, hierarchical nursing regimes, they admired the British nurses' dedication to their work and praised the excellent, thorough training they received. Furthermore, with their British (post-)colonial education and middle-class background they were well equipped to handle the Victorian nursing environment and challenge the limitations that it presented. Having been reared to abide by Victorian social norms and forms of conduct, they were well versed in the type of behavior expected by the senior nursing staff. Some even claimed that they spoke "better English than everybody" except for the matron and some of the senior staff, and that the matron appreciated their good manners and proper appearance. Marilyn, for example, said she was the "matron's favorite" because she was "capable," "mannerly" and in general "knew what she was doing". Moreover, being brought up in a rather disciplined and controlling family environment they were used to respecting seniors and to strict rules in the home. Indeed, Helena related, "I remember writing my mother, thanking her, you know, for the upbringing which made it so easy for me to fit in into England. [...] I think our being a British colony, certain standards were passed down to us." The self-assurance that this colonial upbringing bestowed upon these women moreover gave them the confidence to pursue further education despite the discriminatory practices that many were subjected to during their initial training. Thus, all but a handful of those who had been placed in the practical nursing, mental health or fever nursing programs succeeded at receiving further training, to qualify as registered nurses to enter other professions, or to obtain higher education at universities.[5] If the British matrons managed to recruit hardworking, disciplined and well-educated workers in the West Indies, the recruits were not satisfied with being confined to doing menial labor at the bottom of the nursing hierarchy.

[5] One became ill and had to retire from nursing at a relatively young age, others preferred to do mental nursing. Fever nursing was phased out. See also Olwig (2017).

Leisure Time: The Nurses' Other Life

The matrons attempted to shape the nurses' leisure time in ways that they considered appropriate for nurses. The sitting room in the nurses' home was equipped with, for example, newspapers, magazines and a piano where the nurses could unfold their musical talents and where they might be allowed to hold parties, with soft drinks and finger food, and it was possible to play music and dance. The matron would usually make her appearance during the evening to say hello and check that everything took place in an orderly fashion. Some matrons also distributed free theater or concert tickets that had been donated to the hospital, and they accepted invitations for the nurses to attend dances at nearby universities or military bases. Matrons furthermore sought to keep a check on the student nurses' whereabouts during weekends. Nurses who wanted to stay out late had to receive special passes that usually gave them only an extra two hours, and at some hospitals those who wanted to stay overnight with relatives had to introduce them to the matron and give her their address and phone number so that she could check on them—which she might do at any time.

While the nurses appreciated the matrons' concern for their well-being, and participated in the organized activities at the hospital, they cherished their leisure time mainly for the opportunity it offered to do things on their own. They enjoyed the friendship they developed with the other student nurses and their informal get-togethers in the nurses' home that often included West Indian cooking and dancing to loud music—at least until the home sister complained about the noise. And most of all, they enjoyed modern life outside the Victorian nursing regime at the hospital. Yvette explained:

> I felt the freedom in that I knew I had two days off a week, and those two days off were up to me how I spent them—whether I chose to study, whether I chose to go and explore Kent, or the town, or whether I chose to go into London [...] Now I was in England, I could make those decisions for myself—what clothes I wore, whether I wore make-up, you know, whatever. Whether I go to the cinema, what pictures I see at the cinema, I go clubbing … if I choose to stay out late or not, etc. It seems simple, but it was important to me at the time. (Yvette)

Miriam pointed to the importance of being able to see different people of one's own, not the parents', choosing:

I will say that was the beginning of my independence, living away from home and associating with people from all over the world so to speak.

Key to this sense of freedom and independence was the nurses' sense of being in charge of their own life. "I never slept from about Friday until about Monday morning, and that was the truth", Corinne claimed and added, "You're young, you're away from home, no parents, you know." Many nurses recalled various more or less successful attempts at evading the strict curfew that curtailed their ability to enjoy leisure activities outside the hospital grounds. Selma, for example, related how they would make up their beds so that they looked as if someone was sleeping in them and arrange for a fellow student to open a window so that they could get into the nurses' home when they came back late. This was met with severe sanctions, however, if discovered:

> I can't remember which of the girls went out, and when she came back, nobody could get up to open the window, because Sister Rush was sitting there! So when she got through the window, she landed in Sister Rush's lap! [LAUGHS] So all of her time out was taken away for a couple of months or so.

Some student nurses, however, opted to stay away from clubbing, drinking in pubs or going to dance halls, explaining that they never would engage in such things in the West Indies and saw no reason to do so in Britain.

The ability to make independent choices was a whole new experience for most of the nurses, and Lornette noted, "I remember the first time I realized, I don't really have to ask anybody for permission, I can just do my own thing!" At the same time, however, she realized that such freedom, or independence, was not unconditional, but necessitated a new form of self-control:

> And it was just as if something was holding me back, you know. You really control your own self and you have to have your standards, there is nobody looking at you doing it for you. It is that sort of thing, it is that freedom that really struck me that I never had before.

Such self-control required switching between two modes of self-expression as the nurses moved between the spatially and temporally separated, yet coordinated, subsystems of Victorian nursing and modern youth culture that were essentially "existing apart together" (Brose 2004: 16) in British society. The matrons were aware that most of the young nurses had a modern social life in their leisure time, yet they did not interfere with it, as long as it took place outside the hospital within the allotted time frame. They did not tolerate any trace of this other life, however, when the young nurses were back at the hospital. Joan recalled, "I had nail varnish on once and the matron said she doesn't want to see me [...with nail varnish. The nails] had to be natural. She said, 'why did you wear it'? I say I went out and I came in and I had forgotten to remove it. She said 'right, don't do it again'." More seriously, Lornette recalled that one of her fellow students was fired immediately when the matron found out that she had had a miscarriage. At another hospital the matron allowed a student nurse pregnant out of wedlock to continue her training, but only after she had given birth and placed the child in foster care.

If professional life as a nurse and social life as a young woman were to be negotiated successfully, it was crucial the social life did not get the upper hand. As Clarissa explained, there were those who were "too free with themselves, they got pregnant, and [had] abortions and [were] set back in their work as well, having to ... instead of doing the exams with us, did it later on." Some were even forced to give up their training, which would result in an involuntary return to the West Indies if they had entered Britain on a special visa for nurses. The nurses were well aware that if they came back "with nothing", they would be regarded as failures, a scenario that was to be avoided, not only for their own but also for the family's sake. Indeed, the nurses were generally careful to maintain an image of themselves in their West Indian community of origin as responsible women who pursued training in a highly esteemed profession. They wrote regularly to their family, sending postcards from the hospital where they trained as well as photographs of themselves in the nurses' uniform, and when they had finished their training they often traveled back home to visit their family and show their credentials as nurses. The obligation to live up to the family's expectations thus was a strong motivating factor keeping their social life in check.

The nursing subsystem was not completely uniform, however. The training hospitals in the rural areas tended to be more conservative than the urban ones and those who trained later in the period generally described less rigid nursing regimes, more in accord with modern British society. This gradual adjustment seems to have occurred as a reluctant response to the desperate need for nurses. The West Indian nurses played a part in this push to modernize nursing. It was not before the early 1960s that the matrons gave up on enforcing "the unwritten rule in the profession that nursing and marriage did not mix" (Hardy 1983: 159), yet Jean, who arrived in the mid-1950s, married a year after beginning her training. She did so despite strong discouragement by the matron who told her that she would "have difficulty carrying on in nursing, because if you're married [... and] have babies you have to stay home and look after your children." The interviewed West Indian nurses arrived mainly in the latter part of the 1950s, when marriage was becoming accepted, but they did not stop working when they had children, thus insisting it was possible to combine married life with a professional career. During the 1960s, the West Indian nurses contributed to reforming gender roles and acceptable morality even further. Thus in 1961, Glenda was admitted for training as a nurse at a London hospital, even though she against all advice had included information on her status as a single mother on the application form. The matron, apparently hard pressed to recruit a sufficient number of nurses,[6] told her that she did not mind her having a child but asked her to keep it a secret. Glenda left her child with her grandmother in the West Indies and promised not to "broadcast" that she was a mother, but kept a picture of her son in her room and told close friends that it was not her nephew, as they assumed, but her son. Ten years later, it seems to have become fairly acceptable for unmarried nurses to have children. Thus when Georgette became pregnant in 1973 she did not consider marrying the father, noting merely "he wasn't worth it, you know."

The West Indian nurses also claimed the right to divorce if their marriage did not work out, often due to the husband seeing other women when they worked on the evening shift. Such womanizing was quite common in the West Indies, where it was generally tolerated by middle-class women who depended on a husband for their economic mainstay and social status in the local community. The West Indian nurses, who enjoyed the social and economic security of their profession and benefited from living in a modern society where divorce was relatively common, were not so accepting. Lornette, who divorced her husband, explained, "he messed about with women all over the place [... and] didn't realize that I am not afraid to be an independent woman." This achievement of independence

[6] The hospital had a severe lack of nurses that resulted in the matron "exploring every avenue in the recruitment of nurses", as a contemporary report stated (Wingfield 2003: 75).

was, actually, in accordance with the wishes of the parents, especially the mother. Thus, at the same time that parents promoted nursing as a high-status, respectable profession, they also valued that it would give the daughter something to fall back on, should her marriage not work out, thus recognizing the problematic practices taking place behind the facade of middle-class propriety. This view of nursing as a profession that would enable women to create a life of their own outside the constraints of the home was, of course, much in line with the Victorian perceptions of women during the late nineteenth century when the profession was first established. But notions of what such a life might entail had changed by the late twentieth century.

CONCLUSION: HISTORICALLY HETEROGENEOUS TIMESCAPES AS CHALLENGE AND OPPORTUNITY

Inspired by theoretical and philosophical considerations concerning the coexistence of historically heterogeneous phenomena, this chapter has argued that certain forms of migration must be understood within the context of the prevalence of complex timescapes. Insofar as the continued existence of backward-oriented institutions in a modernizing society is often associated with a segment of the population attempting to maintain a privileged position rooted in the past (Bloch 1977 [1932]), such institutions can be dependent upon migrant workers who regard the occupational niches offered within the subsystem as a possible avenue of socio-economic and personal mobility, as well as a means of gaining access to modern life in the wider society. This is exemplified by this case study of the migration of West Indians for training in nursing in the post-WWII period. At this time, British institutions of nursing were physically and socially separated from the rest of society and organized according to their own gendered subsystem (cf. Brose 2004: 16). This subsystem was controlled by single middle-class British women who were intent on maintaining their privileged status based on Victorian social norms, gender roles and class relations. As they experienced increasing difficulty attracting young student nurses in the modernizing British society, where a wider range of opportunities was becoming available to women, they began recruiting nurses from former British colonies where societal institutions continued to be tied to Victorian social norms and cultural values and opportunities for women remained severely restricted. For West Indian women training as a nurse in Britain was attractive because it would enable them to qualify for a coveted profession that conferred high status in the local West Indian communities and gave them a certain modicum of social and economic security. At the same time, it was a respectable way for the young women to leave home and gain access to the offerings of modern British society outside the hospitals while experiencing a kind of independence that would not have been possible in the West Indies.

Whereas the British nursing regime was successful at using migrants to maintain a well-organized, separate Victorian subsystem within a modern society in the short run, it was not able to keep modern society at bay in the long run. With a shortage of well-educated women willing to train in the nursing profession, it was necessary to accede to the young nurses' increasing expectations of enjoying a modern life and the freedom and independence that went with it. Furthermore, it proved impossible to use the West Indian nurses as only low-ranging handmaidens for the privileged senior nurses. While the West Indian women generally liked nursing, most regarded it as a stepping stone in their socio-economic mobility as well as their own personal development. Many therefore sought further education, and those who found nursing at the hospitals too rigid, and resistant to promoting black nurses in the hierarchy, opted for career paths in, for example, community health, social work, teaching or research. While historically heterogeneous phenomena may coexist successfully if they are contained within "the boundaries of their respective subsystems and organizations" associated with different kinds of lived time, as Brose (2004: 16) suggests, this study shows they will not be unchanged as people move between the various subsystems. This is especially true if these people gain some bargaining power, for example by obtaining needed skills that are not readily available otherwise.

The close relationship between historically heterogeneous timescapes and migration has implications beyond this particular case study, and thus the point of this article is not only to present a general argument, but also to raise questions that can be pursued further in future research. The West Indian nurses' situation of being recruited to work in a separate, gendered subsystem associated with a former era is not unique. The chief migration opportunity for women, for example, has long been found in the need for care work in private homes.[7] Such homes can be viewed as comprising a

---

[7] The literature on care work migration is extensive. For an overview of some of the main issues, see Williams (2010).

separate subsystem that often remains organized according to a 'traditional' gendered division of labor, frequently supported by various state policies, while the wider society has undergone rapid change. Being employed in the private sphere, many care workers have limited legal rights. Indeed, au pairs often have no formal workers' rights, the receiving host families being expected to offer a supportive and protective environment for the young migrant women (Dalgas 2015), like the nurses' homes at the British hospital. Unlike the West Indian nurses, however, care workers do not acquire any formal qualifications on the job. They may attempt to improve their situation by appealing to the personal relations they develop with their employers, but these ties are often fickle. Furthermore, as there are a large number of women eager to migrate for domestic work, they are easily replaced if they become too demanding. They may thus end up merely enabling the continued existence of a gendered subsystem tied to complex power structures. From this perspective, the Victorian nursing regime, despite its harsh discipline and rigid hierarchy, offered the West Indian women a privileged position vis-à-vis many women working in the present-day care sector.

References

Abel-Smith, Brian. 1977 [1960]. *A History of the Nursing Profession*. London: Heinemann.

Adams, Mary. 2009. Playful Places, Serious Times: Young Women Migrants from a Peri-Urban Settlement, Zimbabwe. *Journal of the Royal Anthropological Institute* 15 (4): 797–814.

Baly, Monica E. 2002 [1973]. *Nursing and Social Change*. London: Routledge.

Baxter, Carol. 1988. *The Black Nurse: An Endangered Species*. London: National Extension College for Training in Health and Race.

Bloch, Ernst. 1977 [1932]. Nonsynchronism and the Obligation to Its Dialectics. *New German Critique* 11 (Spring): 22–38. Translated by Mark Ritter from "Erbschaft dieser Zeit".

Bredeloup, Sylvie. 2013. The Figure of the Adventurer as an African Migrant. *Journal of African Cultural Studies* 25 (2): 170–182.

Brooks, Jane, and Rafferty Anne Marie. 2007. Dress and Distinction in Nursing, 1860–1939: A Corporate (as Well as Corporeal) Armour of Probity and Purity. *Women's History Review* 16 (1): 41–57.

Brose, Hanns-Georg. 2004. An Introduction Towards a Culture of Non-Simultaneity? *Time & Society* 13 (1): 5–26.

Carpenter, Michael. 1977. The New Managerialism and Professionalism in Nursing. In *Health and the Division of Labour*, ed. Margaret Stacey, Margaret Reid, Christian Heath, and Robert Dingwall, 165–195. London: Croom Helm.

Dalgas, Karina. 2015. Becoming Independent Through au Pair Migration: Self-Making and Social Re-positioning Among Young Filipinas in Denmark. *Identities: Global Studies in Culture and Power* 22 (3): 333–346.

Dingwall, Robert, Anne Marie Rafferty, and Charles Webster. 1988. *An Introduction to the Social History of Nursing*. London: Routledge.

Giesen, Bernhard. 2004. Noncontemporaneity: Asynchronicity and Divided Memories. *Time & Society* 13 (1): 27–40.

Groes-Green, Christian. 2014. Journeys of Patronage: Moral Economies of Transactional Sex, Kinship, and Female Migration from Mozambique to Europe. *Journal of the Royal Anthropological Institute* 20: 237–255.

Hall, Stuart, and Pnina Werbner. 2008. Cosmopolitanism, Globalisation and Diaspora. In *Anthropology and the New Cosmopolitanism*, ed. Pnina Werbner, 345–360. Oxford: Berg.

Hardy, Leslie K. 1983. *An Exploration of the Career Histories of Leading Female Nurses in England and Scotland*. PhD thesis, University of Edinburgh.

Howell, Jessica, Anne Marie Rafferty, and Anna Snaith. 2011. (Author)ity Abroad: The Life Writing of Colonial Nurses. *International Journal of Nursing Studies* 48 (9): 1155–1162.

Hunte, Eleane I. 2009. *The Unsung Nightingales: The Development of Nursing in Barbados 1844–2000*. St. Michael: E.I. Hunte.

Olwig, Karen Fog. 1993. *Global Culture, Island Identity*. Reading: Harwood Academic Publishers.

———. 2010. Cosmopolitan Traditions: Caribbean Perspectives. *Social Anthropology* 18: 417–424.

———. 2015. Migrating for a Profession: Becoming a Caribbean Nurse in Post-WWII Britain. *Identities: Global Studies in Culture and Power* 22 (3): 258–272.

———. 2017. Female Immigration and the Ambivalence of Dirty Care Work: Caribbean Nurses in Imperial Britain. *Ethnography* 19 (1): 44–62.

Salazar, Noel B. 2011. The Power of Imagination in Transnational Mobilities. *Identities. Global Studies in Culture and Power* 18 (6): 576–598.

Williams, Fiona. 2010. Migration and Care: Themes, Concepts and Challenges. Review Article. *Social Policy and Society* 9 (3): 385–396.

Wilson, Peter. 1973. *Crab Antics: The Social Anthropology of English Speaking Negro Societies of the Caribbean*. New Haven: Yale University Press.

Wingfield, Howard. 2003. *The Workhouse and Hospital at Hillingdon (Middlesex) 1744–1967*. The Hillingdon Hospital NHS Trust. https://www.thh.nhs.uk/documents/_About/historyfinal.pdf. Accessed February 18, 2017.

CHAPTER 4

Time at Sea, Time on Land: Temporal Horizons of Rescue and Refuge in the Mediterranean and Europe

Naor Ben-Yehoyada

INTRODUCTION

The international news cycle over the past five summers (2013–2017) has brought reports from the Mediterranean on a weekly basis, yet this recent international attention focuses on a process that started almost two decades ago. Since the creation of the European Union and its unified border regime, people trying to enter the continent aimed for Europe's southern shores. During the first five months of 2016, 1 of every 23 migrants died attempting to complete the Eurobound route in the central Mediterranean.[1] The most famous commentator on the ongoing situation, Pope Francis, christened the Mediterranean "a massive grave" (Traynor 2014).[2] Waves of migration triggered a reinforcement of

---

[1] https://missingmigrants.iom.int/gmdac-data-briefing-%E2%80%93-central-mediterranean-route-deadlier-ever, accessed October 22, 2017.

[2] Earlier, in 2013 Pope Francis chose to conduct his first Pastoral Visitation to the island of Lampedusa, where he decried 'the globalization of indifference' to migrants' deaths at sea.

N. Ben-Yehoyada (✉)
Department of Anthropology, Columbia University, New York, NY, USA

© The Author(s) 2018
P. G. Barber, W. Lem (eds.), *Migration, Temporality, and Capitalism*, https://doi.org/10.1007/978-3-319-72781-3_4

interception attempts. Interception policies deployed more naval vessels at sea, in increasingly large areas. Such interception in turn facilitated and increased migration flows (Ben-Yehoyada 2011).

At first glance, the events in the Aegean Sea and across the Balkans over the summer of 2015 seem like an increase—"unprecedented" as the Frontex report defined it (Frontex Risk Analysis Unit 2016: 8)—in the numbers of irregular migrants. In addressing these issues, advocates, officials and observers have demanded, denied, enacted or judged migration policies under an umbrella of universal hospitality. In this view, whatever the shape taken by Eurobound migration flows, in essence they all impinge on the same contradiction between universal humanity and bounded citizenship, which lies at the core of the European political order (Balibar 2004).[3] Yet while the frequent images of capsized boats adrift and bodies washed ashore have drawn international attention to migrants' plight, the staging of these rescues at sea obscures a set of relationships of different temporal scales—between rescuers and rescued, interceptors and intercepted. These relationships remained mostly untapped until the summer of 2015 and have since arrived at center stage, posing alternative framings for current migration and interdiction.

On 20 August 2015, Barry Malone, an online editor at Al Jazeera English announced that the station "[would] not say Mediterranean 'migrants'" (Malone 2015): "There is no 'migrant' crisis in the Mediterranean. There is a very large number of refugees fleeing unimaginable misery and danger and a smaller number of people trying to escape the sort of poverty that drives some to desperation." While the word 'migration' might have seemed the more politicized companion to the depoliticizing 'mobility' a decade ago, now the debate revolved around whether the same term and its declensions were politicizing enough—whether they did justice to the political aspects of the situation. Meanwhile, the categorical and situational relationship between the two options—refugee vs. migrant, as well as the relationship to others like asylum (seekers), displaced, forced migration—itself came under consideration. Some argued that 'refugee' is a status granted through legal procedure, while others (like the Al Jazeera's piece) claimed so naming a person does not require waiting for legal decision. Some saw the terms as dichotomously

---

The event received global attention (Vatican 2013), which resurfaced after the disaster in Lampedusa three months later.

[3] This has been a running thread of recent writing (Agamben 1998; Mbembe 2003; Fassin 2012; Cabot 2014).

opposed, while others saw one containing the other (Kyriakides 2016; Giudici 2013). In some aspects, this debate echoed an earlier one, which revolved around the question of the proper qualifier for 'migration'—irregular, illegal, clandestine, unauthorized or undocumented, a debate that is unfolding in various European public arenas and media scenes in parallel.[4] For example, the BBC adds this "note on terminology" at the bottom of relevant articles:

> The BBC uses the term 'migrant' to refer to all people on the move who have yet to complete the legal process of claiming asylum. This group includes people fleeing war-torn countries such as Syria, who are likely to be granted refugee status, as well as people who are seeking jobs and better lives, who governments are likely to rule are economic migrants. (*BBC News* 2017)

While the terminological debate had unfolded for a much longer time and in a more general scope (Castles 2003), it was recently triggered by a specific shift of flows and attention, which itself took place in the summer of 2015. Anti-migrant actors sought to depict migrants as driven by "merely" economic reasons, and thus claimed that these should be pushed back (Perraudin 2015). Meanwhile, as the debate about Eurobound people revolved around their motivations—economic or not, such dichotomous considerations did not apply to the EU member states' reasoning. In one example, which was heavily cited, OECD researchers addressed exactly the economic effects of immigration: "In general across OECD countries, the amount that immigrants pay to the state in the form of taxes is more or less balanced by what they get back in benefits" (Keeley 2013). In other words, while less than catastrophic pragmatism was enough to make non-EU citizens unworthy of refuge, the same level of this-worldly rationality did not taint those debating whether or not to grant such refuge. Against that, the decision to use the term "refugees" emphasized that "the overwhelming majority of these people are escaping war" (Malone 2015). Both sides argued that the situation was one of 'crisis'—whether of 'immigration' or of 'refugees'.

In this chapter, I compare two ongoing central scenes of migration—over sea and over land—to reveal how the crux of the current situation resides not in migration as a problem but in the dynamic relationship of migration and its interdiction, specifically in the discrepant temporalities

---

[4] I thank Anne-Christine Trémon for this observation.

(see Introduction) that inform justifications for migration and interdiction. This relationship includes corresponding changes in migration flows, in interception policies and in the framings that politicians, officials, journalists and activists use to understand the situation. Here, I focus on this third dimension: the interplay between the sea of brotherhood and the fields of care.[5] Through this I make several related claims: First, the changes involved a shift not only in number of people but also in kind. Second, the question regarded not only the qualities or characteristics of the persons themselves—migrants or refugees—but also and crucially, the relationship between them and their oft-reluctant hosts. Third, this question therefore permitted a set of relationships of different temporal scopes and their corresponding geopolitical casting orders and potential responsibilities.

To do so, I follow the differences in the framing of migrants' projects between the two routes, which were articulated in 2015. The maritime scene has cast migrants in danger of drowning as the emblems of abstract humanity (Albahari 2015a) and has brought to the fore the obligation of universal hospitality, which requires neither context nor history—'the sea of (abandoned) brotherhood'. On the contrary, the landed Western Balkan route into and across European member states have cast migrants as refugees of war, demanding and meriting (depending on point of view) refuge, aid and hospitality—'the fields of care'; these routes invoked both a context and a history (Kallius et al. 2016). The image of the route itself stretched beyond landfall in Europe and to migrants' paths throughout EU territory. As a result, the obligation that these scenes posed to Europeans and their institutions changed as well: from one of humanitarian benevolence to retributive justice and historical accountability.

This chapter thus seeks to contribute to the volume's articulation of migration's discrepant temporalities an analysis of the tensions and distinctions that the different framings of migration condition. How, I ask, do temporal discrepancies shape the landscapes of migrants' potential ways of action? I address this question in the light of European political cosmology: how does that political cosmology interact with the labor process of migration/mobility on the one hand and with the spatial layout of European Union's shape, on the other? The discrepancies in the question emerge from the two main anthropological setups that circulate regarding the ongoing situation: hospitality and refuge.

---

[5] This chapter continues the argument from my previous two pieces on migration and interception in the central Mediterranean (Ben-Yehoyada 2011, 2016).

Hospitality ritualizes the encounter of host and guest (Pitt-Rivers 2011, 2012; Herzfeld 1987). It is intended to suspend any potential conflict with strangers and replace it with a turn-taking game of honor. In a way, hospitality ritually prohibits equality between host and guest, in the name of their potential equality and reciprocity on a wider temporal scale. As a result, hospitality *turns* equality and reciprocity into what host and guest negotiate. When they do so, they invoke the moral and political on different scales of time and space. Similarly, when people ask and give (or deny) refuge, they invoke notions of reciprocity and potential parity between refugee and would-be protector on different, often shifting scales: as human to human, citizen to citizen, state to state and so on. Yet perhaps because refuge as an institution emphasizes the force involved and the threat avoided, it focuses on the immediate difference in force between refugee-guest and protector-host, with the obligations this relationship entails.

In the current treatments of the situation, hospitality and refuge serve as emblems of two opposing stances regarding migration. The first stance demands universal hospitality regardless of the identity of the person needing it (Shryock 2009). Yet the duration of that hospitality remains temporally and politically elastic. This is mostly because hospitality—as a ritualized setup of political interaction—is supposed to be limited in space and time ("'After forty days', [the Balga Bedouin] say, 'you become one of us'", Shryock 2012: S31), while no such moral demand is framed by the actors who demand it of the European Union or its members. Hence the political power of refuge and protection (Dresch 2012; Dua 2013; Scheele 2015). These terms reside in the same fountain of political imagination from which hospitality comes (Uribe-Uran 2007; Shryock 2009; Candea 2012). Yet in their borrowed form, these terms—refuge and protection—necessarily demand much more stable obligations from the state that extends them (Cabot 2014). And since the bureaucratized borrowed form of 'refuge' demands a justification for granting it as a status, all the considerations that must disappear in the language of 'universal hospitality' come here to the fore. All states are required to grant hospitality to anyone in need regardless of who they are or where they came from. At the same time, a state must consider giving refuge to people who seek it because of who they are and as a result of where they came from (Mann 2016).

While many of the people crossing the Mediterranean and intercepted by naval vessels encounter first the apparatus of 'universal hospitality' at sea and then that of 'refuge' or 'asylum' applications, the different spatio-political layout of routes in the central and eastern Mediterranean foregrounded one of the terms—'universal hospitality' or 'refuge/asylum'—and backgrounded the other, depending on routes. In other words, I suggest we may treat the sets of routes across the central Mediterranean and through Turkey, the Aegean and across the Balkans as two regional constellations in a process of formation. Along these two routes, such a process involved an interaction of cross-border practices and relations with official state or supra-state policies and projects. In this perspective, transnational regions become ever-changing, multiscalar constellations, which are animated by forms of relatedness across difference (conjured up, demanded, debated or rejected). Regions have a specificity that lends itself to an analysis of spatio-temporal complexes and the political imaginaries that they condition (Ben-Yehoyada 2017).

TIME AT SEA

In the ongoing scene of unauthorized migration across the central Mediterranean, boat people's chances at completing their journeys increasingly depend on civilian and military vessels coming to their rescue or, more recently, trying to block such rescue. The temporal discrepancies underlying the dynamics of migration and interception have shaped how boat people's predicament currently unfolds at sea. Since the creation of the European Union and its unified border regime, people trying to enter the continent have aimed for Europe's southern shores. Waves of migration triggered a reinforcement of interception attempts, and interception in turn facilitated and increased migration flows. The dynamics of migration and interception have conditioned a growing overlap between two projects regarding the transnational maritime space of the Mediterranean (Feldman 2011; Andersson 2014). These two projects are the expansion of the EU's de facto sovereignty over European soil and at sea and human rights advocacy for those who try to cross it. Now, sovereignty and human rights may seem opposed political projects; but, together the two have framed the treatment of unauthorized migration *under* universal hospitality and *promoted* the expansion of European interception of seaborne migration. Both the EU and human rights advocates promote a view of universal humanity as a kind of future global order of ubiquitous human rights—an order that is based on panhuman sameness, equality and brotherhood—and one which is yet to be established. This future moral ideal has justified the EU in expanding its control over maritime space under its claim to lead the world in the spread of the same human rights.

To curb clandestine flows, the European Union 'extra-territorialized' border enforcement on 'the high seas' under the umbrella of 'the law of the sea'. The justification for the project also gradually shifted from "the 'fight' against clandestine immigration and terrorism" during the 2000s (Andrade 2010: 312), to the moral obligation to save human lives in danger under the "law of the sea" (Strik 2014). At the same time, human rights advocates use this future ideal to criticize current EU policies as lacking, and the EU as a sort of 'bad host'. As a result, these two conceptual umbrellas gradually 'territorialized' the Mediterranean: they turned it into an abstract space of projected universal rights, individuals in need of care and land-like territorial sovereignty.

For a short while before the onset of the Arab Spring, this set of policies practically emptied the Mediterranean of its (legal) waters, as it were: EU vessels that caught unauthorized migrants before landing in Italy could take them to North African harbors rather than to the Italian shore. Italy and the European Union's border agency justified these "push-back" policies by breaking the hospitality sequence into two parts—rescue and safe harbor. European vessels intercepted migrants' boats under pretense of rescue. But European policies stopped the ramifications of 'universal hospitality' at sea: once the migrants were rescued from drowning, they required no further Italian or European hospitality. This selective application convinced neither Human Rights advocates nor the UN High Commissioner. As a result, in 2012 the European Court of Human Rights condemned Italian and EU "push-back" policies. To do so, the court prolonged the hospitality sequence from the moment of encounter at sea to the relationship and obligation it triggered. Interception brought migrants under Italian jurisdiction, and Italian obligation applied from that moment onwards (Ben-Yehoyada 2016). Refuge entailed hospitality.

A series of disasters at sea, most notably the Lampedusa migrant shipwreck in October 2013, brought the Italian government to deploy a relatively autonomous interception operation in the central Mediterranean, titled *Mare Nostrum* (Albahari 2016). The operation lasted for a year and transformed at the end of October 2014 into a renewed EU-wide Frontex-led operation, *Triton*. Since the end of the *Mare Nostrum* operation in October 2014, the migrants' fate latched onto the rhythmic activities of the seafarers who spotted their boats. The temporal horizons underlying both the moralizing calls to save lives at sea and the postulations of states' and unions' political exigencies fixed the oscillating rhythm of search and rescue and, as a result, of boat people's survival chances. The gradual attention to lives lost at sea has oriented European interception policies seemingly towards an eschatological consideration of the global reach of human rights. At the same time, intra-European institutional debates have paced the changes in these policies according to segmentary dynamics which the European Union itself undergoes, among member states and, more recently, with some non-state and transnational organizations as well.

No More Time at Sea

The reconstruction of the course of events in this segmentary dynamics goes beyond the scope of this chapter.[6] Instead, I will demonstrate how the current situation (summer 2017), though very different in shape, presents a recognizable variation on the same themes. Until recently, migrants encountered two kinds of seafarers: civilian, dissuaded by themselves and by European policies from rescuing migrant vessels in distress; and military, whose standing orders condition rescue upon the possibility of 'pushing back' those intercepted to non-European shores. In the summer of 2107, after the two main rivals in Libya signed a cease-fire accord (Wintour and Stephen 2017), the Italian Navy was set to begin patrols inside Libyan territorial waters (Balmer 2017). Two other kinds of vessels have been navigating the southern parts of the central Mediterranean: NGO-operated vessels that rescue boats carrying migrants (Pezzani and Heller 2017), and European far-right organizations like the French-based group *Génération identitaire* (GI), attempting to stop or interfere with rescue NGO activities (Hakim 2017). These recent developments make the central Mediterranean migration route similar to the situation along the US–Mexico border in terms of the non-governmental organization mobilizing for or against the crossings (Magana 2008; Mezzadra and Neilson 2013). Early in August, deeper interactions emerged between these two opposing groups. In early August, the Public Prosecutor of the Province of Trapani (in Sicily) arrested the ship *Iuventa* of the NGO *Jugend Rettet* (one of five such vessels; D'Amato 2017). An undercover police officer onboard had allegedly documented at least one case in which the *Iuventa* crew communicated and cooperated with migrant smugglers at sea (Palladino 2017). However, it soon turned out that the information was provided by people associated with the far-right organization and its ship, the C-Star. Several days later, Tunisian fishermen in

---

[6] See the reports by Forensic Oceanography (Pezzani and Heller 2013, 2016, 2017).

Zarzis, close to the Libyan border, prevented the same C-Star, "racist criminal migrant-hunters", from docking in their port (AFP 2017).[7]

Through a renewed agreement with Libya, Italy and the European Union have reestablished their attempt "to empty the Mediterranean of its (legal) waters."[8] As with the Berlusconi–Gaddafi 2009 agreement, now a European country has taken the steps necessary to reduce boat people's capacity to demand refuge on the high seas.[9] And it is exactly this attempt to empty the sea-stretch between Libya and Italy from any protection-inducing space that explains the vigor with which the same Italian government is now seeking to curb NGO rescue operations in the same waters. Since Italian vessels can return intercepted boats to Libyan ports, NGO vessels are the only ones conducting a concerted effort to save people and, eventually, bring them to European shores.

Time on Land

The primacy of the Mediterranean in the debate about Eurobound migration continued until the spring of 2015. Since June of that year, international news cycles during the summer have hosted two kinds of images from around Europe and the Mediterranean. The example of the first kind of image—perhaps the most infamous—was of the small body of Aylan Kurdi, from the Kurdish town of Kobani in Syria, on the shore near Bodrum, on the southwestern Turkish coast.[10] The other was of protests, marches and occupations by migrants—many of whom had survived the

---

[7] The call to stop the ship from berthing in Zarzis read on Twitter: https://twitter.com/MadjidFalastine/status/894134880401063937.

[8] https://www.hrw.org/news/2009/06/09/italy/libya-gaddafi-visit-celebrates-dirty-deal, accessed October 22, 2017.

[9] This is the concern that the European Commissioner for Human Rights raised in his letter to the Italian Minister of the Interior; https://www.coe.int/en/web/commissioner/-/commissioner-seeks-clarifications-over-italy-s-maritime-operations-in-libyan-territorial-waters, accessed October 22, 2017.

[10] The image circulated on Wednesday, 2 September 2015, the day it was taken. Three-year-old Aylan Kurdi died together with is mother and 5-year-old brother when their boat capsized between the coast near Bodrum and the Greek island of Kos (Smith 2015): "Greek authorities, coping with what has become the biggest migration crisis in living memory, said the boy was among *a group of refugees escaping Islamic State in Syria*" (my emphasis). The shocking images soon became the topic of conversation as much as the event they captured (Elgot 2015; Istanbul and Toronto 2015; Tharoor 2015).

sea-crossing and were now trying to make it out of places like Italy and Hungary and into places like Austria, Germany and France.[11]

At first glance, these two images belong together—both illustrate the plight of migrants and the obligation and responsibility this plight invokes (or should) of Europeans and their institutions. From this perspective, the central role of refugee mobilization on European soil seems like a continuation of the earlier one of scenes from the sea. This is true in two senses and along two temporal sequences. The first sequence is that of the migration route, which often starts at sea and then continues across several borders on land.[12] The second is in the short history of Eurobound migration, where the current attention to refugees is couched in the humanitarian terms that have accompanied the process throughout. Presented together, these two types of images depict the current situation as a quantitative, if unprecedented, intensification of the 'problem' of migration, a problem which is in essence the same problem.

Yet this view of continuity is misleading. The events of the 2017 summer and autumn introduced a significant change in the dynamics of Eurobound migration over the last decade—a change of not just quantity but kind. The first evident change is that the attention of European authorities and public opinion has turned from a focus on the sea to a combined focus on the Mediterranean and the Western Balkan route. This change in attention is partly explained by the shift in the routes themselves and in part by interception and interdiction efforts.[13] The severity of the perceived threat to European integrity emerged when the German and Turkish governments asked NATO to deploy ships to interdict the migration route in the Aegean in February 2016, lasting until October that year, when it morphed into Operation Sophia (Zhukov 2016).[14]

The second change in the dynamics of Eurobound migration is that the route is considered as ending not upon arrival on EU soil but at the last EU stop in the migrants' projected voyage. The showdown around the Hungary–Austria border, for example, occurred not on the external border of the EU but along that between two member states. This has to do

---

[11] The action that came to be known as 'the march of hope' began on Friday, 4 September, and immediately made the news cycle (Henley and Agencies 2015).

[12] The route across the Aegean and then the Balkan states requires Frontex to count migrants twice—a cause for critique and debate (Frenzen 2015).

[13] See the centrality of that route in the last quarterly report, for example on pages 8–9 (Frontex Risk Analysis Unit 2015).

[14] See also NATO's annual report 2016, p. 53.

with more than geographical difference. Migrants (including applicants for refuge) arriving in Italy have for years declared their wish to continue to countries like Germany and France. Nevertheless, their problem was considered resolved once they were rescued at sea, before their arrival on EU soil—therefore dismissing whatever further goals they might have as irrelevant. Of the various explanations I've heard people in and around Sicily offered for this difference, the two that stood out were that migrants in the Balkan Route were framed as Syrians, that is, Middle Eastern (and even possibly Christians), whereas the emblematic image of migrants in the central Mediterranean route is of sub-Saharan Africans.

Whatever the explanation for this difference, the resulting third change is in the framing of migrants' projects between the two routes: whereas the overarching framing for addressing the Mediterranean situation is that of "saving lives",[15] the paramount scheme regarding trans-Balkans migrants has emerged as the 'refugee crisis' and migrants themselves were often called 'Syrian refugees' (e.g., Tharoor 2015; Albahari 2015b; Chrisafis 2015; Chrisafis and Agencies 2015).

Finally, these differences in the temporal and spatial framing of migration between the central Mediterranean and the Western Balkan routes culminate in the different role of context and history in their treatments. The maritime scene has cast migrants in danger of drowning as emblems of abstract humanity and has brought to the obligation of universal hospitality to the forefront; the demand for action this invokes requires no context or history. Against this horizon of universality, the landed routes into and across European member states have migrants as refugees of war. This framing invokes a different temporal and spatial scheme. The story of migration that it tells includes both a context and a history. In this history, European institutions appear not only as potential saviors or protectors, but also as responsible for the causes for refugees' plight. When advocates, journalists and activists emphasize the wars in Afghanistan, Iraq and Syria, they set the migrant predicament on a spatio-temporal stage that relates European citizens and institutions to those migrants beyond the moment of welcome or trespass. This relationship precedes the moment of rescue,

---

[15] This framing surfaced during 2011 and then stabilized as the basis for critique of EU policies in the Mediterranean "disaster of Lampedusa" in October 2013 (Sunderland 2012; Strik 2012, 2014).

protection or mobilization.[16] The obligation it demands is of retributive justice, not humanitarian benevolence.

The invocation of history carries another effect: it discriminates among European states and institutions according to their perceived role in bringing about the catastrophes that triggered refugees' quest. Here the effects of this year's 'refugee crisis' has on the shape of the EU's operation differ most clearly from those of Mediterranean operations over the last several years. The gradual framing of interception at sea as saving migrants from drowning had a consolidating effect on EU operations. The events of the summer and fall of 2015 seem to have had a reverse effect, at least initially: the political accounting that we are witnessing has opened numerous fronts within the territory and the structure of the EU.

We should hardly expect political office holders to spell out the connections between Euro-American interventions in Afghanistan, Iraq and Syria and refugees' current plight and direction (it is much easier to blame ISIS). Nor does it take a stretch of the historical imagination to see that imperialism, colonialism and capitalism could potentially perform a similar contextualizing work—to link the chains of migrants' preset lives with the past atrocities wrought on their countries by European powers. Yet in the current state of historical political accounting, this is not the case: in this respect, most people start counting at around the year 2001. At the same time, these officials' negotiations over refugee quotas—as during the Brussels summit in late October 2015 (Chrisafis 2015)—imply exactly this temporal and spatial connection between the recent past, the ongoing present and the demand for actions in the future.

References

AFP. 2017. Des Pêcheurs Tunisiens Prêts À Bloquer L'arrivée D'un Navire de Militants Anti-Migrants. *Libération*, August 6, 2017. http://www.liberation.fr/planete/2017/08/06/des-pecheurs-tunisiens-prets-a-bloquer-l-arrivee-d-un-navire-de-militants-anti-migrants_1588459.

Agamben, Giorgio. 1998. *Homo Sacer: Sovereign Power and Bare Life*. Translated by Daniel Heller-Roazen. Meridian. Stanford, CA: Stanford University Press.

[16] This framing has appeared on various platforms (*The Guardian* 2015; "Who Is Responsible for the Refugee Crisis in Europe?" n.d.; "Europe's Refugee Crisis Isn't Only About Syria" n.d.; "The Iraq War: The Root of Europe's Refugee Crisis–Al Jazeera English" n.d.; "Refugee Crisis in Europe Exposes Asylum Policy Shortcomings–SPIEGEL ONLINE" n.d.).

Albahari, Maurizio. 2015a. *Crimes of Peace: Mediterranean Migrations at the World's Deadliest Border.* Philadelphia, PA: University of Pennsylvania Press.
———. 2015b. Europe's Refugee Crisis. *Anthropology Today* 31 (5): 1–2. https://doi.org/10.1111/1467-8322.12196.
———. 2016. After the Shipwreck: Mourning and Citizenship in the Mediterranean, Our Sea. *Social Research: An International Quarterly* 83 (2): 275–294.
Andersson, Ruben. 2014. *Illegality, Inc.: Clandestine Migration and the Business of Bordering Europe.* Oakland, CA: University of California Press.
Andrade, Paula García. 2010. "Extraterritorial Strategies To Tackle Irregular Immigration By Sea: A Spanish Perspective." In Extraterritorial Immigration Control, edited by B. Ryan and V. Mitsilegas, 305–40. Martinus Nijhoff Publishers.
Balibar, Etienne. 1942–2004. *We, the People of Europe?: Reflections on Transnational Citizenship.* English Translation/Transnation. Princeton, NJ: Princeton University Press.
Balmer, Crispian. 2017. Italy Begins Naval Mission to Help Libya Curb Migrant Flows. *Reuters*, August 2. http://www.reuters.com/article/us-europe-migrants-italy-libya-idUSKBN1AI1JC.
BBC News. 2017. Tunisia Fishermen Prevent Far-Right Ship from Docking. August 6, sec. Africa. http://www.bbc.com/news/world-africa-40846151.
Ben-Yehoyada, Naor. 2011. The Clandestine Central Mediterranean Passage. *Middle East Report* 266: 18–23.
———. 2016. 'Follow Me, and I Will Make You Fishers of Men': The Moral and Political Scales of Migration in the Central Mediterranean. *Journal of the Royal Anthropological Institute* 22 (1): 183–202. https://doi.org/10.1111/1467-9655.12340.
———. 2017. *The Mediterranean Incarnate: Region Formation Between Sicily and Tunisia Since World War II.* Chicago: University of Chicago Press.
Cabot, Heath. 2014. *On the Doorstep of Europe: Asylum and Citizenship in Greece*, Ethnography of Political Violence. 1st ed. Philadelphia, PA: University of Pennsylvania Press.
Candea, Matei. 2012. Derrida En Corse? Hospitality as Scale-Free Abstraction. *Journal of the Royal Anthropological Institute* 18 (June): S34–S48. https://doi.org/10.1111/j.1467-9655.2012.01759.x.
Castles, Stephen. 2003. Towards a Sociology of Forced Migration and Social Transformation. *Sociology* 37 (1): 13–34. https://doi.org/10.1177/0038038503037001384.
Chrisafis, Angelique. 2015. European Leaders Discuss Refugee Crisis at Tense Brussels Summit. *The Guardian*, October 25, 2015, sec. World News. http://www.theguardian.com/world/2015/oct/25/european-leaders-discuss-refugee-crisis-at-tense-brussels-summit.

Chrisafis, Angelique, and Agencies. 2015. EU and Balkans Agree Plan for 100,000 Places in Reception Centres for Refugees. *The Guardian*, October 26, sec. World News. http://www.theguardian.com/world/2015/oct/26/eu-and-balkan-leaders-agree-migration-plan.

D'Amato, Alessandro. 2017. Iuventa: l'ONG Tedesca E Le Foto Degli Accordi Con Gli Scafisti. *neXt Quotidiano*, Blog, August 3. https://www.nextquotidiano.it/iuventa-jugend-rettet-ong/.

Dresch, Paul. 2012. Aspects of Non-State Law: Early Yemen and Perpetual Peace. In *Legalism*, ed. Paul Dresch and Hannah Skoda, 145–172. Oxford: Oxford University Press. http://www.oxfordscholarship.com/view/10.1093/acprof:oso/9780199664269.001.0001/acprof-9780199664269-chapter-6.

Dua, Jatin. 2013. A Sea of Trade and a Sea of Fish: Piracy and Protection in the Western Indian Ocean. *Journal of Eastern African Studies* 7 (2): 353–370. https://doi.org/10.1080/17531055.2013.776280.

Elgot, Jessica. 2015. Family of Syrian Boy Washed Up on Beach Were Trying to Reach Canada. *The Guardian*, September 3, sec. World News. http://www.theguardian.com/world/2015/sep/03/refugee-crisis-syrian-boy-washed-up-on-beach-turkey-trying-to-reach-canada.

Europe's Refugee Crisis Isn't Only About Syria. n.d. *Foreign Policy*, Blog. https://foreignpolicy.com/2015/09/18/europes-refugee-crisis-isnt-only-about-syria-iraq-afghans/. Accessed November 7, 2015.

Fassin, Didier. 2012. *Humanitarian Reason: A Moral History of the Present*. Berkeley: University of California Press.

Feldman, Gregory. 2011. *The Migration Apparatus: Security, Labor, and Policymaking in the European Union*. Palo Alto, CA: Stanford University Press.

Frenzen, Niels. 2015. Clarification of Frontex Data On Persons Detected at EU External Borders – Includes Significant Double Counting. *MIGRANTS AT SEA*, Blog, October 14. http://migrantsatsea.org/2015/10/14/clarification-of-frontex-data-on-persons-detected-at-eu-external-borders-includes-significant-double-counting/.

Frontex Risk Analysis Unit. 2015. *Risk Analysis Network Quarterly Report, Quarter 2 – April–June 2015*. 14851/2015. Warsaw: Frontex, European Agency for the Management of Operational Cooperation at the External Borders of the Member States of the European Union. http://frontex.europa.eu/assets/Publications/Risk_Analysis/FRAN_Q2_2015_final.pdf.

———. 2016. *"Annual Risk Analysis." 2499/2016*. Warsaw: Frontex, European Agency for the Management of Operational Cooperation at the External Borders of the Member States of the European Union. http://frontex.europa.eu/assets/Publications/Risk_Analysis/Annual_Risk_Analysis_2014.pdf.

Giudici, Daniela. 2013. From 'Irregular Migrants' to Refugees and Back: Asylum Seekers' Struggle for Recognition in Contemporary Italy. *Journal of Mediterranean Studies* 22 (1): 61–86.

Hakim, Yalda. 2017. Migrant Crisis: 'Hipster Right' Group Trying to Stop Rescue Ships. *BBC News*, July 8, sec. Europe. http://www.bbc.com/news/world-europe-40505337.

Henley, Emma Graham-Harrison Jon, and Agencies. 2015. Hungary to Take Thousands of Refugees to Austrian Border by Bus. *The Guardian*, September 4, sec. World News. http://www.theguardian.com/world/2015/sep/04/hundreds-refugees-march-austria-budapest-hungary-syrians.

Herzfeld, Michael. 1987. 'As in Your Own House': Hospitality, Ethnography, and the Stereotype of Mediterranean Society. In *Honor and Shame and the Unity of the Mediterranean*, A Special Publication of the American Anthropological Association; No. 22, ed. David D. Gilmore, 75–89. Washington, DC: American Anthropological Association.

Istanbul, Joe Parkinson in, and David George-Cosh in Toronto. 2015. Image of Drowned Syrian Boy Echoes Around World. *Wall Street Journal*, September 3, sec. World. http://www.wsj.com/articles/image-of-syrian-boy-washed-up-on-beach-hits-hard-1441282847.

Kallius, Annastiina, Daniel Monterescu, and Prem Kumar Rajaram. 2016. Immobilizing Mobility: Border Ethnography, Illiberal Democracy, and the Politics of the 'Refugee Crisis' in Hungary. *American Ethnologist* 43 (1): 25–37. https://doi.org/10.1111/amet.12260.

Keeley, Brian. 2013. The Impact of Immigrants – It's Not What You Think. *OECD Insights Blog*, June 13. http://oecdinsights.org/2013/06/13/the-impact-of-immigrants-its-not-what-you-think/.

Kyriakides, Christopher. 2016. Words Don't Come Easy: Al Jazeera's Migrant–refugee Distinction and the European Culture of (Mis)trust. *Current Sociology*, August. https://doi.org/10.1177/0011392116658089.

Magana, Rocio. 2008. *Bodies on the Line: Life, Death, and Authority on the Arizona-Mexico Border*. PhD dissertation, The University of Chicago, Illinois. http://search.proquest.com.ezp-prod1.hul.harvard.edu/dissertations/docview/304406567/abstract?accountid=11311.

Malone, Barry. 2015. Why Al Jazeera Will Not Say Mediterranean 'Migrants'. *Reporter's Notebookwar & Conflict*, Blog, August 20. http://www.aljazeera.com/blogs/editors-blog/2015/08/al-jazeera-mediterranean-migrants-150820082226309.html.

Mann, Itamar. 2016. *Humanity at Sea: Maritime Migration and the Foundations of International Law*. Cambridge: Cambridge University Press.

Mbembe, Achille. 2003. Necropolitics. *Public Culture* 15 (1): 11–40. https://doi.org/10.1215/08992363-15-1-11.

Mezzadra, Sandro, and Brett Neilson. 2013. *Border as Method, or, the Multiplication of Labor*. Durham, NC: Duke University Press.

Palladino, Andrea. 2017. I Magistrati Sulla Nave Fermata. *Famiglia Cristiana*, August 3. http://m.famigliacristiana.it/articolo/iuventa-la-nave-fermatadella-ong-tedesca-ma-il-gip-commenta-ma-anche-le-ong-militanti-non-sono-criminali.htm.

Perraudin, Frances. 2015. 'Marauding' Migrants Threaten Standard of Living, Says Foreign Secretary. *The Guardian*, August 10, sec. UK News. http://www.theguardian.com/uk-news/2015/aug/09/african-migrants-threaten-eu-standard-living-philip-hammond.

Pezzani, Lorenzo, and Charles Heller. 2013. *Addendum to the "Report on the Left-To-Die Boat"*. Forensic Oceanography. http://www.forensic-architecture.org/case/left-die-boat/.

———. 2016. Death by Rescue. https://deathbyrescue.org.

———. 2017. Blaming the Rescuers: Criminalising Solidarity, Re-Enforcing Deterrence. In *Forensic Oceanography, Forensic Architecture agency*. Goldsmiths: University of London. https://blamingtherescuers.org/.

Pitt-Rivers, Julian Alfred. 2011. The Place of Grace in Anthropology. *HAU: Journal of Ethnographic Theory* 1 (1): 423–450.

———. 2012. The Law of Hospitality. *HAU: Journal of Ethnographic Theory* 2 (1): 501–517. https://doi.org/10.14318/hau2.1.022.

Refugee Crisis in Europe Exposes Asylum Policy Shortcomings – SPIEGEL ONLINE. n.d. http://www.spiegel.de/international/europe/bild-1051481-894164.html. Accessed September 10, 2015.

Scheele, Judith. 2015. The Values of 'Anarchy': Moral Autonomy Among Tubu-Speakers in Northern Chad. *Journal of the Royal Anthropological Institute* 21 (1): 32–48. https://doi.org/10.1111/1467-9655.12141.

Shryock, Andrew. 2009. Hospitality Lessons: Learning the Shared Language of Derrida and the Balga Bedouin. *Paragraph: The Journal of the Modern Critical Theory Group* 32 (1): 32.

———. 2012. Breaking Hospitality Apart: Bad Hosts, Bad Guests, and the Problem of Sovereignty. *Journal of the Royal Anthropological Institute* 18 (June): S20–S33. https://doi.org/10.1111/j.1467-9655.2012.01758.x.

Smith, Helena. 2015. Shocking Images of Drowned Syrian Boy Show Tragic Plight of Refugees. *The Guardian*, September 2, sec. World News. http://www.theguardian.com/world/2015/sep/02/shocking-image-of-drowned-syrian-boy-shows-tragic-plight-of-refugees.

Strik, Tineke. 2012. *"Lives Lost in the Mediterranean Sea: Who Is Responsible?" 12895*. Parliamentary Assembly, Council of Europe. http://assembly.coe.int/ASP/XRef/X2H-DW-XSL.asp?fileid=18095&lang=en.

———. 2014. *"The 'Left-to-Die Boat': Actions and Reactions." 13532*. Parliamentary Assembly, Council of Europe.

Sunderland, Judith. 2012. *Hidden Emergency – Migrant Deaths in the Mediterranean*. New York, NY: Human Rights Watch. http://www.hrw.org/node/109445.

Tharoor, Ishaan. 2015. A Dead Baby Becomes the Most Tragic Symbol Yet of the Mediterranean Refugee Crisis. *The Washington Post*, September 2. https://

www.washingtonpost.com/news/worldviews/wp/2015/09/02/a-dead-baby-becomes-the-most-tragic-symbol-yet-of-the-mediterranean-refugee-crisis/.

The Guardian. 2015. The Guardian View on the Refugee Crisis: Much More Must Be Done, and Not Just by the UK. September 3, sec. Comment Is Free. http://www.theguardian.com/commentisfree/2015/sep/03/the-guardian-view-on-the-refugee-crisis-much-more-must-be-done-and-not-just-by-the-uk.

The Iraq War: The Root of Europe's Refugee Crisis – Al Jazeera English. n.d. http://www.aljazeera.com/blogs/middleeast/2015/09/iraq-war-root-europe-refugee-crisis-150908151855527.html. Accessed November 7, 2015.

Traynor, Ian. 2014. Pope Francis Attacks EU Over Treatment of Immigrants. The Guardian, November 25, sec. World News. http://www.theguardian.com/world/2014/nov/25/pope-francis-elderly-eu-lost-bearings.

Uribe-Uran, Victor M. 2007. 'Iglesia Me Llamo': Church Asylum and the Law in Spain and Colonial Spanish America. Comparative Studies in Society and History 49 (2): 446–472.

Vatican. 2013. Visit of Holy Father Francis to Lampedusa. La Santa Sede, July 8. http://www.vatican.va/holy_father/francesco/travels/2013/papa-francesco-lampedusa-20130708_en.html.

Who Is Responsible for the Refugee Crisis in Europe? n.d. Global Research. http://www.globalresearch.ca/who-is-responsible-for-the-refugee-crisis-in-europe/5473724. Accessed November 7, 2015.

Wintour, Patrick, and Chris Stephen. 2017. Libyan Rival Leaders Agree to Ceasefire After Macron-Hosted Talks. The Guardian, July 25, sec. World News. http://www.theguardian.com/world/2017/jul/25/france-raises-hopes-of-deal-between-libyan-rival-factions.

Zhukov, Yuri M. 2016. NATO's Mediterranean Mission. Foreign Affairs, February 21. https://www.foreignaffairs.com/articles/europe/2016-02-21/natos-mediterranean-mission.

CHAPTER 5

Conjunctural Reversals, Capital Accumulation and Family Adjustments in Chinese Trans-Pacific Migration

Anne-Christine Trémon

Chinese migration to the Pacific, the Americas and the colonies of Southeast Asia between the mid nineteenth century and the 1930s was one of the largest in human history. As part of this wave, around 5000 immigrants, all originating from Guangdong province, arrived in the Etablissements Français de l'Océanie (today, French Polynesia) between 1890 and 1930.[1] The majority settled on Tahiti, where they formed an urban community in the capital Papeete, but they also migrated to the rural districts and to other islands. They were registered and given a

---

[1] This was the name given in 1881 to the French colony that was composed of the Windward Islands (Tahiti and Moorea) and the Tuamotu and Marquesas archipelagos. The Leeward Islands, the Gambier and the Australs were annexed in the following decades. The colony was transformed into an Overseas Territory in 1946 and renamed French Polynesia in 1957.

A.-C. Trémon (✉)
Laboratoire d'anthropologie culturelle et sociale, Institut des sciences sociales, Université de Lausanne, Lausanne, Switzerland

© The Author(s) 2018
P. G. Barber, W. Lem (eds.), *Migration, Temporality, and Capitalism*, https://doi.org/10.1007/978-3-319-72781-3_5

number upon arrival. These registers show that by 1948 only about half of them had remained in the colony.

France did not apply *jus soli* (citizenship based on birth) in its colonies and overseas territories, which formed a regime of exception within the French Republic.[2] The children of Chinese immigrants born in the colony thus remained Chinese. After immigration came to a halt in the mid-1930s, the Chinese population continued to grow internally, reaching around 6000 in the 1960s. A change occurred only in 1973 when all Chinese were granted French citizenship in accordance with a decree that extended French citizenship law to French overseas territories. This happened just before the reopening of China in 1979 and when France started to grant increasing political autonomy to its overseas territories. The historical period considered in this chapter is marked by a de-hegemonization of the Western-dominated world-system (Friedman 1994), from a situation where Chinese immigrants migrated into a French colonial society to one in which their third and fourth-generation descendants are now members of an ethnic minority in a French overseas territory that has a large degree of autonomy.

Historian Gérard Noiriel, in his work on immigration in France (1988), has offered a comparative model in terms of a growth/crisis alternation that has been slightly refined but remains uncontested (Bruno et al. 2006). At least since the end of the nineteenth century, the French state has always asserted economic liberalism at the same time as it has sought to control the access of aliens to the labor market. In periods of economic recession and political crisis, such as the 1930s to the 1940s, and 1970s to the 1980s, regulations of entry, residence and labor tighten. The colonial context differs in some aspects, yet the policies towards Chinese immigrants and their descendants conform to this periodization in terms of both the control of immigration flows and the granting of citizenship. In the 1930s, the relation between economic crisis and the restrictions brought to policies towards aliens is very clear, as will be shown. From 1960 to the 1970s, in the general context of the crisis of hegemony linked to decolonization, France sought to maintain its control over Tahiti and therefore legally and culturally assimilated the Chinese minority living in this geostrategic territory.[3]

---

[2] Colonies were ruled administratively, rather than legislatively, by simple decrees. In the decrees applicable to the colony, single and double *jus soli* contained within the French citizenship Code (as formulated in the laws of 26 June 1889, 10 August 10 1927, and the 1945 Code) were absent.

[3] The decision taken in 1974 by the French government to halt immigration was less the result of economic slowdown, which started only in 1975 in France, than of the movement

In this chapter, I examine how Chinese migrants and their descendants in colonial Tahiti (today French Polynesia) have mobilized kin transnationally in response to fluctuations both in legal and political immigration regimes and in economic opportunities over several generations, to accumulate capital.[4] I call these practices 'flexible kinship'. Transnational studies (Glick Schiller et al. 1992; Rouse 1991; Smith and Guarnizo 1998; Portes et al. 1999) have been critiqued on several key grounds. In particular, they have been taken to task for overemphasizing a rupture with the past (Waldinger and Fitzgerald 2004; Morawska 2001; Friedman 2004) and for a lack of clarity in defining the specific features of transnationalism. Waldinger and Fitzgerald suggest an alternative approach that emphasizes the interactions of migrants with states: "*states* make migrations international by bounding territories and defining the nations they seek to enfold" (emphasis in original). However, their interests remain in the "constitutive aspects of movement across borders" (2004: 1188).

Yet, examining the intersection between state policies of nation-building and migrant practices involves more than looking at population movement. On the one hand, flexible kinship examines the practices of relocation of family members in different places, motivated by the expected benefits of this varied dispersion. But on the other hand, it encompasses a second set of practices that determine, not their location in space, but their legal status (although one can imply the other). Among the Chinese in French Polynesia, it was, in particular, a matter of legal recognition of family members that amounted to a difference in legal status, that is, in citizenship. As we will see, this practice was especially salient when it came to daughters, who by not being legally recognized, became French nationals. These practices were transnational in that they exploited the legal spaces that articulate birth (and thus kinship) and citizenship, since the latter results largely from filiation.[5] Transnational practices, then, are not

of decolonization in the 1960s (Laurens 2008).

[4] The material presented here is largely drawn from my doctoral research (2000–2005) and two follow-up visits in 2008 and 2013. It also includes a few elements from the new project I have been working on since 2011 in one of the villages of origin of the Tahiti Chinese, in Shenzhen, China. In Tahiti, I carried out participant observation, collected archival material (in the colonial archives and the Chinese associations) and conducted over a hundred interviews mainly with second- and third-generation descendants of Chinese immigrants. These open-ended interviews often took the form of personal and family histories (Trémon 2010).

[5] This is obvious in regimes based on *jus sanguinis* (right of blood) but also in those based on *jus soli* (right of the soil or birthright citizenship) (de la Pradelle 1995). The vast majority

necessarily translocal. In making this distinction, the concept of flexible kinship moves beyond the preoccupation within transnational studies with movement or dispersal in space. The shift highlights the importance of addressing practices that involve not just a spatial extension of networks, but also practices that cross legal boundaries within the host locality itself.

These legal manoeuvres are temporal in that they seek to evade constraints and also to accumulate a variety of resources—different kinds of capital—through the exploitation of differentials in regimes of citizenship and economic contexts. Contexts mutate; studying how transnational families are formed and evolve over time requires focusing on temporal *variation* in economic and political constellations shaping the environment for social action (Waldinger and Fitzgerald 2004: 1188). My aim is to show, from the analysis of family trajectories across several generations and an outline of recurrent schemes of practices, how discrepancies between the temporal horizons of individuals and families and economic and political conjunctures have shaped practices of flexible kinship.

Flexible kinship is also an expansion of Aihwa Ong's (1999) notion of 'flexible citizenship', which she describes as "the strategies and effects of mobile managers, technocrats and professionals seeking to both circumvent *and* benefit from different nation-state regimes by selecting different sites for investments, work and family relocation" (1999: 112; emphasis in original). While her conceptualization of 'flexible citizenship' is extremely valuable in highlighting how relations between kin are used strategically for purposes of capital accumulation, it is built upon a view of kinship that is, paradoxically, 'inflexible'. Ong as well as Greenhalgh (1994) and Nonini and Ong (1997) have levelled a much needed critique of the glorification of 'Confucian' capitalism and particularly of the Chinese family firm, showing how this is at once a discourse that masks and a culturalist explanation that overlooks power differentials and the exploitation of family members—particularly younger sons and women. However, while they stress the instrumentalization of Confucian values, they seem to assume that these remain unchallenged. This is at least the impression that one can derive from their evocation of a "long-standing habitus" of family relations (Nonini and Ong 1997: 21), and of a "cultural logics of transnationality" or "Confucian ethics" on which the "family governmentality" is based (Ong 1999: 118). Greenhalgh for her part acknowledges that her focus is "not on women's

of nationals receive French citizenship at birth as a function of filiation.

agency in resisting structures of domination, but on men's agency in creating and reproducing those structures of domination" (1994: 748).

Flexible kinship is meant to emphasize that not only are kinship relations central to the workings of flexible capitalism, but that kinship itself is adjustable. Moreover, not only do these hierarchies bend according to the circumstances, but the flexible uses themselves have further altered them, especially as regards gender. I therefore start from another direction, by looking at kinship from a practical and processual point of view. A practice-based approach looks at kinship as a resource than can be mobilized in larger social fields (Bourdieu 1990). A diachronic approach further allows exploring how family developments result both from the intentions of their members and from the social and economic environment (Bruguière 2002).

The practices of flexible kinship result from and respond to discrepancies between the migrants' own temporalities, that is, their perspectives, life trajectories and family dynamics across generations; and the global temporality of capitalism and hegemonic relations in the world-system, which influences local regimes of citizenship and policies towards migrants and their descendants. I analyze how, over several generations, these practices have served strategies of capital accumulation in response to shifts in immigration policies and citizenship regimes as well as in economic opportunities. I further argue that successive changes and reversals in conjunctures have shaped a habitus that maximizes economic and legal security for families and individuals, especially women.

In the first section I examine the rupture during the Great Depression and its consequences in terms of the arrest of immigration flows and discrimination towards the Chinese. In the second, I consider the familial adjustments in the 1960s resulting from the economic boom, the facilitation of naturalization and assimilation, and tightened French Metropolitan control over the colony. This moment of temporary normalcy was soon challenged by the rise of the Tahitian pro-independence movement and the reopening and mounting hegemony of China. Finally, I indicate how these practices of adjustment have shaped flexible management of family members, visible in a set of practices that continue even though the descendants of migrants are now all French citizens. They are explained by the current political and economic crisis in French Polynesia as much as by the internalization of the possibility of politico-economic reversals as experienced in family histories.

THE RUPTURE OF THE 1930S: ESCAPING DISCRIMINATION

Following a widespread pattern in the history of Chinese migration in the second half of the nineteenth century, the introduction of some 400 contract laborers or 'coolies' in the mid-1860s triggered a larger wave of migration, based on recruitment by the Chinese themselves. From the 1890s, the colonial administration allowed Chinese immigrants to enter the territory freely (rather than on contract) because it considered them as tools for developing the colony without governmental intervention. The Chinese brought labor and capital into a colony in which the native population had sharply decreased during the nineteenth century and attempts at developing a plantation economy had failed (Panoff 1997). The migrants spread from Papeete to the rural districts and other islands, and developed a network of shops based on a system of credit and patron-client relationships (Moench 1963). Although the colonial elite's representatives put pressure on the administration to restrict Chinese immigration and slow down their economic progress, the administration refused, and practiced a 'laissez-faire' politics. The colonial administration viewed the Chinese as an instrument of balance between the native Tahitians, who were not willing to work on colonial plantations, and the elite of Euro-American origin, who increasingly formed an economic oligopoly and expressed demands for a political role beyond the consultative role to which they were confined.

The migrants' goal was to accumulate sufficient economic capital to return home and reconvert it into social and symbolic capital. As "sojourners" (Wang 2000), they kept close connections with their villages in China and often travelled back and forth, until the 1930s. By 1948, only about half of the Chinese who had entered the colony or were born locally had remained.[6] During that period, flexible kinship consisted mainly of spatial localization of family members linked to patterns of immigration and oriented towards the continuation of the family line in China. Several brothers migrated to the same destination, one after the other. It was usually the eldest who opened a shop and then sponsored his younger brothers who, each in turn, worked in the enterprise until they had repaid their ticket and could open their own shop. It was also usually the eldest who was the first to return to the home village in China.

---

[6] Between 1904 (the year when a new count started) and 1948, there were 5404 registered Chinese; 2927 departed, making a net gain of 2477. Among them, about a third were born in the colony.

From the 1920s to the mid-1930s, immigrants also sent back their children to China, mainly their sons. There was a high rate of intermarriage between Chinese men and Tahitian women in the first generation (and with part-Tahitian women in the next generations). Only the big merchants in the urban centers had the means to bring over a Chinese wife. Many who settled in the rural districts and islands spent their entire lives with Polynesian women. From the 1920s to the mid-1930s, first-generation immigrants often sent back one or two of their eldest sons to China, at around the age of 8 or 9, to be raised by the immigrants' parents, elder uncles and/or legitimate wives in China. This was intended to prepare the father's own return, but its main aim was to provide a proper Chinese education, especially for those born from a Tahitian mother. Although my research uncovered a few cases in which daughters were sent back as well, the dominant pattern consisted in sending back sons.

The economic downturn of 1929–1930 led to a change in policy towards Chinese migrants at the same time as it modified, by force of circumstances, the behaviour of migrants in terms of land acquisition. Until then, buying additional land in their home village was one of the migrants' aims, rather than acquiring land in the host country. In 1927, the number of Chinese landowners was only an estimated 250. The global market crash in the early 1930s followed a boom (in vanilla, especially) in the 1920s, during which Tahitian clients had accumulated huge debts towards the Chinese shopkeepers. This led to several bankruptcies of large exporting firms, owing to the pyramidal system of credit; this, in turn, led Chinese shopkeepers to reclaim debts to their clients. Insolvent clients therefore started repaying their debts with land. The equilibrium the colonial administration had so far preserved threatened to collapse. It is thus no coincidence that in the following years the colonial administration took two measures aimed at restricting the economic power of the Chinese. In 1931, a decree imposed a duty to all people "of Chinese race exercising a commerce, industry, or profession" to pay an additional tax on a basic trading license.[7] A 1932 decree subjected any transfer of real estate to administrative authorization—in principle without any distinction as to citizenship or status, but colonial correspondence makes clear that this regulation targeted the Chinese. In the following years, the administration also took several measures to halt Chinese immigration.

---

[7] The use of the term 'race' is normally absent from French law; this is one of many examples of France's derogatory and differentiating policies in its colonies.

These measures led to a slowdown in transnational flow and mobility, but they entered in conflict with the changing orientations of the migrants. Because of the Japanese invasion of China in 1937, and later the Chinese civil war and the loss of their savings in the economic crisis, Chinese migrants started conceiving of their presence in Tahiti less as a temporary sojourn then as an undetermined period of residence without a clear plan for return to China.

Not only did they stop sending their children back to the homeland, but the Chinese started devising strategies that would allow their children to escape discriminatory taxes and prohibition on land acquisition. From the 1930s onwards, and well into the 1950s, they frequently used fraudulent means—such as false names—to operate businesses and buy land. Along with these subterfuges they registered shops or lands in the name of daughters, and more frequently wives, who held French citizenship. Whether the mother was Tahitian or Chinese, couples were not legally married according to French civil law, and therefore the only way to prove filiation was by the legal recognition of one's children. In almost every family history I collected, I found one or several second-generation female children (and even all in some families) whose parents had not legally recognized them at birth. They thus gained French citizenship. When the father was Chinese and the mother Tahitian, only the mother recognized these daughters; in families with a Chinese father and mother, parents asked friends or neighbours to recognize these daughters in their place, or with the note "father and mother unknown". The non-recognition of a daughter so as to allow her to hold French citizenship acted as the equivalent of a dowry—in legal rather than economic capital. Indeed, daughters born to Chinese families but holding French citizenship were in high demand. This explains why such a practice was more common among the poor majority than in wealthy families, whose fathers could endow their daughters in cash.

In most situations, wives were used as 'straw-women' to buy land or register shops. The history of the Hong[8] family is interesting in this regard. This family arrived among the last wave of migrants, in the mid-1930s. Two of the eight children were daughters; the eldest was married away as the family transited through Malaysia. The father earned a meager salary

---

[8] All patronyms and first names cited in this text are fictitious. They reflect the original names' Chinese, Tahitian or French consonance.

as a teacher at the Kuomintang school. The two eldest sons started working when they were 12 years old as odd-job boys in a shop owned by Americans. It was they who initially provided the family's livelihood. Their work allowed the family to pay for the schooling of their younger brothers in a French Catholic school after they had attended a Chinese school. (All urban Chinese families paid for these extra schooling years as soon as they could, because mastery of the French language was considered indispensable for business and dealings with the administration.) The fourth son and last daughter worked for the third son, who had managed to open a shop with the help of the elder brother's income. At that time, the family economy was inclusive; it had not yet been divided.[9] The income of the third son's shop and the salaries of the two eldest were put together in the family budget, meals were taken together, and each son received a small amount of pocket money for personal expenses. Fabien Hong, the son of the fifth son, explained to me that it was this third brother (and not the eldest) who became the official family leader after their father died, but that he had already been the chief before his father's death: "[He] spoke French better than the two eldest brothers (...) And also because his wife, Amélie, was the only Frenchwoman in the family at that time. And this is how we got the shop license from the trade registry." The shop was named 'Amélie', after her. The family business thus grew around this shop: "Everyone worked in the shop Amélie except the two eldest."

The history of this particular family shows how the general habit of not recognizing girls among the Chinese in Tahiti was part of a larger family strategy, whereby the entire familial workforce was used to achieve economic success by 'investing' in one asset—one particular family member. It also reveals how the family's authority structure changed. The third son took over the role of 'chief' as dispatcher of family income and manager of the company employing his brothers and sister because the trade license was drawn up in the name of his wife, an unrecognized daughter of Chinese immigrants and thus a French citizen. As the Hongs—and many others—tried to escape their difficulties as aliens and obtain maximum profit from their family business, the family's authority structure changed.

---

[9] The 'family', *jia* in Mandarin, has been defined by Myron Cohen as "the group of persons who not only have kin ties to each other, but also a series of claims of one sort or another to the *jia* as an estate" (1976: 59). They can proceed to *fenjia*, family property division. This is the axis around which the family cycle develops (Cohen 1970, 1976).

DISPERSION AND RETURNS: THE NUCLEAR BOOM
AND ACCESS TO FRENCH CITIZENSHIP IN THE 1960S

Although some among the first generation stood out by building fortunes early in the twentieth century, the second and third generations benefited most from the economic opportunities that multiplied in the 1960s. The opening of airlines promoted tourism, and the transfer of France's nuclear testing from decolonizing Algeria to French Polynesia in 1962, was accompanied by massive investments and the growth in consumption of imported goods due to the increased presence of French soldiers, civil servants and salaried employment. While the first generation of Chinese immigrants included many shopkeepers and farmers, their children turned towards commerce, services and especially imports. It is also during this period that access to French citizenship was first facilitated and then became automatic. There is, therefore, an overall convergence between the descendants of migrants' aims and orientations and the field of political and economic possibilities. I emphasize how seizing these opportunities has both pre-supposed and accelerated family fragmentation and the generalization of conjugal families.

While most of the second generation, particularly girls, had only a Chinese primary education, some could attend private French schools after their Chinese schools, and a very small minority were able to study at high schools and universities abroad. In less wealthy families, only the youngest siblings could go abroad, owing to the elders' work. Thus, in the Hong family, the work of the four elder sons and the daughter paid for the last two sons' studies. They went to France to earn a *baccalauréat* (high school) and higher education diploma. Around the mid-1950s, when the two youngest sons returned from France after completing their studies, the father divided the family estate. Fabien Hong explained:

> The company was overcrowded, and so my grandfather decided to scatter the family. So in family council it was decided that my father, who had learned farming, would go to Brazil, so there, Brazil. My uncle [the last son] was told, 'You go back to France.' And then the family actually split, and the estate was shared. Each one of them left with his share to set up his own business.

Here we see that the Hongs' international dispersion coincided with family division and reflected different types and degrees of investments in each sibling. Such a strategy is a typical response to "the petty accumulation trap" (Nonini 2003, 2005) that Chinese petty capitalists face as a result of demographic reproduction and the pressure which the increase in population puts on small-scale businesses by the principle of equipartibility among sons. The Hong family's division tried to exploit the workforce as much as possible; an inclusive economic unit would have left them 'overpopulated' and underemployed. The dispersion was also meant to enable each to exploit his capacities, especially the two youngest, who held higher degrees and had specific skills. And indeed, both siblings did very well; one, after working as an agronomist in Guyana, came back to Tahiti, where he set up a flourishing import business in agricultural tools and machinery; the other came back to set up a business that imported cars from a major French manufacturer. He eventually became the exclusive supplier of the French army in Tahiti.

The case of the Hongs illustrates how the family development cycle accelerated in this context. This resulted from the decisions that were made in the 1950s and 1960s, once the second generation reached adult age, to proceed to the division of family property in order to maximize opportunities. The economic boom in the early 1960s happened when many second-generation Chinese had become adults or reached maturity and had to take care of their own children's future. This tendency towards fragmentation went against the ideal of the extended family and joint complex of companies, which only some families in Tahiti were able to reach. Several sons of some of the wealthiest families, who had settled in the United States after their studies, started in business by creating U.S.-based import-export or tourism companies in association with their families in Polynesia. But most families had already divided by the time the economic boom would have made such arrangements profitable.

Paradoxically, strategies of geographic dispersion across borders, like that of the Hongs, were soon followed by returns to Tahiti. These returns not only sought profit from the phenomenal economic boom of the 1960s, they also responded to the less stringent naturalization criteria of the period. This issue, which had until then not attracted much interest, became urgent when France established diplomatic ties with the People's Republic of China (PRC) in 1964. The nuclear testing program made the prospect of a Chinese Communist presence in this strategic French overseas territory unacceptable. Indeed, since 1943 the French Polynesian Chinese had been under the legal jurisdiction of the Republic of China (ROC). A consul of the ROC represented them even after China's exile of Taiwan in 1949.

Stories of hardships faced by those who had returned to China at the end of the war, the hostility towards overseas Chinese 'capitalists' (Fitzgerald 1972: 55), and the closing of China's doors after 1949, changed how the Chinese perceived their status in French Polynesia. Beginning as sojourners, they had become permanent residents. This rooting was stronger among second-generation members born in the colony and notably among those of the elite who went to study in France. When sons of the wealthiest Chinese families came back from France in the mid-1950s, they took part, with several successful young businessmen, in the foundation of an association campaigning for mass naturalization.

The granting of French citizenship was all the more desirable for many Chinese because it offered political and civil rights and removed the discriminatory taxes still levied on foreigners. Many Chinese experienced being citizens of a republic in exile, combined with the feeling of being rejected by the People's Republic of China, as a situation of statelessness. And although the ROC Consul had pressured France into suppressing its additional tax on commercial licenses in 1948, the Chinese still had to pay a residence tax and a tax on the delivery and renewal of the 'identity card for alien traders' created in 1940. The Chinese therefore perceived naturalization as the resolution of a legal limbo and a normalization of their status, putting an end to the discrimination they faced.

Furthermore, the 1960s was a decade of mounting opposition by the autonomists to the pro-France De Gaullian party that formed the majority at the French Polynesian territorial assembly. The members of the association who campaigned for naturalization argued that it would turn them into loyal pro-French voters. As the autonomists openly took anti-Chinese stances, the Chinese saw the control of the territory by France as a warrant that would allow their continued presence. This positioning was in accord with the French authorities' search for a means to keep control of the territory. The law of 1973 extended *jus soli* to France's overseas territories and a decree immediately followed that granted French citizenship to all those born in the territory.

The fragmentation into conjugal families was accelerated due not only to strategies of economic and cultural capital accumulation, but also to naturalization—the acquisition of legal capital. Naturalization was an individual act, and the 'Frenchification' of Chinese names was part of the procedure. It consisted in reworking the names according to French phonetics or even changing them to something altogether different. Thus the name *Lan* could become *Lanne*, or, as rewritten by some zealous clerks, even the very common *Dupont*. Some adopted the first name of their wife, after which they had named their shop, such as the third Hong son, who took the patronym Amélie. As the authorities proceeded case by case, siblings and cousins bearing the same original Chinese surname often obtained very dissimilar French surnames. This 'dispersal' of surnames often came up during interviews as an example of individualization, in contrast to an earlier golden period where families were more unified and solidary. While perceived as radical break from the past, the case of the Hongs demonstrates how this fragmentation was actually the very result of the strategies followed by the families.

This is most clearly shown by the ways in which the practice of using women as nominal owners led to unwanted consequences. At the time of the division of the family estate, dissent appeared among brothers on the one hand and between brothers and sisters on the other. First, the son married to a French wife could often slight his brothers at the time of the split. The Hong brothers felt that the monetary compensation they had received at the time of division, from which they had to start from scratch, was less than the part received by the third brother who kept the shop. Second, once all had become French citizens, daughters could claim a share of the estate registered in their name, even though their parents had not intended to give them anything at all. Some even took action in court, in spite of this being seen as a disreputable move in the community. Women thus challenged Chinese gender hierarchy in the name of French law, which mandates equal inheritance between all children. Among the third and fourth generations, sons and daughters inherit equally from their parents, in conformance to the legal dispositions of the French civil code. This further generalized the conjugal family.

In the meantime, the regime change in China led to the split of the family estate that was once bilocal. Owing to confiscations of land and property accumulated by successful overseas Chinese that took place as soon as the Communist Party took power, and to the collectivization of land that occurred in the early 1950s, the family estate in the villages of origin generally shrank to the house inhabited by returned members of the family or held in trust by fellow villagers. This loss of property led to a recentring of the family estate in French Polynesia that favoured those who had not gone back—the younger siblings. Many of those who had gone to China managed to flee to Hong Kong at the end of the 1950s and early 1960s. Many others migrated again from Hong Kong to other destinations in the Americas and Europe. Those who came back to Tahiti found themselves dependent on their younger brothers, or on their father's younger brothers, contradicting the hierarchical logic that had led to their return to China in the 1930s. Moreover, the Chinese education they had received was of no use at a time when success in business and access to French citizenship were highly dependent on French cultural capital.

ANTICIPATING FURTHER REVERSALS

In the space of two decades, the 1960s and 1970s, French Polynesia saw a radical transition from a dual economy based largely on subsistence and partly on exports to an economy based on the nuclear rent. This made the post-nuclear reconversion that started in the 1990s extremely difficult. The French Polynesian economy is now still extremely dependent on financial aid from France. Its debt has become huge and this makes its trajectory, in spite of its specific history as a French overseas territory, quite similar to that of many formerly colonized developing countries. The French authorities have attempted to boost investments through a politics of generalized tax exemptions. In the absence of income, wealth and inheritance taxes, inequalities are particularly pronounced, and 27% of the population lives below the poverty line (Herrera and Merceron 2010: 23). On the island of Tahiti, the contrast in standards of living between the well-to-do and the poor is striking: the former live in villas with lagoon views on the heights; the latter, increasingly, in housing projects and slums. These inequalities clearly intersect with ethnic divisions between the Tahitian, Chinese and French. Following Barth's (1988) logic of ethnic boundary maintenance, the Chinese are overrepresented in private business, even though many have entered the public sector as school teachers or civil servants.

The ethnicization of identities in Tahiti has also been fostered by the competition between the rising independence party and the autonomist party and can be seen as an effect of the dehegemonization of the Western-dominated world system in the 1970s (Friedman 2004: 82). Furthermore, and as part of this same global process of 'hegemonic transition', the promotion of multiethnicity through the branding of the 'Chinese community' has been used to establish diplomatic relations with the People's Republic of China (PRC). These efforts have met those of the PRC, which has, since the early 1980s, reconnected with its diaspora's communities in French Polynesia and elsewhere, using an enlarged definition of 'Chineseness' (Nyíri 2002; Dirlik 2004).

In this unstable, uncertain political and economic context, practices of 'flexible kinship' take the form of a search for the diversification and securitization of economic assets simultaneously with an exploitation of the opportunities that French Polynesian residence continues to offer. These practices by descendants of Chinese migrants pertain to a diasporic rather than a migratory transnationalism in the sense that they are less oriented to the country of origin than to other destinations. Although the reopening of China from 1979 encouraged those of the first generation who were still alive and the second generation (especially those sent back during childhood) to visit their villages of origin, on the whole there was a distancing, if not a breakup, of family ties (as also argued by Hoe 2005). Furthermore, while many entrepreneurs make frequent trips to China to supply their import businesses, family ties rarely frame business relations.

There is a constant concern for adaptation and anticipation of further reversals even today among descendants of migrants who hold French citizenship. A set of widespread transnational practices is the internationalization of economic, legal, and cultural capital by means of exporting savings, accumulating citizenships, and getting degrees abroad. We will see, however, through the Lin family, that these are not necessarily systematic and can conflict with localized identities.

The Lins, born in the 1950s, are third-generation descendants of Chinese immigrants. Jean-Pierre grew up on the island next to Tahiti, Moorea, where he inherited half of his father's business (a grocery-bakery). Eliane grew up on Tahiti in the urban Chinese community, where she went to the Chinese school. After briefly studying in France, she came back and found employment in the enterprise of her maternal uncle, the last son of the Hong family (she is the only daughter of the Hong's younger sister). After her marriage, she moved to Moorea to work together with Jean-Pierre in the grocery shop. When their first daughter, Marina, reached legal majority, they registered their enterprise as a limited liability company under Marina's name (Marina is officially the manager) and themselves as employees of their daughter. This brought two advantages: the first, it evaded the corporate tax and led them to be taxed at a very low level.[10] The second is that it allowed them to contribute to a retirement

---

[10] Corporate tax varies from 35% to 45% of profit. In France, enterprise heads can opt for a single proprietorship, which is normally subjected to income tax. As there is no income tax in French Polynesia, these types of enterprises are taxed on transactions, which amounts to only 5% of the sales revenue.

pension scheme for employees that was more favourable than the one for enterprise heads. This legal arrangement, which profits from the low tax regime specific to French Polynesia, is extremely widespread among Chinese shopkeepers. It relies, evidently, on relations of trust and authority between parents and their children. "It works if children do not rebel", as Marina told me. We find here a continuation of flexible kinship practices, although this particular type is not strictly transnational.

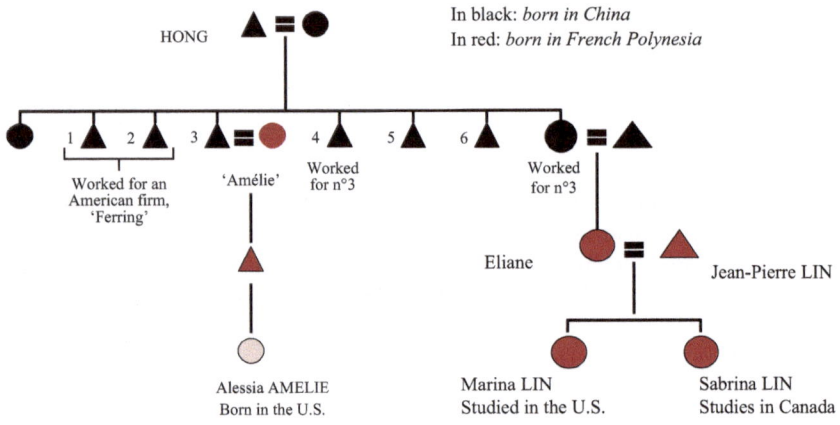

Marina herself is employed, and so is her husband William; they work for the local airline company and a bank. They will not take over William's parents' shop, nor Marina's parents'. They are not willing to wake up at 4 a.m. and work all week without a day of rest, as their parents did, "and anyway, you cannot make as much money out of a shop nowadays", said Marina. However, she recognizes that, as employees, they will never be able "to accumulate as much" as their parents did.

Marina's and William's parents belong to the generation that was born Chinese and became French in 1973, and which has largely benefited from the economic growth that continued until the 1990s. From the moment they obtained a French passport, the members of this generation have been able to travel easily internationally. This generation has strongly resorted to 'birth tourism', a practice consisting in travelling (with a tourist visa) to a *jus soli* country for the purpose of giving birth, thereby granting their child birthright citizenship or enhancing his future chances of getting citizenship. In one case a couple gave birth to four children, all in different countries (Australia, New Zealand, Canada and the United States). Accumulating a wide range of citizenships within a family increases the legal capital of the family and of each member. In the same vein, third-generation parents generally influenced their children's choices of location for studying abroad, encouraging each to select a different destination. As one informant put it, the idea is that "one should not put all eggs in one basket". Birth tourism is part of this same rationale, since children born in a given country will have better chances of admission and are more likely to choose schools there.

Unlike her rich cousin Alessia, the granddaughter of the third Hong son, an American citizen by birth who chose to follow her boyfriend to France (to her mother's dismay), Marina herself was born in Tahiti but opted for studies in the U.S. Her parents did not have the means to practice birth tourism, but her mother did push her in that direction. Marina believes she would have chosen France if the decision had been her own, but her mother argued that an American degree and the English language were a backup. America is "a plan B", she said, "because we already have the French citizenship, which is a good one, it is part of the European Union". In other words, what is at stake is a diversification of different forms of capital, and hence, options for the future.

Since Marina's return from the U.S., in 2002, French Polynesia has gone through a sharp economic crisis because of the impact on tourism of the World Trade Center attack, and now the world economic crisis. There has also been a deep political crisis since the accession to power, for the first time in 2005, of the independence party. This has increased the tendency among Tahitian Chinese to place their savings and assets abroad, in bank deposits and real estate.

In 2014, Marina's mother, Eliane, bought two apartments in Montreal's Côte des Neiges neighbourhood. She chose Montreal because it is the place where her second daughter, Marina's sister Sabrina, has been studying biology for several years, more recently as a PhD candidate. Marina's mother gave the information about this opportunity to several people, all very close female friends, who purchased apartments in the same building. Eliane's parents did not own a shop and placed nothing in her name; however, she strongly bears in mind the situation of her mother, the last Hong sister, who was the "slave" of her brothers all her life and received nothing at the time of family division. Eliane told her daughters that she had sworn to herself to give her own daughters everything they needed and never act as the "elders" did in the old times; she calls this "acting as a civilized Chinese". The two apartments in Montreal are in the names of Marina and Sabrina.

Buying real estate abroad is Eliane's decision, which Jean-Pierre does not support. Recently, his decision to buy an additional piece of land on the island of Moorea led to a huge dispute between them, to the point at which Marina thought they were about to divorce. What structures their debate on whether to invest locally or abroad is the prospect of the country's gaining independence, but also in a shorter term, their retirement plans. In case of independence, Eliane proclaims she would leave at once, while Jean-Pierre states he would defend his property with a rifle. Jean-Pierre sees himself spending his old age fishing in the islands.[11] His father had bought an apartment in China in preparation for his own retirement, but died before he left, and Jean-Pierre told me, "Honestly, I don't give a damn about China." Neither does Marina's mother. However, in contrast to Jean-Pierre, she envisions herself spending half of the year in Montreal upon retirement. She reasons that now that Sabrina has Canadian citizenship, she could sponsor them in case they decided to make the move.

While the difference between Jean-Pierre and Eliane is clearly linked to their socialization in different settings, the purchase of the Montreal apartment together with several women, and her own family history, also suggest that transnational flexible kinship practices may be continued by women more than by men because of the central role they play in family arrangements and the way this has enhanced their economic roles.

CONCLUSION

Throughout this chapter I have shown the discrepant temporalities between, on the one hand, immigration and citizenship policies, which fluctuate along with global economic conjunctures and reconfigurations of hegemony in the world-system, and, on the other, the orientations of migrants and their descendants. The reversal in policy of the 1930s and the restriction brought to immigration and economic latitude of the Chinese

---

[11] Jean-Pierre grew up on Moorea, two of his sisters are married to Tahitian men, and he likes practicing hobbies associated with islander lifestyle. For a discussion of different milieus of socialization and contrasts in lifestyles between rural districts and islands and the Chinese in Papeete, and corresponding 'localization' and 'cosmopolitanization' of identities, see Trémon (2009).

intervened at a moment when immigrants postponed their return plans because of the economic slowdown and the war in China. This orientation continued and increased after the advent of the communist regime in 1949 and even more in the 1960s, a decade of rapid growth and facilitated access to French citizenship at a time when the members of second generation, born between the 1920s and 1940s, reached adult age. This concordance between French politics towards the territory and the wishes of the Chinese did not last, however. The 1970s and onward saw the rise of aspirations for independence and the ethnicization of politics. Although descendants of Chinese migrants were henceforth nationals of the country they inhabited, they were still a distinct ethnic minority.

These discrepancies have nourished the practices I call 'flexible kinship'. Flexible kinship depends on the organization of the kin unit—the dynamics of its development cycle—and on its internal relations—the hierarchy based on birth, generation and gender. It involves strategies of spatial and legal localization that consist in the crossing of national borders by some of the families' members with the aim of evading constraints and benefiting from opportunities. Of course, kinship may always be flexible. The practices described are an accentuation of processes already present within the very logics of family dynamics itself. Although this may make the notion seem redundant, flexible kinship draws attention to the specific uses that are made of kinship in the context of migration and diaspora: the adjustment to cultural, political and legal borders that lead to changes in family forms and in the relations between kin. The form the family takes and the nature of the relation between its members are the product of these adjustments.

It involves strategies of spatial and legal localization that consist in the crossing of national borders by some of the families' members with the aim of evading constraints and benefiting from opportunities. Families thereby adjusted to and profited from differences (in space and time) in cultural, political, economic and legal regimes and conjunctures. The differentiated strategies and investments in family members were intended to profit the family as a collective unit. These flexible arrangements, requiring members to make sacrifices by investing in some individuals for the benefit of all, stimulated division, accelerating the family development cycle. If the 'cultural logics' of the Chinese family have framed the transnational practices of flexible kinship, the latter have also modified these logics and brought changes to the relations between kin. On the one hand, the Confucian hierarchy that underlay the relations between kin has been bent, adjusted to reach the desired benefits. On the other hand, these adjustments have sometimes led to unintended consequences for the families' organization and internal relations.

Furthermore, flexible kinship involves a processual approach to kinship. In this regard, a multigenerational perspective shows how discrepancies between successive changes, reversals in policies, over the *longue durée* of family history, and the history of the adjustments to them have produced a habitus of security maximization, possibly even more among women. It is visible in the constant concern for adaptation and anticipation of further reversals that continue today among descendants of migrants who hold French citizenship. This concern appears throughout a set of practices of accumulation and dispersion of legal, cultural and economic capital. The practices described among the first and second generations continue in new forms, in birth tourism and the choice of different destinations for studying abroad in the same family. However, the discrepancy internal to the Lin family as it is expressed in disagreements over retirement plans also points to the tension between the localization of identities and the fragility of the descendants of migrants' place in French Polynesian society as a result of past history and the present uncertain conjuncture. Practices of flexible kinship are thus an ideal locus at which to observe the discrepancies between migrants and their descendants' projects and the ordering and disordering effects of state policies and global capitalism.

Acknowledgments This is a shortened and modified version of a paper that appeared under the title "Flexible Kinship. Shaping transnational families among the Chinese in Tahiti" in the *Journal of the Royal Anthropological Institute*, 2017, 23, 1, 42–60.

References

Barth, Fredrik. 1988. *Ethnic Groups and Boundaries, the Social Organisation of Culture Difference.* Prospect Heights, IL: Waveland Press.

Bourdieu, Pierre. 1990 [1980]. The Social Uses of Kinship. In *The Logic of Practice* , trans., R. Nice, 162–199. Cambridge: Polity.

Bruguière, André. 2002. Les sciences sociales et la notion de solidarité familiale. In *Les solidarités familiales en question*, ed. D. Debordeaux and P. Strobel, 19–40. Paris: Maison des Sciences de l'homme.

Bruno, Anne-Sophie, et al. 2006. Jugés sur pièces. Le traitement des dossiers de séjour et de travail des étrangers en France (1917–1984). *Population* 61 (5): 737–762.

Cohen, Myron. 1970. Development Process in the Chinese Domestic Group. In *Family and Kinship in Chinese Society*, ed. M. Freedman, 31–36. Stanford: Stanford University Press.

———. 1976. *House United, House Divided*. New York: Columbia University Press.

De la Pradelle, Géraud. 1995. La distinction entre droit public et droit privé en matière de nationalité. In *C.U.R.A.P.P., Public/privé*. Paris: PUF.

Dirlik, Arif. 2004. It Is Not Where You Are from, It Is Where You Are at: Place-Based Alternatives to Diaspora Discourses. In *Worlds on the Move*, ed. J. Friedman and S. Randeria, 141–166. London: I.B. Tauris.

Fitzgerald, Stephen. 1972. *China and the Overseas Chinese: A Study of Pekin's Changing Policy 1949–1970*. Cambridge: Cambridge University Press.

Friedman, Jonathan. 1994. *Cultural Identity and Global Process*. London: Sage.

———. 2004. Globalization, Transnationalization, and Migation. In *Worlds on the Move. Globalization, Migration and Cultural Security*, ed. J. Friedman and S. Randeria, 63–90. London: I.B. Tauris.

Glick Schiller, Nina, Basch Linda, and Blanc-Szanton Cristina. 1992. *Towards a Transnational Perspective on Migration: Race, Ethnicity, and Nationalism Reconsidered*. New York: New York Academy of Sciences.

Greenhalgh, Susan. 1994. De-Orientalizing the Chinese Family Firm. *American Ethnologist* 21 (4): 746–775.

Herrera, Javier, and Sébastien Merceron. 2010. *Les approches de la pauvreté en Polynésie française*, Working Paper Series No 103. Paris: Agence française de développement.

Hoe, Yow Cheun. 2005. Weakening Ties with the Ancestral Homeland in China: The Case Studies of Contemporary Singapore and Malaysian Chinese. *Modern Asian Studies* 39 (3): 559–597.

Laurens, Sylvain. 2008. '1974' et la fermeture des frontières. Analyse critique d'une décision érigée en *turning-point. Politix* 82: 67–82.

Moench, Richard U. 1963. *Economic Relations of the Chinese in the Society Islands*. PhD thesis, Unpublished Manuscript, Harvard University.

Morawska, Eva. 2001. Immigrants, Transnationalism, and Ethnicization: A Comparison of This Great Wave and the Last. In *E Pluribus Unum? Contemporary and Historical Perspectives on Immigrant Political Incorporation*, ed. G. Gerstle and J. Mollenkopf, 175–212. New York: Russell Sage.

Noiriel, Gérard. 1988. *Le creuset français: histoire de l'immigration XIXe–XXe siècles*. Paris: éditions du Seuil.

Nonini, Donald M. 2003. All Are Flexible, But Some Are More Flexible Than Others: Small-Scale Chinese Businesses in Malaysia. In *Ethnic Business: Chinese Capitalism in Southeast Asia*, Routledge Curzon Studies in the Growth Economies of Asia, 50, ed. K.S. Jomo and B.C. Folke, 73–91. London, New York: Routledge Curzon.

————. 2005. Toward a (Proper) Postwar History of Southeast Asian Petty Capitalism: Predation, the State, and Chinese Small Business Capital in Malaysia. In *Petty Capitalists and Globalization. Flexibility, Entrepreneurship, and Economic Development*, ed. A. Smart and J. Smart. Albany, NY: State University of New York Press.

Nonini, Donald M., and Aihwa Ong. 1997. Introduction: Chinese Transnationalism as an Alternative Modernity. In *Ungrounded Empires: The Cultural Politics of Modern Chinese Transnationalism*, ed. A. Ong and D.M. Nonini, 1–33. New York: Routledge.

Nyíri, Pal. 2002. From Class Enemies to Patriots. In *Globalizing Chinese*, ed. Migration P. Nyíri and I.R. Saveliev, 208–241. Aldershot: Ashgate.

Ong, Aihwa. 1999. *Flexible Citizenship: The Cultural Logics of Transnationality*. Durham: Duke University Press.

Panoff, Michel. 1997. The French Way in Plantation Systems. *The Journal of Pacific History* 26: 206–212.

Portes, Alejandro, Guarnizo Luis, and Landolt Patricia. 1999. Introduction. Pitfalls and Promise of an Emergent Research Field. *Ethnic and Racial Studies* 22 (2): 217–238.

Rouse, Roger. 1991. Mexican Migration and the Social Space of Postmodernism. *Diaspora* 1 (1): 8–23.

Smith, Michael P., and Luis E. Guarnizo, eds. 1998. *Transnationalism from Below*. New Brunswick and London: Transaction Publishers.

Trémon, Anne-Christine. 2009. Cosmopolitanization and Localization. *Anthropological Theory* 9 (1): 103–126.

————. 2010. *Chinois en Polynésie française. Migration, métissage, diaspora*. Nanterre: Société d'ethnologie.

Waldinger, Roger, and David Fitzgerald. 2004. Transnationalism in Question. *American Journal of Sociology* 109 (5): 1177–1195.

Wang, Gungwu. 2000. *The Chinese Overseas: From Earthbound China to the Quest for Autonomy*. Cambridge: Harvard University Press.

CHAPTER 6

Migrating for a Better Future: 'Lost Time' and Its Social Consequences Among Young Somali Migrants

Anja Simonsen

This chapter explores the tension between time and existential uncertainty as young Somali male migrants make the risky journey toward Europe. 'Migrant', in this chapter, is an all-embracing term, defined in such a way as to make clear the argument that movement becomes a way to survive, physically and socially, for everyone, despite what they are moving away from. Many young Somalis find themselves in a state of existential uncertainty in the sense, as one reported, of a constant state of "mind or minding, when we are unable to predict the outcome of events or to know with assurance about something that matters to us" (Whyte and Siu 2015: 19). For Somalis, this uncertainty is created by insecurities such as not knowing which future steps might enable them to move ahead in their lives; what moves, physically and socially, these steps involve; and when to attempt to undertake them. For young Somali men wanting to migrate, this experience of uncertainty as a constant state is closely linked to the notion of *wakhti lumis* ('losing time', present tense) or *wakhti lumay* ('lost time', past tense)—which refers to an

A. Simonsen (✉)
Department of Anthropology, University of Copenhagen, Copenhagen, Denmark

© The Author(s) 2018
P. G. Barber, W. Lem (eds.), *Migration, Temporality, and Capitalism*, https://doi.org/10.1007/978-3-319-72781-3_6

inability to make sense of the time spent in the past and the present. It was exactly when they had nothing but time that they referred to time as 'lost'. Put differently, they lost time by having too much of it. Losing time involved a certain kind of meaningless waiting, with little if any control over what was coming and a feeling of making no progress in life. Individuals made constant attempts to minimize the experience of 'lost time', yet the success of their efforts was conditioned on events and on relations with others that were beyond their control. Their lives, in other words, were characterized by a context of insecurity related to both their distant and close physical and social surroundings.

Young Somalis described the country in which they grew up as one in which they had lost time. The urge to migrate was one of the important ways they attempted to gain time. In Somali migration is defined as *tahriib*, referring to the geopolitical framework that defines this way of moving as 'illegal migration', along with the existential experience of uncertainty regarding 'the journey into the unknown' (Simonsen 2017). En route to a desired future, however, experiences of insecurity and of losing time continued, followed by various attempts to minimize them. In this chapter, I discuss my interlocutors' experiences of lost time, starting in Somaliland and moving on to Turkey. My analysis is based on fieldwork with Somali men in Somaliland, Turkey and Greece. It was when the young Somalis were stuck, physically and socially, that I could reach them, drink tea with them and try to grasp the sociality surrounding 'lost time'. My main argument is that my interlocutors attempted to change their location as a way to gain time—a time that was measured and experienced socially. Locations therefore signified not only geographical places, but social and economic landscapes as well. Gaining time and/or not losing time was thus a way to manage the existential uncertainty felt in Somaliland, Turkey, Greece and in between, whereas losing time was the embodied experience of not being able to spend time pursuing desired futures. Hence, by examining the everyday lives of young, undocumented Somali migrants en route, I show how experiences of 'lost time' created certain kinds of strategies, including attempts at onward migration that were all embedded in the sociality of time. I will begin by setting the theoretical scene.

The Sociality of Time

Emile Durkheim's studies of religion and religious life were foundational to the conceptualization of time in the social sciences (Gell 1996 [1992]). Durkheim emphasized time when he argued that ideas of time "dominate all intellectual thought", perceptions of time being "the solid frame which encloses all thought" (Durkheim 2008 [1915]: 9). Giving the example of the way we, as human beings, divide time into days, weeks, months and years, Durkheim argued that these divisions are the products of collective and social events in society such as rites and public ceremonies. Thus, the use of a calendar illustrates how time is shaped by society, while simultaneously being integral to society's regulation (Durkheim 2008: 10–11). According to Durkheim, we cannot think of time without dividing it into bits and pieces. In line with Durkheim's suggestion that time is universal, social and collective, classic anthropologists like E.E. Evans-Pritchard (1969) in his study of the Nuer proposed that time can take two forms: "oecological time" and "structural time". Time, as an ecological rhythm, is organized in years that are divided into a cycle following the ecological rhythm of rain and drought (Evans-Pritchard 1969: 93). Structural time, on the other hand, takes place within the context of the social structure through which people relate to each other, thus enabling "a reflection of relations between lineages ... a looking backwards, since relationships must be explained in terms of the past" (1969: 108).

Evans-Pritchard's (1969) definition of the experience of time among the Nuer can be criticized for being static and unchangeable (Whyte 2009: 238). Both Durkheim and Evans-Pritchard nevertheless made important contributions by pointing out that time is experienced as embedded within a particular context; in other words, it is a form of sociality. Newer anthropological work builds on the conceptualization of time as relational. Mains (2007: 667), for one, argues that "time is taken as a measure of human activity, but it is used to measure and quantify relationships rather than labor and its corresponding monetary value". The close association between time and sociality, I argue, is key to understanding Somali migration. As I illuminate throughout this chapter, it was the experience of time within the context of being young persons, neither children nor adults (cf. Mains 2007), that made my interlocutors migrate, for example, of not being considered a mature man able to make important decisions within the family or the clan, not being able to finance a good education, find a job, get married, provide for the family who had cared for them since their childhood, etc.[1] In other words, it was the

---

[1] See Simonsen (2017), which situates the social being of the younger generation within Somaliland.

inability to live up to both their own hopes as well as the surrounding community's expectations for their present and future time that led to the decision to migrate. In moving on from Somaliland, time continued to be experienced through the contingency of various others, understood not only as human beings, but as family, friends, brokers, strangers, their own health or the environment—or, to use Evans-Pritchard's (1969) term (and spelling) 'oecological time'. When snow and ice had covered the landscape, movement became more difficult. At the same time, certain periods of time were better to move in, as they would follow the rhythm of others who had moved 'legally', which could make the passage of borders more feasible. Though time is not divided as neatly and as structured as Evans-Pritchard (1969) proposes, my interlocutors' experiences of time did involve a form of relationship to the environment, both seasonally and socially.

It is through this analytical lens of sociality that I will approach the experience of time among young Somalis. I will take my point of departure in Somaliland, first with an exploration of what it means to be young in Somaliland and how that is connected to the experience of losing time. This will be followed by the story of Jabriil. Focusing on his attempts to move through the geographical and social landscapes that surrounded him in an attempt to gain time, I will show what strategies he used as he went from having nothing but time to having very little spare time, a move which the majority of my interlocutors dreamed of making, but could not. Secondly, I will explore the way that waiting, in the form of drinking tea, became a symbol of temporal stagnation. Thirdly, through the case of Habaane, a young Somali migrant in Turkey, I will show how losing time can be experienced in a so-called transit country,[2] thereby illuminating how tempo impinges on time.

---

[2] See Simonsen (2017), in which I criticize the term itself, as well as the categorization of countries such as Turkey as 'transit countries'. Some of my interlocutors never made it out of Turkey alive, but tragically lost their lives on inflatable boats sailing towards Greece. Others managed to leave Turkey, but only after various periods of time spent waiting, in different ways and with different costs. Finally, some were in Turkey as students, others as refugees and some as laborers. In other words, they had very heterogeneous backgrounds, profiles and categorizations attached to them, which the term 'transit migration' did not seem to capture. For similar and more in-depth critiques, see Bredeloup (2012), Collyer and de Haas (2012), Düvell (2012), İçduygu and Yükseker (2012) and Schapendonk (2012).

SOMALI YOUTH: IN SEARCH OF THE RIGHT KIND OF TIME

In order to understand why young Somali men migrate as a way to gain time, it is important to paint a picture of the social setting from which they migrate. What expectations follow them as they become older, not only from the surrounding society, but also from themselves, and how does this create a sense of losing time?

According to the Constitution of Somaliland, the category of youth is defined as falling between the ages of 18 and 24. Discussing the concept of *dhalin yaro* ('young generation') with my interlocutors, they would argue how social and cultural perceptions differed from political ones. Debating who belongs to *dhalin yaro*, they agreed that it started at the age of 18, but differed with regard to when it would end by citing anything between 32 and 40. What seemed to matter was the belief that when a person left the category of youth behind him and became a man [*nin*], he would be mature and have the capacity to be responsible, as Cabdirahman, a young man with whom I spent the majority of my time in Somaliland, explained to me. Answering my questions about the difference between youth and adulthood, Cabdirahman explained:

> In adulthood, the person is treated as a great person, and he will solve problems and conflicts between his clan and others; while the person is in youth, he/she has not enough intelligence to solve critical issues. That's the difference.

In other words, leaving the category of youth behind was very much about being taken seriously, about being able to make decisions and take part in more serious matters within the clan. With age came wisdom, as is the case throughout Somalia (Glascock 1986: 56). I was often presented with this form of association between age and wisdom through the example of the president. The young men often stated that in Somaliland, one has to be at least 40 years of age to run for the presidency, as this is when a person is considered capable of making mature decisions. Similarly, to run for Parliament, one needs to be 35 years of age or older, though, as Cabdirahman explained, this depended on culture and not facts, which meant that younger people would also be found as MPs and ministers, despite their age, due to them having the right clan affiliations, experience from abroad or other circumstances that would increase their sense of maturity and thus enable them to enter politics. This led to a search for life experiences such as becoming part of the diaspora, which would more easily qualify them to be considered mature and respected men as well as indicate their dissatisfaction with the way society was structured. In conversation, Egal, a young Somali man who was living in Turkey until he could migrate further on, shed light on the constraints felt by young people in Somaliland like himself in achieving influence in society and obtaining his future goals. He wanted, like others among my male interlocutors, to become the president of Somaliland, but added: "In Somaliland the presidents are old, 120 years old, that is dominating, but other countries, when they are 70 years old, they finish the policy." Egal was referring to the current structural constraints felt by young people. In Somaliland, it was mostly the elderly who had the decision-making power in politics.[3]

Among my male interlocutors, this wish to become someone important, symbolized through the status of being president, often clashed with the lack of ability to enact this dream of social visibility due to the rather gerontocratic system that treated being young as a form of limitation. It illuminated a period of "restriction rather than opportunity, making youth a social moratorium" (Vigh 2007: 96). As Vigh argues (cf. ibid.), it was a lack of access to resources and thus social mobility which led my interlocutors to try to escape the category of youth.

Age was thus closely related to the achievements of the individual. As Ali argues (2016: 15), marriage is one of the ways in which you measure adulthood, as a young man who is married is considered more of an adult than an older, but unmarried young man. Many of the young men I followed suffered from not being able to marry due to the lack of means to finance their lives as a married man. Cabdirahman, for example, lost his girlfriend of the past four years to a young Somali man from the diaspora who was believed by his (ex-)girlfriend's family to be better off financially. As Taban, who was the older brother of Cabdirahman's good friend, explained during an interview conducted in Somaliland, it was difficult being young and moving rapidly towards adulthood, but not being able to fulfil the social obligations that came along with adulthood. This had led him to become a labor migrant in Saudi Arabia:

> My mother brought me up, since my father died when I was very young, and when I grew up as an adult I was thinking how to sponsor [i.e., support] my mother who brought me up, because at this stage I cannot expect [more] from my mother. Since I could not get a job from here, I decided to leave and get better life conditions over there [Saudi Arabia].

[3] For an exploration of the role of elders in the Somali society, see, among others, Höhne (2007).

Taban's worries about not being able to take care of his mother reflects what, in the anthropological literature, has been conceptualized as 'the intergenerational contract', a theme that has been widely discussed in different geographical and socioeconomic contexts (Barakat 1985; Stafford 2000; Alber et al. 2008; Pedersen 2011, 2013). Pedersen (2011: 128) defines the intergenerational contract as that economic and moral bond between parents and their children where the roles of provider and provided are expected to shift as the child grows into adulthood. What many of my young male interlocutors experienced, however, was a clash between on the one hand how time passed and how they became of age, and on the other hand how the restrictions of their surroundings did not allow them to live up to the expectations of their actual age. Instead, it became a race to catch up with time. One way to do this was by migrating.

While most young Somalis were keen to enter adulthood, some of my interlocutors also dreamed of "extending their youth" (Wulff 1995: 7). Some Somalis would explain how they dreamed of freedom, referring to a situation in which they would be beyond the reach of their parents' control. They described to me how, in Europe, young people lived in apartments by themselves and were thus not controlled by their parents to the same extent as they were. Therefore, there was a mixture, I argue, of wanting to become adults, with the respect and social visibility that followed, and thus of moving faster and not being stuck in the experiences of youth; and of dreaming of living a life without responsibilities and control that shaped their experience of 'being' in Somaliland, which would allow them to be the kind of youth they dreamed of and thus extend their time within it. This speaks to the two major approaches within anthropology, one in which being young is defined as a period of transition, a form of liminality (Mead 1928; Henry 1965; Turner 1967), and one in which young people were categorized as a group in their own right that needed to be taken seriously by introducing the concept of 'youth culture' (Parsons 1964). Neither situation, however, was within the reach of most of my interlocutors, and this made many of them decide to migrate in an attempt to not lose time.

'It's Not Like Before': Gaining Time in Somaliland

It was around noon when Jabriil and I met in one of the oldest hotels in town in Hargaysa, the capital of Somaliland. The sun was already burning, and I could see small pearls of sweat on Jabriil's face as I entered the hotel, where he was already sitting with his laptop and that day's newspaper. We sat down together, and Jabriil opened his laptop, in which he had stored his CV, and then the newspaper, which had a section for job vacancies. This week there were five jobs that Jabriil could apply for. Jabriil showed me on his laptop two applications he had written, one he had already sent off to an employer, and another that he wanted to send that day.

Jabriil, a Somali man in his early twenties, belonged to the 95 percent of men and women aged 15–24 years old in Somaliland who had no gainful employment.[4] For them, getting a job in Somaliland had therefore become all but something they could only dream about. Jabriil would spend his days searching for opportunities to maintain himself and his family. When he was not searching the newspapers or internet for vacancies, he would sit and drink tea with his friends in the market or the local neighbourhood. He, along with many of my other interlocutors, would describe his situation through statements such as: "Waxa halkan nagaga lumaya waqtiga." ("We are losing our time here.") Like the other young Somalis in Somaliland, Turkey and Greece with whom I did fieldwork, Jabriil was occupied with minimizing what they defined as *wakhti lumis* ('losing time'). This speaks to a time in the present that is not used properly according to social norms—a general time that can refer to anything from wasting your time in front of the TV to being imprisoned. Using the notion of *wakhti lumis* thus means passing time by, for example, spending a great deal of time drinking tea as Jabriil and his friends did, since they did not have any job with which to occupy themselves. *Wakhti lumay*, the past tense of *wakhti lumis*, thus always refers to time that has been lost because it was not used in a satisfying or fulfilling way. *Wakhti/waqti* comes from Arabic and has been incorporated into the Somali vocabulary used by the younger generation. For Jabriil, as for all my interlocutors, dissatisfaction with both the past and the present, and not knowing how or whether they would be able to create a desirable and satisfying life for themselves in Somaliland in the near future, led to migration. He hoped to be occupied through a job, but not just any job. Jabriil was looking for a position that followed the social laws that surrounded him, which, as he often explained to me, meant that, having entered university, only office jobs or other so-called white collar jobs were acceptable. In this way, the tempo of time was very much embedded in the sociality of my interlocutors' surroundings, as time spent in the wrong way would not be defined as time gained, but

[4] These figures are based on the International Labor Organisation's (ILO) survey conducted in Somaliland in 2012. See Hall (2015).

rather the opposite—time lost. When I met Jabriil in June 2013, he had already attempted to migrate in an attempt to gain time, but had been unsuccessful. On the border between Ethiopia and Sudan he had been imprisoned by the authorities and tortured for three days: "We were in jail for three days, like animals, you know; that is why I don't like to go back. They were beating us with the back of their guns. Sometimes they might put you in a cell and put water up your mouth and nose." Jabriil had promised himself never to attempt to migrate again. He had had high hopes when he had decided to migrate:

> After graduating, I got a job for three months as a teacher in the primary school. Then I left it because, you know, in the primary, the salary is very low and you cannot make it with that commission, so that is why I left it. When I left the job I tried to migrate from here. My hope and expectations were really high. When I left from here, I would get higher education, proper education like master's and PhD, because here you don't get that, so because of that and lack of job I left here.

Having a job with a low salary did not fit in with Jabriil's vision of the future, and thus he decided to migrate. The present time and the imagination of a certain kind of future time clashed. The decision to migrate was taken at what Johnson-Hanks (2002: 871) in another context has called "a nexus of potential social futures: a vital conjuncture":

> These are the moments when seemingly established futures are called into question and when actors are called on to manage durations of radical uncertainty. Conjunctures are navigated in reference to their horizons—the imaginable futures that are hoped for or feared. (Johnson-Hanks 2002: 878)

My interlocutors all had specific individual experiences that had made them decide to migrate. Certain events or periods of hardship had convinced them that their dreams of a decent life in Somaliland would be unattainable, as in the case of Jabriil, who, because he was not able to find a job that could provide sufficiently for himself and his family, had developed a sense of losing time. Spending the time wisely thus referred to being able to live up to the responsibilities and expectations my interlocutors encountered in their social surroundings. In general, they would describe the time they spent in Somaliland in sentences such as, "There is nothing to do here." Xalaane, a well-educated young man from Somaliland who had migrated to Turkey by means of a scholarship, said, "The only thing that is good in Hargeysa [the capital of Somaliland] is security. All others are not good. There [in Somaliland], there is nothing to do, just get up and sleep, get up and sleep, nothing else." Time passed, according to the majority of my interlocutors, without anything to do. Jabriil's way of coping with the sense of losing time focused on his surroundings. He was a young man aiming to acquire a sense of the future by obtaining a master's degree, a PhD and a job. This, he argued, could not be found in Somaliland, and so he left. He attempted to gain time by moving through the geopolitical landscape of Ethiopia and Sudan, only to find himself abruptly stopped by the border police, who imprisoned and tortured him—in other words, he was thrown back in time.[5] Being back in Somaliland after a failed attempt at migrating, he struggled to gain time by concentrating his efforts on something he considered valuable, rather than spending his time on nothing or on events defined as lacking in value. Thus, when I met him for the first time in 2013, he was constantly trying to negotiate the loss of time by searching for good jobs:

> I'm hoping to get a job here in Hargaysa because at this current time, I don't have [one]. Life here is very good, but I'm looking for a job every day. There is a lack of job opportunity here. I look at websites or local journals or the civil commission where the government posts are posted. I'm looking these areas. Many times I made it to the short list and I made some interviews, but still my chance did not come.

The lack of opportunities, not only in jobs, but more broadly in things such as marriage, freedom (not being so constrained by the control of their parents or social norms in society) and education, led my interlocutors to make constant attempts to minimize the experience of lost time, yet the success of their efforts was seen as being conditional on events and relationships with people beyond their control. Their lives, in other words, were characterized by what Whyte and Siu (2015: 19–23) have termed 'social contingency', understood as individuals' particular dependency on circumstances that are largely unknown. As Jabriil explained, "his chance did not come".

When I returned to Somaliland in 2015, Jabriil had succeeded in finding a job. When I contacted him upon my arrival, his time was therefore

---

[5] See Geeldoon (2016), who describes in vivid detail his experiences of torture and imprisonment during *tahriib*.

limited, and I could no longer just call and expect to meet up with him. We had to compare our diaries and did not manage to find a time when we could both meet. As Jabriil said, "It's not like before", referring to the summer of 2013, when time was all he had. His time was now following the tempo of the more successful people surrounding him, and the tempo of his time had increased, leaving little time for me, the anthropologist, who depended on the abundance of time of young people who had no jobs. Jabriil had gained time, and his time had become valuable, as he filled it by doing a job through which he could maintain himself and his family. He had gained time because time had become scarce, and drinking tea had become a luxury in a busy life in Somaliland. But many were not as lucky as Jabriil: some lacked the education to pursue white collar jobs, while others had the education but still formed part of the high unemployment rate. For them, drinking tea became a symbol of losing time, as the following section will illustrate.

Drinking Tea: Symbols of Temporal Stagnation

For my male interlocutors such as Jabriil during my fieldwork in 2013, their days were, as already noted, characterized by hopes of employment, success, marriage, etc. Waiting for these things to happen implies an expectation of something more (Hage 2009: 1). The days of waiting would be passed in going to the mosque for prayers, spending time in tea shops at the market, applying for jobs as Jabriil had done, returning home to have lunch prepared by their mothers or sisters, and then sleeping until the afternoon. They would then get up again and make it to the tea shops to meet their friends and discuss the day's news and their overall concerns. They would debate the current political issues in their country and the problem of tribalism—a reference to a society which in many ways is based on clan and family relations—as well as the job sector, which, many of them argued, had a big influence on unemployment. Some would also go to the university for classes during the day or in the evening. I also spent my days drinking tea with Cabdirahman[6] and other young Somali men, who found themselves stuck in a condition that did not allow them to connect the present with a future horizon in which waiting for unfulfilled hopes was not eternal. Drinking tea became the symbol of not moving ahead socially.

---

[6] One of my interlocutors in Somaliland.

We would often meet at hotels because it was more acceptable for me as a woman to join the tea-drinking sessions there. This meant that the tea would cost double, that is, 2000 Somaliland schillings instead of 1000 (tea that I would offer them), which in its own way was an indicator of the present condition they were in and the places they could afford to spend their time in which was in smaller teashops rather than at the big and beautiful hotels. For the young people I followed, drinking tea became the symbol of a temporal stagnation and thus developed into a way to endure the waiting, but it was also a constant reminder of the lack of social mobility they felt in life in general. One afternoon at the end of June 2013, Cabdirahman gathered four of his friends for a group interview in one of the smaller hotels in Somaliland. The four of them all wanted to migrate. I asked them what made them decide to leave. One of the four young men replied:

> My friends contacted me by phone and asked, 'Are you still at the place where we used to drink tea', and that was a big disappointment for me. And there is a big economic problem in the country, and the ones of my friends who come back here have bought big houses and fancy cars, and people are hunting them, welcoming them, while they don't consider me.

The question posed by his friend was a constant reminder of the time Cabdirahman's friend was losing. Waiting in the form of drinking tea highlighted a paradox, or rather two contradictory characteristics which were inevitably intertwined. First, time passes, whether we like it or not, whether we act in one way or another, minute by minute, hour by hour. The time with which we calculate exists before our actions within it (Hage 2009: 8). My interlocutors would, while waiting, see time pass in a time-frame that was beyond their capacity to change. They could not pause time until they had found a job or got married, as a way to catch up with it. As a Somali proverb states, "Time and tide wait for no one." At the same time, however, drinking tea created a certain kind of waiting that, while embedded in men's social habits of going out to drink tea, broke social norms because it was all they did, one of the few ways in which they could pass time. They could not provide for their families, get married or provide for clan members in need of help, as social custom normally prescribed. Thus, waiting created a certain kind of temporality that both coincided with and deviated from social norms. As a result waiting could, as Hage (2009) argues, mistakenly be defined as passive, but though Jabriil, Cabdirahman and the other young men were not moving physically while they were drinking tea,

I will argue, along with Hage, that waiting, trying to engage with the expectations and fears of the future by either taking the decision to move or deciding not to engage in certain kinds of actions, was a way to act in the world.[7]

Mahad, a friend of Cabdirahman's, explained how the experience of waiting and attempting to create a consistency between one's present situation and one's future horizon formed part of the daily tea discussions: "Some say we must migrate, some say we might stay and struggle for our lives." Their discussions in the tea-drinking sessions arose out of their current situations, which were characterized by what Hage (2009: 4) has called 'stuckedness': "[B]y definition a situation where a person suffers from both the absence of choices or alternatives to the situation one is in and an inability to grab such alternatives even if they present themselves." The lack of opportunities, or absence of choices, to fulfil the goals they had set for themselves took place in two different scenarios: either to migrate or to stay and 'struggle for' their lives, and in some instances both, as in the case of Jabriil. Hage (2009: 1), in his approach to stuckedness, focuses on those who, to use Mahad's words, "stay and struggle for our lives". Through images of a climber who survives a landslide in Australia or of the survivors of 9/11, Hage focuses on what society has defined as the heroes or the good citizens, who, he argues, "wait it out". Instead of searching for existential mobility through movement, they endure social immobility, waiting for the obstacle that has entered their lives to be lifted. Waiting it out is passive, he argues (2009: 4), but still imbued with agency: the "heroism of stuckedness lies in this ability to snatch agency in the very midst of its lack", as when a person survives a natural disaster, or what Hage defines as 'endurance'.

Linking this to the wider political context of Europe today, in which borders are being reinforced to keep migrants at arm's length, young people like Jabriil, who wait it out and actually manage to get a job whereby they can maintain themselves, symbolize success. In Somaliland, however, the hero was more often than not portrayed, by young people and others, as the individual who could endure obstacles while on *tahriib*, or rather, who was moving in the right direction, *tahriib* symbolizing exactly that. Stories would constantly be shared about experiences during *tahriib*, with

---

[7] Ghassan Hage's work is inspired by Pierre Bourdieu's approach to time, an approach that depicts a non-time or a dead time (2000: 222–223) for people who are socially stuck, with all the time in the world, surrounded by busy people who have very little time.

most seeing Libya as the route taken by the 'tough men', implying those who could endure the most. However, some of the difficulties encountered during this form of travel were not mentioned, rape, for example, being a taboo topic. Nonetheless, as Mahad explained, waiting it out by drinking tea became a symbol of stagnation. Thus, the slow tempo at which the tea-drinking sessions moved and the lack of direction they involved became a negative way to measure time. In this way, *tahriib* symbolized gaining time, as it was associated with moving fast in the direction of wealth and success. But what happened, then, to the actual experience of losing time when young Somali men were en route? Did physical movement erase the experiences of losing time?

Losing Time en Route

Young Somalis en route would more often than not travel through what they hoped would be mere transit points, but turned out to be places of waiting. For my interlocutors, Turkey was just such a place where they got entangled in what Andersson (2014: 12–13) has defined as "the doubleness of waiting". By using this term, Andersson argues how, on the one hand, waiting is a technique imposed by institutions such as the state or people in power on those with less power, such as undocumented migrants turning their time into a kind of non-time in which they feel stuck. Making migrants wait thus becomes a technique. As Andersson also argues, places like Ceuta and Melilla have turned into traps of time, places of temporal control that affect the experience of time among migrants. On the other hand, people who experience this timely entrapment most often find ways to make the waiting time count or ascribe it some kind of valuable meaning. This 'doubleness of waiting' characterizes my interlocutors' experiences in Turkey. The young Somali men continued to use the term 'lost time' to describe the uncertainty of waiting, of having lost control and having very few options to choose between. They described the time of doing nothing, of again being slowed down in tempo, to a pace in which nothing was available but time—something they had tried to escape by leaving Somaliland behind. This lost time was caused by the surrounding authorities imposing a pause in the migrants' movement through increased border police, among other things. I sat one day with Habaane, a young Somali man in his early twenties, married and the father of one, in the usual café, drinking Turkish tea. Habaane explained how the agent (i.e., the broker) kept telling them, *them* referring to himself and the many other migrants who wanted to move to Greece, that they would be leaving Turkey "tomorrow, tomorrow, tomorrow" and moving to Greece. Habaane explained that the Somalis in Turkey had an agreement with the Kurds, who were arranging everything, and that the Somalis were just waiting for the call telling them they were leaving. "Maybe the Kurds are in trouble or something, I don't know", he added, and explained that he wanted to go to the city where the boats left for Greece because he was losing too much time in the place where he was staying. "Tomorrow, tomorrow, tomorrow might be one month", he said. Hearing the phrase 'lost time' constantly, I asked Habaane to tell me what it meant to lose time. He replied:

> Maybe you are here for five years, much time you could have married or got an education. Instead, you sit in the house and do nothing. The time is lost. One day you are sitting in your room not doing anything. That time you could do other things like writing, reading, meeting your friends. When I was at the university [in Somaliland] I was thinking that my time was lost, but I did not want to disappoint my mother. All my time was not lost. When I was young, I liked education. I went to a middle-class University.

In saying this, Habaane is referring to the fact that he did not want to migrate while still in education, as this would have disappointed his mother, who he respected and cherished. Habaane also draws our attention to the existential uncertainty of which lost time is a sign, not knowing which step to take next and when. This uncertainty also characterized the way I spent time with Habaane. Like Habaane, I would never know if we would meet again. We would arrange to do so the next day, but he would always say that he might have left, since the agent (the broker) would say 'tomorrow', or 'Monday', and so his days, along with my own, were always premised on a lack of control over both present and future time. He was in a constant position of waiting, which for some lasted months, for others years and for yet others an eternity. Hence, Habaane defined the time he spent in Turkey as waiting, losing his time—similar to the experience he had felt in Somaliland, but characterized by a hope that things would change. This recalls the other aspect of Andersson's concept of waiting, in which being stuck in time is converted into something meaningful, in this case the hope of departing soon. Moving physically as a way to gain time socially, however, was a very uncertain practice. This not only became apparent during the physical travel through surrounding insecurities such as border guards, but was experienced in a more bodily manner.

When Night Turns into Day

The 'doubleness of waiting', whether through enforcement (by people in power) or tactics (by people such as my interlocutors), resulted in changes in the experiences of time in a very practical sense. While occupying themselves in these temporal traps, my interlocutors experienced a new construction of the daily rhythm of time. Day and night were turned around so that the majority of my interlocutors would sleep during the day, wake up late midday and stay up all night. They would explain that there was nothing to do during the day, and thus time was spent during the night. The longer I did fieldwork, the more I became embedded in this rhythm of night turning into day. The same was true for new arriving Somalis, who would similarly become accustomed to these different rhythms of time. Getting up between 2 and 4 p.m., they would go to internet cafésthat were affordable, where they would talk and chat with friends, stand on the street constantly looking for opportunities to talk to brokers who could get them out of Turkey, or sit in the houses in which they had rented a mattress and tell each other stories, mostly of migration experiences. And so I, along with them, spent my time like this. I would know never to go to the area early, as most of my interlocutors would not be present anyhow.

This change in their daily rhythm was related, I argue, to their very insecure situations. As Habaane indicated, the majority of the young Somalis in similar situation as him spent their days waiting. They never knew when brokers would announce the time of departure and thus were not in control of their own time, despite the fact that time was one of the few things they had an abundance of. At the same time, friends and family members who lived in Europe, Canada, the US or elsewhere and who had jobs or were getting an education had little time during the day, as they were busy. In addition, many people who went through extreme experiences, such as three Somali men whom I met on my first visit to what became my fieldsite in Turkey, explained how, during one of their attempts to flee Turkey, they had been caught on a boat that had been floating in the water for four days. Finally found by the Greek police, they were arrested, stripped naked and punished. Then they were returned to Turkey only to try again. Many with similar experiences of being caught by border guards, being arrested and beaten, suffered from a lack of sleep and nightmares, which also produced a changed rhythm and experience of time. The protracted waiting periods often led to very bodily transformations. Many of the young Somali women and men I met in Turkey and

Greece would show me pictures taken before they had departed on *tahriib*. A lot of them had lost a considerable amount of weight during *tahriib*, and others had become ill both physically and mentally along the way. Thus, the experience of time was in many ways a bodily experience, physically as well as mentally.

Conclusion

We seldom hear about experiences and social understandings of time among migrants before they venture out on dangerous journeys, or how time turns many people into temporal prisoners fighting a system that seeks to throw them back, physically. In this chapter, I have set out to fill this gap by exploring, through fieldwork in Somaliland and among Somalis in Turkey, notions of the sociality of time in which movement becomes a way to catch up with time, and deportation, in whatever form, is experienced as being thrown back in time in a world that moves faster and faster.

I have argued throughout the chapter that moving through precarious landscapes becomes a way to manage the existential uncertainty of losing time. Being unable to spend his time in a valuable way by having a job that would sustain a living for himself and his family, Jabriil set himself in motion with a sense of direction by migrating. He was brutally stopped by imprisonment, however, and forced to return to the place where there 'is nothing to do', as Xalaane pointed out. Time, tempo and direction increased as he succeeded in finding a job. His time became valuable, as he was able to fill it with a job with which he could maintain himself, a job with a sense of future direction in which the tempo follows the flows of people working. Time became scarce. Jabriil's story, therefore, has shown how the tempo of time is always measured against its social surroundings when losing and gaining time—what I call 'homo-velocity' (Simonsen 2017). 'Homo-velocity' refers to time as embedded in a sense of direction that is moving forward according to social norms. Habaane takes this notion a step further and shows us how the experience of losing time is not erased by moving physically, but keeps being deeply embedded in the constant insecurity of the tempo and direction of time for young Somali women and men en route and how it is experienced through a change not only of location, but also physical, bodily changes and rhythm.

Adopting a broader perspective, this chapter has added to the understanding of time when uncertainty is a context rather than a brief moment.

Time is universal in the way that it passes everywhere in the world, hour by hour, minute by minute. However, time is also a social, embodied experience that, when detached from the hope of a prosperous future, creates uncertainty in the life-worlds of young Somali migrants.

REFERENCES

Ali, Nimo. 2016. *Going on Tahriib: The Causes and Consequences of Somali Youth Migration to Europe.* Kenya: Rift Valley Institute Research Paper 5.

Andersson, Ruben. 2014. *Illegality Inc. Clandestine Migration and the Business of Bordering Europe.* Oakland, CA, Berkeley: University of California Press.

Barakat, Halim. 1985. The Arab Family and the Challenge of Social Transformation. In *Women and the Family in the Middle East: New Voices of Change,* ed. Elizabeth Warnock Fernea, 27–48. Austin: University of Texas Press.

Bourdieu, Pierre. 2000. Social Being, Time and the Sense of Existence. In *Pascalian Meditations,* 206–245. Cambridge: Polity Press.

Bredeloup, Sylvie. 2012. Sahara Transit: Times, Spaces, People. *Population, Space and Place* 18: 457–467.

Collyer, Michael, and Hein de Haas. 2012. Developing Dynamic Categorisations of Transit Migration. *Population, Space and Place* 18: 468–481.

Durkheim, Emilie. 2008 [1915]. *The Elementary Forms of the Religious Life.* Mineola, NY: Dover Publications Inc.

Düvell, Franck. 2012. Transit Migration: A Blurred and Politicised Concept. *Population, Space and Place* 18: 415–427.

Evans-Pritchard, Edward Evan. 1969 [1940]. *The Nuer: A Description of the Modes of Livelihood and Political Institutions of a Nilotic People.* New York: Oxford University Press.

Geeldoon, Mohamed Hussein. 2016. *We Kissed the Ground: A Migrant's Journey from Somaliland to the Mediterranean.* Kenya: Rift Valley Institute.

Gell, Alfred. 1996 [1992]. *The Anthropology of Time: Cultural Constructions of Temporal Maps and Images.* Oxford, Washington, DC: Berg.

Glascock, Anthony. 1986. Resource Control Among Older Males in Southern Somalia. *Journal of Cross-Cultural Gerontology* 1: 51–72.

Hage, Ghassan. 2009. *Waiting. Melbourne.* Melbourne: University Press.

Hall, Samuel. 2015. *Investing in Somali Youth: Exploring the Youth–Employment–Migration Nexus in Somaliland and Puntland.* Nairobi: Commissioned by IOM Somalia. http://www.iom.int/sites/default/files/press_release/file/IOM-Investing-in-Somali-Youth-2015.pdf. Accessed November 6, 2017.

Henry, J. 1965. *Culture Against Man.* New York: Vintage Books.

Höhne, Markus Virgil. 2007. From Pastoral to State Politics: Traditional Authorities in Northern Somalia. In *State Recognition and Democratization in Sub-Saharan Africa: A New Dawn for Traditional Authorities?* ed. Lars Buur and Helene Maria Kyed, 155–182. New York: Palgrave Macmillan.

İçduygu, Ahmet, and Deniz Yükseker. 2012. Rethinking Transit Migration in Turkey: Reality and Representation in the Creation of a Migratory Phenomenon. *Population, Space and Place.* 18: 441–456.

Johnson-Hanks, Jennifer. 2002. On the Limits of Life Stages in Ethnography: Toward a Theory of Vital Conjunctures. *American Anthropologist* 104 (3): 865–880.

Mains, Daniel. 2007. Neoliberal Times: Progress, Boredom, and Shame Among Young Men in Urban Ethiopia. *American Ethnologist* 34 (4): 659–673.

Mead, M. 1928. *Coming of Age in Samoa.* New York: William Morrow and Company.

Parsons, T. 1964. *Essays in Sociological Theory.* Chicago: Free Press.

Pedersen, Marianne Holm. 2011. "You Want Your Children to Become Like You": The Transmission of Religion Practices Among Iraqi Families in Copenhagen. In *Mobile Bodies, Mobile Souls: Family, Religion and Migration in a Global World,* ed. Mikkel Rytter and Karen Fog Olwig, 117–138. Aarhus: Aarhus University Press.

Pederson, Marianne Holm. 2013. *Iraqi Women in Denmark: Ritual Performance and Belonging in Everyday Life.* Manchester and New York: Manchester University Press.

Reynolds Whyte, S., E. Alber, and S. van der Geest. 2008. Generational Connections and Conflicts in Africa: An Introduction. In *Generations in Africa: Connection and Conflict,* ed. E. Alber, S. van der Geest, and S. Reynolds Whyte. Berlin: Lit Verlag.

Schapendonk, Joris. 2012. Migrants' Im/Mobilities on Their Way to the EU: Lost in Transit? *Tijdschrift voor Economische en Sociale Geografie* 103 (5): 577–583.

Simonsen, Anja. 2017. *Tahriib: The Journey into the Unknown. An Ethnography of Mobility, Insecurities and Uncertainties Among Somalis en Route.* PhD dissertation, The University of Copenhagen, Copenhagen.

Stafford, Charles. 2000. Chinese Patriliny and the Cycles of Yang and Laiwang. In *Cultures of Relatedness. New Approaches to the Study of Kinship,* ed. Janet Carsten, 35–54. Cambridge: Cambridge University Press.

Turner, V. 1967. *The Forest of Symbols.* Ithaka, NY: Cornell University Press.

Vigh, Henrik. 2007 [2006]. *Navigating Terrains of War: Youth and Soldiering in Guinea-Bissau.* New York, Oxford: Berghahn Books.

Whyte, Zachary. 2009. *In Process: An Ethnography of Asylumseeking in Denmark.* PhD dissertation, Wolfson College, University of Oxford.

Whyte, Susan Reynolds, and Godfrey Etyang Siu. 2015. Contingency: Interpersonal and Historical Dependencies in HIV Care. In *Ethnographies of Uncertainty in Africa: Anthropology, Change and Development,* ed. Elizabeth Cooper and David Pratten, 19–35. London: Palgrave Macmillan.

Wulff, Helena. 1995. Introducing Youth Culture in Its Own Right: The State of the Art and New Possibilities. In *Youth Cultures: A Cross Cultural Perspective,* ed. Vered Amit-Talai and Helena Wulff, 1–18. London, New York: Routledge.

CHAPTER 7

"Wait, and While You Wait, Work": On the Reproduction of Precarious Labor in Liminal Spaces

Catherine Bryan

In a small town in rural Manitoba, Canada, a group of temporary foreign workers from the Philippines wait. In the Philippines, so too do their non-migrant kin. For both groups, this waiting corresponds to the hoped for completion of the migration project; added to the routine waiting, they manage the physical distance and time differences that separate them. This chapter draws on several examples from my multi-sited ethnography of this group of workers in Manitoba and their families in the Philippines. In it, I argue that these forms of waiting produce particular kinds of value for the small hotel that employs them, and that this occurs even as, for most of these migrant kin groups, this waiting eventually comes to an end. Following the exploitative tendencies of guest worker programs globally and in Canada (Binford 2013; Foster 2012; Fudge and MacPhail 2009; Lenard and Straehle 2012; Nakache and Kinoshita 2010), but filtered through the unique opportunity for permanent residency offered by the province, the hotel manipulates the timelines to which its workers are subject through a strategic and adaptive use of two immigration programs,

C. Bryan (✉)
Social Work, Dalhousie University, Halifax, NS, Canada

© The Author(s) 2018
P. G. Barber, W. Lem (eds.), *Migration, Temporality, and Capitalism*, https://doi.org/10.1007/978-3-319-72781-3_7

123

each with its own temporal characteristics and time-based objectives: the Manitoba Provincial Nominee Program, which offers permanency, and the Temporary Foreign Worker Program, which facilitates the short-term recruitment of temporary migrant labor.

Recruiting and retaining workers through these two programs, the hotel capitalizes on their distinct temporal logics, and as such on the manifold waiting of their migrant workers, and the depth of feeling and emotion (sadness, loneliness, but also boredom) these logics produce. In what follows, I elaborate these forms of waiting as they unfold and are experienced in the liminal spaces occupied by migrants and their non-migrant kin. Within the discipline of anthropology, liminality is used to signal the quality of ambiguity or disorientation that occurs in the middle of a ritual event (Turner 1967). During the liminal stage, participants find themselves at a threshold between old and new forms of identity, ways of understanding, and forms of belonging. For many migrants globally, this liminal stage is protracted. Often, they find themselves stalled at that threshold— unable to move forward toward a new identity or backward to the old. This is because labor migrants, as Aguilar Jr. (2014) argues, are liminal in relation to the place of origin (from which they are absent and from where others wait) *and* in relation to the site of employment and potential settlement. From this double liminality, the labor migrant "finds the self in a sort of suspended state of animation" (p. 159)—they wait, but what they wait for is unclear. Such an understanding and application of liminality denotes intense pause. Chu (2010), for example, draws on such a conceptualization of liminality in her work on transnational mobility amongst Chinese migrant workers. The liminal spaces she draws our attention to are not those of transition but immobility; her participants are stalled, held in place by systems and structures beyond their control.

For the migrants at the Hotel and their non-migrant kin in the Philippines, liminality is impermanent, but it is malleable, shaped by their employer in collaboration with the state which capitalize on it, and more precisely, on the intensity of feelings it produces. And yet, even as it is emotionally taxing, liminality and waiting are often articulated by the migrants as an exercise in patience as they wait for permanent residency. As a result, it is purposeful, born of longing and commitment, but also hope and anticipation. Such an exercise is, however, demanded by the various states with which they interact, and their employer, whose adaptation of the Manitoba Provincial Nominee Program has extended their waiting. Moreover, it reflects of the realities and dynamics of low-waged, low-status precarious overseas work, and it is generative of the kinds of migrant subjects required of that work. Indeed, the more these families wait, the more they grow accustomed to waiting. And as such, their waiting and indeed their liminality are central to the material reproduction of the Hotel—a small-scale capitalist enterprise in a tenuous rural economy.

The chapter is organized in three sections. The first offers a brief sketch of the policy context that these migrants and their employer occupy, as well as the ways in which the Hotel strategically uses both federal and provincial immigration policy to produce and reproduce its workforce. Sections two and three are organized around two narratives of waiting and liminality centred on two migrant kin groups. In section two, *waiting in minutes and hours*, Rosalinda tries (in vain) to reach her children on her 39th birthday. She has only just arrived in Manitoba and will not become a permanent resident for another two years, at which point, her children will be able to join her in Canada. In section three, *waiting in months and years*, Lillibeth, John and Shelly participate in a shared project of transnational social reproduction: Lillibeth from Manitoba, where she works at the front desk at the Hotel; John, Lillibeth's husband, who has remained in the Philippines with the couple's children; and Shelly, the family's *yaya* (or paid helper), who tends to the household's localized reproductive labor: cooking, cleaning, and caring for John and the children. From their various positions, each wait—but experience that waiting differently. These vignettes illustrate the waiting these migrants and their families endure. The chapter concludes with a discussion of how these forms of waiting are mutually constitutive and reinforcing. In it, I suggest that both augment the Hotel's capacity to extract value from its migrant workforce, which while increasingly permanent, retains some of the qualities of a temporary workforce.

THE POLICY CONTEXT

This section focuses briefly on two immigration programs, which were utilized between 2009 and 2014 by the Hotel in its recruitment of labor: the Federal Temporary Foreign Worker Program and the Manitoba Provincial Nominee Program. Temporary at its inception but now increasingly permanent, the Hotel's migrant workforce is reproduced at the intersection of these two programs. However, given these programs' competing objectives, the Hotel's migrant workforce is shaped by a dual intention: the recruitment of temporary, precarious labor on the one hand, and the long-term retention of new immigrants on the other. These policy objectives, and their adjoining programs, initiate two temporal processes to which the migrants at the centre of this work and their families are subject.

Between 2009 and 2012, all of the 44 migrant workers recruited by the Hotel arrived on temporary work permits through Canada's Temporary Foreign Worker Program. Despite its decades-long history and ongoing development and expansion, the expressed objective of the multi-faceted Temporary Foreign Worker Program has remained consistent: to facilitate the short-term employment of foreign nationals by Canadian employers who are temporarily unable to find appropriately skilled Canadian residents. Impermanency is, thus, embedded in the program in two ways. It refers, at once, to the status of the workers and to the nature of the vacant positions. Yet, reflected in the persistence of these initiatives is the unspoken permanency of temporary foreign labor in Canada. As Goldring (2010) argues in her work on precarity, rather than a stopgap measure, as articulated by program policy, the recruitment of temporary foreign labor is an ongoing and near-permanent strategy of both the Canadian state and employers. Indeed, the only thing temporary about temporary foreign labor in Canada are the workers. This ambiguity is critical, as it is the temporary configuration of these programs in conjunction with their long-standing dominance within specific labor markets (notably, agriculture, care and, more recently, food services) that underpin and reinforce their most problematic features and give employers the flexibility to minimize their commitments to labor.

And yet shortly after their arrival, the workers recruited by the hotel were informed by management that they could apply for permanent residency through the Manitoba Provincial Nominee Program (MPNP). The Program and its adjoining initiatives represent an attempt to reverse longstanding trends of depopulation through the recruitment of new immigrants to the province. The first of Provincial Nominee Programs, the Manitoba Program began as a Pilot Project in 1996. The Nominee Programs represent the initiation of provincial jurisdiction over immigration as stipulated in Section 95 of the Constitution Act (1982) (Carter et al. 2008; Dobrowolsky 2011). By way of a series of bilateral agreements with the federal government, the PNPs give provinces the authority to 'nominate' individuals who meet their respective PNP criteria, which correspond to each province's unique economic and labor market needs. 'Nomination' refers to the final step in the PNP application process, whereby having approved an application, the province nominates the applicant for settlement to their jurisdiction. That person then applies for permanent residency to the federal government, which includes their nomination. Between 2009 and 2014, during the five-year period this study focuses on, this application was submitted to Citizenship and Immigration Canada (CIC) (renamed Immigration, Refugees and Citizenship Canada in 2015). Final responsibility for selection—effectively approving of the nomination—rested with CIC, which was the sole authority for the issuance of admission visas in Canada (Carter et al. 2008).

For the once-temporary labor migrants at the Hotel, the Manitoba Provincial Nominee Program dramatically altered their long-term strategies of familial survival and reproduction. They would continue to be financially responsible for non-migrant kin (notably, parents), but their employment would no longer be dependent on foreign labor markets. Moreover, those who had partners and/or children would be reunited with them in Canada. In other words, life would become far more localized and far less uncertain. Given their protracted labor migration histories, this was a highly sought-after outcome. For the first few cohorts, the process was expedient. Typically, transition through the Nominee Program process occurred six months after arrival through the Temporary Foreign Worker Program. If hotel management was satisfied with the worker, a permanent position would be offered. The Hotel would write a letter of support that included a job offer, which would be included in the nominee application. During the first few years, all temporary migrants who worked at the Hotel passed through this process, with the exception of one, who had, after a few months, returned to her previous job in Singapore.

Over time, the Hotel's use of the Nominee Program shifted. While hotel management still used the program to ensure permanent residency for its initially temporary workers, they also began using it to recruit new workers. An innovative and progressive development in the recruitment of overseas workers, it allowed the Hotel to circumvent the Temporary Foreign Worker Program altogether. In these cases, the Hotel would work with their migrant employees to identify friends, family, and former co-workers with the requisite training and education and who were interested in employment in Manitoba. Such a use of the Manitoba Provincial Nominee Program was beneficial, then, for the Hotel, their increasingly permanent Filipino workforce, and the new recruits. For the Hotel, it meant a reduction in the costs associated with foreign worker recruitment.

For the migrant workers, it meant the re-establishment of existing networks of support. And finally, for new recruits, it meant that permanent residency was ensured, and moreover, that it would be secured prior to or shortly after landing in Canada. Moreover, for the province of Manitoba, it meant that new immigrants would be arriving with full-time permanent employment secured. This, coupled with the presence of friends and family in the town, would increase the likelihood of long-term retention—one of the government's primary objectives. These goals have largely been realized. The Hotel has access to its existing workforce's large, social and family networks for recruitment purposes; the members of that workforce benefit from the arrival of friends and family; and new recruits become permanent residents faster. That said, while most of the migrant workers recruited between 2009 and 2014 remain in the town and at the Hotel, 20 have resigned their positions, approximately half finding employment elsewhere in the town or in Manitoba, and the rest leaving the province.

Once permanent, migrant workers are no longer bound to their employer as when under the conditions of the Temporary Foreign Worker Program. They, like Canadian citizens and other permanent residents, are free to seek out other job opportunities and are able to move out of the province. That said, even as it is not enforceable, the province prefers if 'nominees' (as they are referred to) remain in Manitoba. Nominations are issued to TFWs with the implicit understanding that the individual will remain with their employer, and more explicitly, that they will remain in Manitoba. Given restrictions on how many nominations the province can issue annually, each is highly valued. And while there is no legal requirement that, once permanent, nominees remain, the province invokes a rhetoric of moral obligation to dissuade newcomers from leaving the province. In other words, while all resignations are disruptive for the Hotel, when the worker leaves Manitoba they are regarded as particularly problematic. In an effort to limit the number of resignations, but more precisely the number of newly permanent migrants leaving the province, the Hotel, with the support of the Manitoba Provincial Nominee Program, modified the timeline according to which temporary workers could transition to permanent residency. Whereas earlier cohorts could begin the process after 6 months of employment, those who arrived after 2013 had to wait until they reached 18 months. Furthermore, they were called upon to more rigorously defend their interest in remaining in Manitoba throughout the application process.

Importantly, the switch from 6 to 18 months did not affect rates of transition through the Manitoba Provincial Nominee Program, and the Hotel continued to support the vast majority of its temporary workers in becoming permanent residents. Despite this continuity, however, the extension of the period between landing as a temporary worker and the initiation of the nominee process prompts workers eager to become permanent residents to submit to labor practices and expectations that exceed the conditions of their work permits. Moreover, even in the absence of such practices—as in the case of the Hotel—workers continue to be a source of considerable and additional surplus value, in that their productivity and on-the-job outputs continue at rates higher than other, local workers. The threat of deportation, so acutely felt by temporary foreign workers globally, merges, in this instance, with the promise of permanency, which is offered as a reward to those who are diligent, careful in their work, and loyal.

A parallel and mutually reinforcing dynamic occurs in the context of the Hotel's use of the Manitoba Provincial Nominee Program to recruit from within the social and family networks of its existing migrant workforce, whereby the Hotel, like the province, invokes powerful discourses of obligation and reciprocity to compel retention. At the same time, longer-standing migrant workers, to increase the likelihood that they too will be reunited with friends and family (other than dependents and spouses/partners), work hard to retain favour with the Hotel, tolerating working conditions, they otherwise might not. In this scenario, pressure is exerted downward with the Hotel's newest nominated recruits bearing most of it. To retain these newcomers, the province exerts pressure on the Hotel, and the Hotel, not wanting to jeopardize its ability to use the Nominee Program, exerts pressure on its workers, who—anxious to bring in additional friends and family—in turn, exert pressure on new recruits, who despite their permanency and its adjoining freedom of mobility, feel compelled to stay for the duration of their "contracts" (which are non-binding, given their permanent status). Permanency has, thus, become a central, if somewhat amorphous, element of the Hotel's labor recruitment and retention strategy. It is harnessed practically, but also, discursively, as a means of retaining workers who would be otherwise free to resign, and of ensuring the complacency of those who wish to one day become permanent or, who wish to utilize the program to bring in overseas family. Put differently, while permanent residency appears a clear solution to the exploitative dynamics of temporary foreign worker recruitment, as it is operationalized by the Hotel as a means of labor recruitment and reten-tion, it takes on the features of those dynamics. In all of this, time—con-tracted or prolonged according to the actions of the Hotel, and experienced in manifold ways by the Hotel's migrant workers and their non-migrant kin—figures centrally as workers come to be positioned along a contin-uum of temporary, potentially permanent, almost-permanent, nominated and permanent. These designations are reflective of conditions and gen-erative of outcomes both material and temporal in nature. In the following sections, these conditions and outcomes are illustrated through a detailed reading of waiting in the liminal spaces that extend between the town and the Philippines.

WAITING IN MINUTES AND HOURS

What is life like in Manitoba? This question is almost always met with polite laughter. Though immediately qualified and contextualized, some variation of "boring" is typically offered: "I like Manitoba, but compared to Singapore, there's very little to do here"; "all I do is work and go home"; "I work, I eat, I sleep, I chat online"; "I come home, I cook, I wait for my husband to wake up in the Philippines"; "I miss my family"; "I miss the mall"; "I miss the pollution [in Manila]". It is not for a lack of organized outings, impromptu parties, or contact with friends and families in the Philippines via Skype or instant messaging that boredom persists as a condition of migrant life in the town; but rather, that moments of intense sociability and interaction punctuate lives, otherwise, described in terms of boredom, listlessness, longing, and loneliness. And yet, echoing Bruce O'Neill's recent exploration of boredom amongst homeless populations in Romania (2014, 2017), theirs is not a privileged boredom; rather, it is a boredom indicative of economic uncertainty and social instability. It is grounded in the transnational strategies employed by the migrants to redress those realities, and it is symptomatic of the various kinds of waiting undertaken by the Hotel's Philippine workers.

Rosalinda, a new Filipino recruit, has been working at the Hotel since March 2014. Rosalinda is still relatively new to the Hotel. Moreover, and perhaps more significantly, she is new to working overseas. She is adjust-ing. She is trying to make sense of a reality completely foreign to her: she is out-of-sync with her children. Four months in, she is still developing the skills required to navigate the distances, both spatial and temporal, between her basement apartment in Manitoba and her home in Philippines.

She has only just started to fill those spaces; to attune her life to that of an overseas worker, separated from her family, implicated in this transnational project that maybe wasn't all it was touted to be. In the town, like in other sites of migrant labor, parenting, intimacy and negotiation with spouses, and the overseeing of household finances come to be transmitted through a collection of communication technologies: instance messaging, Facebook posts, and emails. In the private spaces of bedrooms and apartments, these technologies alleviate some of the stress of waiting and some of its sadness. They also, however, have the tendency to accentuate both. Indeed, in the moments following contact, or when contact goes unrealized, that absence is often felt most acutely.

On her evening of her 39th birthday, Rosalinda and I stand in her bedroom. She shares a basement apartment with three other women, each has her own room. There is common space upstairs, shared by all the tenants in the building, all of whom work at the Hotel. From upstairs, the sound of footsteps and laughter. Rosalinda's birthday party is in full swing. "Don't you want to go upstairs?" I ask. But on her birthday, all she really wants is to talk to her children—her daughters. She hasn't been able to reach them. She will continue to try until she succeeds, and she would prefer to stay downstairs until then. Nothing will dissuade her, not the unreliable internet connection, not the music, not the laughter, not the food, not her new friends and certainly not me. "I'll be up soon", she offers kindly but firmly. She does not come up soon. Instead, Rosalinda spends most of the evening in her room by herself. Perhaps it is the sudden influx of mobile devices upstairs, all of which now vie for limited bandwidth, or perhaps it is a problem with the Wi-Fi in the Philippines, but she cannot connect to her children.

Boredom for those migrants at the Hotel may be an outcome of separation from family, or it may be an outcome of a different pace of life, but it is almost always discussed alongside waiting. Boredom is often is synonymous with waiting, while at the same time it is an outcome of waiting. "Boredom", Lars Svendsen argues, "is the 'privilege' of modern man [sic], and while there are reasons for believing that joy and anger have remained fairly constant throughout history, boredom seems to have increased dramatically" (2005, p. 21). The democratization of boredom—that is, the infiltration of boredom into the everyday lives of ordinary people (notably in the Western world)—reflects a series of related material and intellectual processes originating in the nineteenth century. Rather than a reflection of some characteristic of 'human nature', boredom, then, emerges as a particularity of modern life. That said, boredom, while 'accessible' by all and experienced by most, is not evenly distributed, nor is it equally or similarly experienced.

For the Hotel's migrant workers, boredom is multi-faceted. It is an outcome of separation from family. It is a symptom of their migration. And it is a consequence of service work—its repetitive and manual nature and its consistency from one day to the next, coupled with a generalized process of deskilling that many of them, following from their high levels of training in the Philippines, experience. Indeed, with rare exception, the work undertaken at the Hotel is regarded as less challenging, less stimulating and less rewarding than work undertaken elsewhere—even if that work, be it in the Philippines or in the context of other overseas employment, had been within the service and hospitality sector. Some of the migrant workers attribute this to the rurality of the hotel, and subsequently, the slower pace of work. Others describe the limited opportunity for professional advancement, an outcome of the Hotel's small size. Furthermore, for those who had been engaged in supervisory or managerial work in the past, the return to the 'shop floor' is challenging. In a similar vein, several of the Hotel's line cooks and fast food counter attendants had trained and worked as chefs, managing their own kitchens in hotel restaurants. Still others find that the Hotel was less than exacting in its implementation of standards. Particularly for those who had worked in high end hotels and restaurants, the basic level of services offered to hotel and dining guests is viewed as curtailing their ability to use their skill set, transforming work that many had taken pride in performing into a series of monotonous tasks.

Some workers, however, experience this monotony more acutely than others. Housekeepers, for example, engage in a series of similar tasks repeatedly until their assigned rooms are completed. In quick succession, the bed is stripped and remade, the carpet is vacuumed, surfaces are wiped down, the bathroom is disinfected, and the garbage is emptied. In contrast, those at the front desk are assigned a greater number of responsibilities, which, while repeated over the course of a shift, vary in substance. That said, while all workers are expected to abide by the Hotel's 'no phone' rule, which prohibits them from using their phones at work (except on their breaks), some are better able to avoid detection when they do. The housekeepers, in the seclusion of their work, have greater sustained access to communication technology throughout the day. This is facilitated by the Hotel's robust wireless internet, which is often more reliable than the internet in staff accommodation where the majority of workers live for their first two years in Manitoba. Those at the front desk or who serve in the restaurant or bar or who work as counter attendants at the coffee shop or sandwich counter are far more visible and, as such, less connected during working hours. Additional variation follows from shift work and changes in seasonal capacity. So that when they work the night shift, even those at the front desk may use their mobile devices without being noticed; moreover, during periods of customer downturn, managers and supervisors are more tolerant of mobile phone use on shift.

More often, however, slow business has the effect of reducing hours, in particular for housekeepers. So, while the front desk must always be staffed, housekeepers are often asked to leave early once they have completed cleaning and preparing their allotted rooms. This is significant. Boredom sets in most acutely in the hours outside of paid work, leaving some workers—like the housekeepers—more vulnerable to the effects of waiting. That said, even for those working a 40-hour week, with limited opportunity for overtime, nonworking hours represent 75 percent of the week (128 hours). Of course, some of this is spent sleeping. But sleep, often used as a strategy to counter boredom and loneliness, does not always come easily. Moreover, as the migrant workers remain attuned to the rhythms and routines of kin in the Philippines, sleep is often staved off—avoided to facilitate contact with children, parents, siblings, partners and friends.

Communication technologies are routinely deployed within these transnational spaces and around the edges of waiting, both short- and long-term. These technologies allow for what Parreñas (2005) labels *transnational communication*. Here, she refers to the flow of ideas, information, goods, money and emotion so critical to the reproductive strategies of migrants, and to sustaining the relationships at the centre of those strategies. Indeed, as Barber (2010) comments these technologies provide powerful means of "sustaining transnational ties to 'home' allowing for a 'stretching of intimacy' and an 'absent presence' over the time and space displacements in migrant's transnational families" (p. 150). These transnational strategies of reproduction are not naturally occurring, as Saskia Sassen reminds us, nor are they self-generative. Rather, they must be "produced, and such a feat of production requires capital fixity, vast concentrations of very material and not so mobile facilities and infrastructures" (2000, p. 217). Moreover, as Parreñas argues, "social and geographical inequalities shape the quality of [and indeed, the very possibility of] intimacy in transnational family life" (2005, p. 318). The capital fixity demanded of such infrastructure is distributed according to patterns of global hierarchy—patterns in which the Hotel's migrant workers are doubly positioned. In periods of crises or, reflecting Rosalinda's experience on her birthday, moments of inaccessibility, the extent of this dual-positionality comes to be revealed. Physically in Manitoba though emotionally connected to the Philippines, as these migrants wait in the uneven spaces created by capital, they experience the full force of the systems and structures that compel and require their mobility.

Waiting in Months and Years

The waiting that occurs in between contact with family in the Philippines is overlaid with a more persistent waiting: the outcome of the promise of permanency offered by the Manitoba Nominee Program and, more broadly, of the desire held by most to be permanently reunited with family. As the migrants at the Hotel wait, they work, and as they work, they wait. As they clear tables and strip beds, as they greet guests and prepare sandwiches, these workers wait—they wait for the completion of their migration projects, articulated in terms of permanent residency and reunification with family. When I met Lillibeth, who had arrived in late 2012, she was looking forward to submitting her application for permanent residency through the province. She had learned of the possibility of permanency shortly after arriving in Manitoba, such that though her departure from the Philippines was marked by the anxieties associated with a more protracted separation from family, those anxieties were redressed in relatively short order.

As the principal applicant on the family's Nominee application, Lillibeth orients her waiting to the long term. Lillibeth feels the separation from her children intensely, but the intensity of separation is tempered by the potential of permanent residency and reunification in Canada. Surrounded by a growing number of once temporary and now permanent migrant workers, Lillibeth is more secure in the possibility of these outcomes. She speaks mostly in terms of *when*. From the Philippines, her husband, John, in contrast less certain of the process, speaks primarily in terms of *if*. He misses his wife, and even as his days are busy, he describes them as aimless and unfocused. John's waiting is most acutely experienced in the hours, minutes and even seconds between contact with her. His phone always close at hand, he makes himself available to talk or to text throughout the day and night.

For Shelly, whose seven-year employment with Lillibeth and John has meant living away from her own family, this period of waiting is experienced differently. Rather than anticipating reunification, she is bracing herself for yet another separation. Although Shelly would like to go to Manitoba, given her training (a one-year course in aesthetics) and the informality that characterizes her work with the family, it is very unlikely that she will accompany John and the children when they join Lillibeth in Manitoba. Shelly does not meet the requirements of the Manitoba Provincial Nominee Program, nor those of what was then the Live-in Caregiver Program. Moreover, where the latter is concerned, even if she did meet the requirements, reflecting their Canadian-bound class status as service workers, Lillibeth and John would not qualify as employers under the Live-in Caregiver Program. Shelly's experience of waiting, then, is far less focused than that of Lillibeth and John as her future remains undetermined.

While the wait for permanency was unexpected for Lillibeth, like for many others it was certainly welcomed. Indeed, for many the waiting required of the Manitoba Provincial Nominee Program represented, at least in theory, the final leg of the migration project. Once permanency in Canada is granted, long-term settlement would begin, and separation and its adjoining complications would be remedied. *Wait and while you wait, work* is the message the Hotel's migrant workers implicitly receive from both the Manitoban state and their employer. In addition to boredom, the experience of waiting is often described in terms of longing. They miss their families; they imagine what life will be like after they become permanent residents; they look forward to the future. In this way, waiting is aligned with anticipation of a more secure and less precarious future. Waiting, then, occurs within a present that is characterized by uncertainty tempered by hope. And following from this, the boredom and longing referred to by the Hotel's workers, though ubiquitous, is not melancholic. Instead, boredom and longing—manifest in waiting—is experienced as an essential part of the broader projects of reproduction and immigration. And so, rather than serving as a register of inadequacy, waiting and boredom, and indeed, their liminality, are purposeful, signifying the migration project and the intentions embedded therein.

In the Philippines, the profound longing for migrant family members is palpable and sustained. There are noticeable absences. Sometimes these are shapeless, carried in the private thoughts and memories of non-migrant friends and family, revealed in comments like, "I think about her all the time, but I simply try to focus on work." And, "I stay busy, but I'm always thinking about him." Other times, they are more tangible. In the moments immediately following contact (via cell phone or internet), the weight of separation hangs heavily. When the voice and image of the loved one has just filled the room, their absence is more noticeable. And still at other times, this longing and absence assumes a shape. It is made visible through the uncanny nature of a system that prompts separation and then commodifies it, allowing for physical proximity only through the circulation of money and material goods.

For the migrants at the Hotel and their non-migrant spouses/partners and dependents in the Philippines who pass through the Nominee program, waiting is impermanent, but it is malleable, shaped by their employer, in collaboration with the state to capitalize on it, and more precisely on the intensity of feelings that it generates. And yet, even as it is emotionally taxing, waiting is often articulated by the migrants as an exercise in patience as they wait for permanent residency. As a result, it is purposeful, born of longing and commitment, but also hope and anticipation. This exercise, however, is demanded by the various states with which they interact, and by the Hotel, whose adaptation of the Manitoba Provinical Nominee Program has resulted in more waiting and uncertainty. Still, for those migrants recruited by the Hotel this period is one of protracted transition rather than perpetual uncertainty. This, as revealed in the example of Lillibeth, John and Shelly is a privileged (relatively speaking) position. Informed by and indicative of their respective class positions within globalized hierarchies of mobility and migration, Lillibeth, John and Shelly experience waiting and its outcomes differently. Shelly's life and future are determined by the agenda of the Hotel vis-à-vis labor recruitment, and that of the province of Manitoba vis-à-vis the retention of new immigrants, but she benefits from neither. She waits according to the time frame established by the migration project of her employers and the immigration programs with which they interact, but the liminality she experiences, unlike John and Lillibeth's, is not one of transition; rather, it is ongoing. It is, as described by Chu (2010), one of stasis and immobility.

Conclusion: On the Value of Waiting

The adaption of the Manitoba Provincial Nominee Program to include a waiting period of 18 (rather than 6) months is an illustration of the ways in which waiting, and the liminal states in which waiting occurs, can be adjusted to meet the requirements of states and employers. This is not lost on the workers themselves. Dennis, for example, arrived late in 2013, and as such was subjected to the extended waiting period initiated by the Hotel and the province. Because he knows of the policy change, Dennis feels the weight of this *extra* time. At the same time, this protracted exercise in patience (on the part of the migrants) generated new opportunities for accumulation for the Hotel. In their delivery of reproductive labor to the Hotel's guests, the Hotel's migrant workers engage in affective performances dependent upon the management of their emotions. They do this to generate the effect of hospitality central to the production undertaken at the Hotel. The Hotel takes advantage of the emotional labor necessary for this production in two ways. This labor underpins the interactive quality of the services provided, wherein workers come to embody the Hotel's intentions toward their clients. The profound and often fraught emotions that accompany migration—those that must be managed on the shop floor—also serve as a mechanism through which the higher than average value of Philippine workers comes to be realized. In other words, the Hotel capitalizes on the intensity of the workers' feelings, generated through separation and waiting, to ensure a high degree of productivity and loyalty in the face of exploitative working conditions. Engendered by the inequalities of low-skilled labor migration and harnessed by the Temporary Foreign Worker Program, these conditions have the effect of generating additional capital for the employer. Motivated, at once, by their separation from family and their desire to be reunited, Dennis explained that workers "keep it together".

In the context of prolonged waiting, "keeping it together" becomes more arduous and more vital, as prolonged time away from family encourages the ongoing emotional self-discipline required of hospitality. From the vantage point of the Hotel, then, waiting is not only a necessary outcome of the migration process, but also a productive component of the labor process. Perhaps, paradoxically, the more the Philippine workers at the Hotel wait, the more inclined they are to wait; the closer they feel to the completion of their migration projects, the less likely they are to jeopardize it. The more they wait, the more they work (in the interim at least), tolerating conditions that they perhaps otherwise would not. At the same time, if workers are able to repress the feelings generated by separation and waiting in their performances of hospitality (if they manage to "keep it together" on the floor), it is because they are constantly reminded of the stakes each time they go online and each time they check their phones.

Through their willingness to wait and through the strategies they deploy to minimize the immediate effects of waiting, these migrant workers adapt to the requirements of their employer. Thus, waiting serves as a mechanism of accumulation, and as such it underpins the Hotel's material reproduction. When viewed through such a lens, the experience of waiting, imbued with emotion, offers more than simply insight into the hardship of separation, revealing something of international labor migration. As the Hotel capitalizes on the moments of intense pause, boredom and longing generated by the Temporary Foreign Worker Program and the Manitoba Provincial Nominee Program, waiting as described here is about power, and it is a critical dimension of the political economy in which it operates. Migration as a strategy deployed by states, employers and families, then, is as much about time as it is about space. And that just as those implicated in projects of migration (states, employers, the migrants themselves and their families) navigate and negotiate the complications of physical distance, so too must they contend with time in various iterations.

References

Aguilar, Filomeno V., Jr. 2014. *Migration Revolution: Philippine Nationhood and Class Relations in a Globalized Age*. Singapore: NUS Press.

Asis, Maruja Milagros B., Shirlena Huang, and Brenda S.A. Yeoh. 2004. When the Light of the Home Is Abroad: Unskilled Female Migration and the Filipino Family. *Singapore Journal of Tropical Geography* 25 (2): 198–215.

Barber, Pauline Gardiner. 2010. Cell Phones, Politics, and the Philippine Labor Diaspora. In *Class, Contention, and a World in Motion*, ed. W. Lem and P.G. Barber, 138–160. New York: Berghahn Books.

Binford, Leigh. 2013. *Tomorrow We're All Going to the Harvest: Temporary Foreign Worker Programs and Neoliberal Political Economy*. Austin, TX: University of Texas Press.

Carter, Tom, Margot Morrish, and Benjamin Amoyaw. 2008. Attracting Immigrants to Smaller Urban and Rural Communities: Lessons Learned from the Manitoba Provincial Nominee Program. *Journal of International Migration and Integration/Revue de l'integration et de la migration internationale* 9 (2): 161–183.

Chu, Julie Y. 2010. *Cosmologies of Credit: Transnational Mobility and the Politics of Destination in China*. Durham, NC: Duke University Press.

Dobrowolsky, Alexandra. 2011. The Intended and Unintended Effects of a New Immigration Strategy: Insights from Nova Scotia's Provincial Nominee Program. *Studies in Political Economy* 87 (1): 109–141.

Foster, Jason. 2012. Making Temporary Permanent: The Silent Transformation of the Temporary Foreign Worker Program. *Just Labor* 19: 22–46.

Fudge, Judy, and Fiona MacPhail. 2009. The Temporary Foreign Worker Program in Canada: Low-Skilled Workers as an Extreme form of Flexible Labor. *Comparative Labor Law and Policy Journal* 31: 101–139.

Goldring, Luin. 2010. Temporary Worker Programs and Precarious Status: Implications for Citizenship, Inclusion and Nation Building in Canada. *Canadian Issues, Special Issue of Temporary Foreign Workers* (Spring): 50–54.

Lenard, Patti Tamara, and Christine Straehle, eds. 2012. *Legislated Inequality: Temporary Labor Migration in Canada*. Kingston: McGill-Queen's Press-MQUP.

Nakache, Delphine, and Paula J. Kinoshita. 2010. The Canadian Temporary Foreign Worker Program: Do Short-Term Economic Needs Prevail Over Human Rights Concerns? *IRPP*.

O'Neill, Bruce. 2014. Cast Aside: Boredom, Downward Mobility, and Homelessness in Post-Communist Bucharest. *Cultural Anthropology* 29 (1): 8–31.

———. 2017. *The Space of Boredom: Homelessness in the Slowing Global Order*. Durham, NC: Duke University Press.

Parreñas, Rhacel Salazar. 2005. *Children of Global Migration: Transnational Families and Gendered Woes*. Palo Alto, CA: Stanford University Press.

Sassen, Saskia. 2000. Women's Burden: Counter-Geographies of Globalization and the Feminization of Survival. *Journal of International Affairs* 53: 503–524.

Svendsen, Lars. 2005. *A Philosophy of Boredom*. London: Reaktion Books.

Turner, Victor Witter. 1967. *The Forest of Symbols: Aspects of Ndembu Ritual*. Vol. 101. Ithaca, NY: Cornell University Press.

CHAPTER 8

Migration Across Intersecting Temporalities: Venezuelan Migrants and 'Readiness' in Montreal

Turid Fånes Sætermo

INTRODUCTION

The quiet street in the newly developed residential area in central Montreal is lined with neat terrace houses. It is late spring 2010, and I have come to interview Eva and Eduardo, a middle-class couple in their 50s, about their experiences of migrating from Venezuela to Montreal, Canada. We sit around the living room table talking about how, after having submitted their application to Canadian immigration authorities in 2004, they prepared for migration. Eduardo says:

> In this interim, for a couple of years, you have this insecurity. Because you prepare for leaving without knowing if you will. The decisions you make while you are there, you make them thinking that you are leaving, but there is always this doubt. If the answer is no, you will feel like you have lost these years of your life, because your life is already a function of the decision to migrate. You are already detaching yourself from the country.

T. F. Sætermo (✉)
Department of Neuromedicine and Movement Science,
Norwegian University of Science and Technology, Trondheim, Norway

© The Author(s) 2018
P. G. Barber, W. Lem (eds.), *Migration, Temporality, and Capitalism*, https://doi.org/10.1007/978-3-319-72781-3_8

Eva and Eduardo are among the growing number of migrants that have come to Canada from Venezuela since 2000. As a group, they represent among many other things the travelling of skills, which makes them attractive for countries that seek to attract the highly educated (Cohen 2006; Kuptsch and Pang 2006; Simmons 2010). Emigration from Venezuela is also a classed phenomenon and it is predominantly middle-class individuals who leave. Class is an important element in social identity in Venezuela, since society is strongly divided along class lines (Ellner 2008). Many middle-class individuals feel that they have become the targets of the socialist government in power since 1999 and that they have been deprived of the futures they envisioned before. In contrast, Canada's skilled worker policy cast them as wanted and welcome. The decision to migrate, then, also carries the anticipation that the lost ways of living and projected futures can be restored.

The connection between immigration management and labor market-driven demands has deep roots in Canada (Knowles 1997; Kelley and Trebilcock 2010). In an historical perspective, the priorities and strategies of immigration authorities have shifted between the idea of the desired immigrant as the "right citizen" or as the "right worker" (Hawkins 1972). However, migration has increasingly become viewed in terms of its economic role. A separate category of immigration based on skills and education was introduced already in 1976, and in 2002—also under a Liberal government—a point-based selection system was developed which was intended to be more effective at singling out immigrants who would succeed economically. After 2006, a series of neoliberally informed reforms pursued by the Conservative government of Stephen Harper (in power from 2006 to 2015) sought to make the immigration system faster, more flexible and more strongly focused on "fuelling economic prosperity". The explicit goal is to attract immigrants who have the ability to integrate and become productive fast and, ideally, without the need for social or economic support in the process (Simmons 2010; Root et al. 2014; Sætermo 2016). With this emphasis on 'winning time', a temporal reckoning has come to dominate migration into Canada. For example, the new Express Entry system, introduced in 2015 is based on faster processing of applications for applicants wanted by employers instead of the former practice of processing applications according to the chronology of their submission (CIC 2012).

The interim Eduardo refers to is an unintended consequence of the 2002 reforms' objective of singling out the "most preferred" skilled immigrants.

The goal of the skilled worker program is to mold an immigration stream that matches Canada's current labor market needs; however, the procedures put in place in 2002 produced a temporal paradox: The extensive verification of each applicant caused lengthy processing which could last around two to three years. The process involved verification of the documents supplied by applicants, assessment of their personal suitability through an individual interview, and a check of their health condition, criminal record and financial situation. During this period, as Eduardo notes above, the lives of prospective migrants were in many ways a function of the decision to migrate, as they were subjected to temporal forces of both Canada and Venezuela. Social relations, family ties, economic priorities, career decisions, time use and so on were all influenced by and negotiated in the light of the upcoming possible departure. "It destabilizes you emotionally", Eva commented, "because in many ways you are neither here nor there."

This chapter focuses on this interim, which I shall refer to as the 'pre-migration period', exploring how different temporal forces and orderings combine to construct, structure and influence migrants' experiences and trajectories in this period. In particular, the chapter considers Canadian authorities' attempts at speeding up immigration processes and 'winning time' by urging immigrants to arrive 'already ready' to become productive workers. The interim thus reflects temporal discrepancies and their articulation in terms of the policies of neoliberal capitalism. The chapter draws on interview data from my ethnographic research on Venezuelan immigration to Montreal between 2008 and 2013, to discuss how political, social and bureaucratic processes in both Canada and Venezuela imposed themselves onto the everyday lives of these migrants-to-be in ways that extended beyond formal bureaucratic procedures, and that were sometimes at odds with other temporal frames, including the migrants' own life projects. The discussion centers on migrants' personal experiences of the temporal discrepancies, as presented in their narratives. These narratives illustrate how individual migrants negotiate various temporal forces in real life and create strategies to cope with the ambivalence and dilemmas they represent with regards to their personal life projects. I will first briefly present some theoretical concepts that address the ways in which migrants engage with and are constrained by temporalities of different societies simultaneously. Second, I will present the empirical case of middle-class emigration from Venezuela and discuss how migration was cast as a way to recuperate middle class ways of living and the 'lost' futures of the past for the informants in the study. In the third part I elaborate on the political-historical moments in which the migration unfolded; on the one hand, with regards to political, economic and social developments during Hugo Chavez' rule in Venezuela, and on the other, with regards to developments in Canada's skilled migration policy. The final part of the chapter discusses these policies further, focusing particularly on the Harper government's attempts at manipulating the temporalities of the immigration system to produce faster results with regards to immigrants' labor market integration; it argues that this produced a shift that involved a temporal reframing of processes associated with integration and resettlement.

NARRATIVES AND TIMESCAPES

A central motive behind the emerging literature on temporal dimensions of migration has been the recognition that these have usually been left invisible in our analysis, and that there are few examples of studies that explicitly focus on temporality (Griffiths et al. 2013; Robertson 2014). Yet, the multiplicity, heterogeneity and complexity of time have long been acknowledged by social scientists (see for example Cwerner 2001; Adam 2004). Migration studies bring new questions to the field, such as for example how migrants engage with and are constrained by temporalities of different societies simultaneously (Griffiths et al. 2013). The present chapter engages with this question through a focus on the lived experience of 'multi-sited' temporalities. I suggest that focusing on individual narrated experience is a useful way to gain insights into the workings of different temporal frames. Experiences of discrepancies between these manifest themselves in migrants' lives as temporal dilemmas and contradictions, which unfold in everyday settings related to, for example, family life, friendship, work, leisure, economy or dwelling. Narratives elucidate how and when temporal frames intervene in individual trajectories and the ambivalence and predicaments this may cause. They also shed light on migrants' strategies vis-à-vis temporal constraints and contradictions, and contribute to contextualize these. Finally, narratives provide us with concrete examples of time experienced as frenzied or stagnant, scarce or in abundance, occupied or empty—sometimes simultaneously, and with regards to different aspects of one's life.

Several scholars have put forward analytical concepts that seek to capture the complexity of time and temporalities. For example, Adam (1998) proposed the notion of 'timescape' to bring together quantitative time, the connections between space and time, and the multi-dimensionality of time experienced at different levels. The multi-dimensionality of time encompasses individually experienced time, social and cultural time, and time as an historical dimension. The notion of timescale has also been used in ethnographic research as a way to analytically connect the macro level of global political economy, the meso level of migration regimes, and the level of the individual (Robertson 2014). Robertson (2014) employs this notion in combination with the concept of 'time track' which seeks to capture movement that happens over time, but not necessarily in a forward, linear way. Rather, the notion of time track encompasses the "dynamic senses of beginnings and endings, disruptions, withdrawals, accelerations and decelerations" (Robertson 2014: 4). Notions such as of timescape, time scales and time track compel us to consider time and temporality as complex and multiplex, and to go beyond simply treating time as a "neutral medium in which events take place", as Adam (2000: 126) put it. With these insights in mind, I will consider the multiple temporal frames at work in the pre-migration period for my interviewees, and discuss these in relation to the migrants' individual situations and life cycles.

RECUPERATING THE FUTURES OF THE PAST

Eva and Eduardo and the other migrants I interviewed settled in Montreal during the first decade of the twenty-first century and were part of a rise of emigration from Venezuela that commenced in the early years of the presidency of Hugo Chavez. When my interviewees made the decision to apply to Canada, Venezuela was experiencing societal and political polarization, and serious and growing problems of crime and insecurity, corruption, shortages of basic goods and high inflation. Yet, in this moment emigrants claimed to be leaving because of uncertainty with regards to the future, not because of material want. Eduardo says:

> When we were young and had the children, we dreamt that they would grow up in a country that continued to develop, with its values. With its limitations, too, but with its grandness [*grandeza*]. Unfortunately, forces came into play that we could not control.

Decisions to migrate are often understood as motivated by aspirations for the future (Halfacree 2004; Vigh 2009). Related to this is the notion of agency as informed by the past and orientated to the future (Emirbayer and Mische 1998), of seeing one's life in a direction, imagining and projecting futures (Rapport 2004). These elements were central in the narratives of the immigrants I interviewed. A significant driver in their decisions was the desire to recuperate futures they had imagined, but that had been 'lost', such as, for example, formerly predictable career paths that had now been rendered insecure. In the present moment in Venezuela, they thought that the 'lost' future could only be realized elsewhere. As mentioned in the introduction of this chapter, their middle-class background played a significant role here; their narratives of Venezuela and their own emplacement in Venezuelan society were largely articulated through the trope of class. They would, for example, frequently mention the years they had invested in acquiring competences that would benefit the country and express bitterness with regards to the political and ideological developments in Venezuela that had made them (the middle class) symbols of inequality, self-interest and undue privilege. Venezuela was described as a country where it was no longer possible to lead a meaningful life nor imagine a future, a description often set against an image of the peaceful and stable country it had been. For example, Daniel said:

> It was a slow deterioration, slow but constant. I remember that until I was 10, no, 15, I had not heard of such problems, this violence. Attacks, robberies. But there is no particular moment where you can say, here, this is when it changed. It's been happening slowly. When the politics are bad and the economy, then poverty increases, and these things proliferate. Now I would describe it as chaos. Everyone do as they please.

Daniel interpreted the situation as so bad that it had no foreseeable solution; according to his estimates, it would take many years to restore a "normality", and he did not think that he would live long enough to experience any significant improvement. This assumption had played an important role in his decision to migrate: his own life was limited in time, as he himself put it, he therefore could not afford wait. Thus from Daniel's point of view, the political regime administered potentially unlimited time, whereas for him, living once and living now, time was a scarce resource.

Most of the migrants I interviewed were in the phase of life associated with early careers and founding families, the majority of them in their 20s and 30s, and when they submitted their application, they envisioned Canada as a place where they would raise their children, spend the rest of their working years and live their social lives. Migration was imagined spatially as an A to B movement and temporally as a long-term project. Their migration should also be seen in the light of a desire to recover lost social and economic positions, which was also set in a long-term perspective. They claimed to have been aware that their skills and class would not be immediately convertible in Canada, and from that perspective the process represented a temporary set-back. However, the expectation was that in a longer temporal perspective this 'lost' time would be recaptured, so that migration represented a sort of "going back in order to go forth". Such ideas illustrate that migrants do not necessarily imagine the time track of migration as a process moving forward in a linear way.

A WINDOW OF TIME

Migration trajectories should be understood as imagined and configured at the juncture of political-historical moments in both source and destination countries. The immediate context of the decision to migrate for the migrants I interviewed was the unfolding social, economic and political developments in Venezuela. It is significant that in this moment emigration was both contested and increasingly common (Paez 2015). The interviewees were part of an avant-garde in the sense that their emigration represented something historical new, a break with the country's past. In fact, Venezuela distinguishes itself from many Latin American countries in that prior to the present wave it did not have a history of emigration (Pellegrino 2001), rather, it was traditionally a destination for immigration. Several of the migrants I interviewed mentioned this fact, locating their own migration as untypical in Venezuela's history, and thus also underlining the abnormality of the country's present situation. With Chavez' rise to power the country had become divided into *chavistas* (supporters) and *nonchavistas* (opponents), and in this climate of political polarization, emigration was inevitably understood as a political and moral statement. Migration, then, was set in the cleavage between those who experienced the present as disquieting and those who saw promising futures in it. Such differing views also affected family relations and social networks for some of the migrants. For example, Eva's parents were strongly in favor of Chavez and thus could not understand why she had wanted to leave Venezuela. Eva says:

> According to them, the country is experiencing its best moments. So my mother and father protested. They said, 'You are abandoning us and we are getting old'. I told them, 'You abandoned me when you continued to vote for a president that is mad!'

Some had friends who reacted negatively upon hearing about their plans to migrate, accusing them of "leaving the ship" instead of staying and fighting. Michelle told me that when her plans of migrating became known, she was accused of abandoning her country:

> You feel like a traitor because, you know, they'd say that 'if all the good people leave we surrender the country to disaster'. But they've had to leave too. Because either you change and begin to work for the government, or else you find yourself in an extremely difficult situation.

The highly politicized and controversial nature of emigration in Venezuela meant that many chose to be discreet about the project. Some of my informants even kept the decision to migrate secret during the entire period after the decision was made and until they received their visa, even for close family members and friends. Ana says:

> You cannot say that you are leaving; you have to pretend as nothing, even though it is the only thing on your mind.

One crucial dimension here is that the new emigration is to a large part composed of highly educated individuals, and that the exodus is understood as triggering further emigration. In this perspective, emigrating would contribute further to draining the country of much-needed competence, which produced very mixed emotions in some of the migrants I interviewed. At the same time, the political and social developments produced a sense of growing urgency. For example, when Michelle and her husband submitted their application, she said they had seen it as their "plan B", in case things would get worse in the country:

> We didn't know if we would get a visa, or if we would even use it. But by the time the visa arrived two years later we had become desperate to leave, it was all we wanted.

The sense of urgency was also linked to the perceived window of time containing the possibility of leaving. Some feared that it would become increasingly difficult to leave the country in an orderly and legal way, especially since the outflow was largely composed of highly educated individuals and thus represented a problematic human capital flight. The government had imposed restrictions on the amount of foreign currency individuals could possess, and rumors wanted that the government would begin to withhold passports. There was also the fear that Canada would change immigration rules and that it would become more difficult to obtain residency in Canada, or that immigration authorities would seek to curb immigration by, for example, relocating visa offices or conducting migration interviews less frequently, or begin to require proof of language proficiency in advance. Sometimes there was a short timespan between not even considering migration and deciding to leave. Eva:

> At that time we didn't think about migrating yet. We were thinking about maybe buying a new car. When we migrated, we were the first among our friends. Two years later, all of them had left the country.

"Already Ready" Migrants

Canada's skilled immigration program made it a potential destination for Venezuelan in this period, and the migrants in this study conformed very much to Canadian immigration authorities' ideas of 'ideal immigrants', as mentioned above. The immigration authorities therefore realized several recruitment missions in Venezuela to woo these skilled individuals. The notion of skills, it should be noted, is also a momentary matter. As Freitas et al. (2012) have pointed out, skills are not neutral and universal, but dependent upon specific socioeconomic and political contexts. The link between labor market needs and type of skills of wanted immigrants is also politicized. For example, Faraday (2012) argues that immigrants in professional, managerial or other occupations designated as skilled are cast as beneficial for Canada and offered permanent residency, whereas migrant workers in occupations that require less formal education are cast as likely economic burdens and constructed as temporary migrants, even if labor shortages in these occupations might be chronic.

Over the last decade, Canadian immigration authorities have had as primary objective to make the immigration system more responsive to the immediacy of labor market needs. Present policies therefore prioritize formal qualifications combined with personal skills associated with the ability to obtain, keep and switch jobs in a fast-changing labor market. The ideal migrant in this picture should be flexible, independent, goal-oriented and ready to become productive fast (Barber 2008; Root et al. 2014). The former Canadian Minister of Immigration described them as "immigrants who will hit the ground running". I employ the notion of 'readiness' to frame the connection between the lived consequences of the temporal frames imposed on prospective migrants and the manipulation of time in concordance with neoliberal agendas more generally. The notion of readiness, I suggest, brings together the goal of immediacy that the immigration system seeks to achieve, and the real or felt expectations on applicants to conform, perform and prioritize in certain ways during the application process, in order to demonstrate their suitability with regards to this goal. The notion thus works to illuminate how the migration system imposes its temporal frames on applicants in the pre-migration period.

The narratives presented here show that the expectations combined with the formal bureaucratic obligations structured and influenced migrants' lives in many ways. With the submission of the immigration application they embarked on a path of obligatory steps that were fixed in chronology but not in time. The process thus advanced through relatively unpredictable shifts between dead time and rushes, which in turn needed to be negotiated into already busy lives. Persons who wish to immigrate to Québec must first apply to the Québec Ministry of Immigration (provincial level) and then to the Canadian Ministry of Citizenship and Immigration. After submitting their application to Québec, the next step was the immigration interview, which would take place somewhere between 6 to 12 months after submitting the application. Candidates either passed or failed the immigration interview and the decision was immediate. Those who passed would after some time receive a Québec Selection Certificate, with which they could apply to Immigration Canada for a permanent residency visa. This step involved a second round of filling in forms, supplying requested documents and paying fees. When Immigration Canada was done with the processing of the application, a medical exam was required, along with an updated transcript of one's police certificate.

The applicants did not know when the next step would take place and thus had to cope with speeds and rhythms of procedures that were sometimes in conflict with their own temporal patterns and expectations. One could suggest that from Canadian authorities' point of view, flexibility with regards to shifts between 'fast' and 'slow' time, and the ability to cope with unpredictability, could be perceived as a useful personal skill in a highly flexible labor market. Several migration researchers have studied how time can work as a disciplinary practice of the state, for example, that immigration authorities manipulate time as a form of control to regulate immigration (see for example Robertson 2015). Although the protracted processing time could work to ward off 'unserious' candidates, it was generally considered a problem for Canada, since it could also demotivate the wanted applicants, especially considering that these were sought also by other countries. A related problem was the unpredictability of the process, which also frustrated applicants. While the progression from step to step was clear, the pace and speed of the process was experienced as unpredictable and shifting, and this would at times cause great stress or disappointment. According to Eva:

> The first step of the process was Québec. That one passed fast. After 3 months, we were notified that we had been accepted. We were surprised and though that it would go fast and that soon we would be leaving. We announced for our family and all our friends that we were soon going to migrate. We did not know that the process would take much longer that we had imagined. Afterwards it lasted very much longer, the federal part.

The immigration interview was narrated as a stressful event given its vital importance. In the interview, the feasibility of their migration projects was assessed, including their economic situations, work experiences, language skills, adaptability and personal suitability. The evaluation of the latter was based on for example their general knowledge of Québec, knowledge of the job market and living expenses, and their plans when it came to career and integration. The numerous online migrant blogs were useful in the preparations of the interview, with their real-time, insider information, including lists of common interview questions. Preparations were also guided by assumptions about the kind of immigrants Canada was looking for, ideas that were quite explicitly communicated on the authorities' websites. For example, the official immigration webpage of Québec addresses candidates seeking to "achieve their goals, push their limits and expand their horizons". Several interviewees commented that they had wanted to come across as determined, competent, motivated, well-organized and realistic. These qualities had to be demonstrated in the interview and performing convincingly was understood as crucial for their chances of being selected. As Karen said:

> We lived nearby, but I got up super early to iron my blouse and my skirt. The papers were already in my handbag, I had prepared that the evening before. I knew that whichever they asked for, I could take it out easily, not having to search for it. I knew all the important dates by heart. I was confident that I would make a good impression; the only thing that worried me was the French. What if I began to trip over the words? What if I had forgotten an important word?

The migrants, I suggest, also sought to present themselves as the 'right immigrant' through their management of their application and the migration project, as some of them called it. This concern translated into them striving to submit a flawless application demonstrating their ability to understand and accomplish tasks, organize time, respect deadlines and otherwise comply with formalities. Approaching the migration project with the same assiduity and resolution as he had done with his university studies, Felix was convinced that this effort had been remarked:

> I am enterprising [*soy emprendedor*]. When I begin something, I complete things. When I started the process of migration it was as if the decision was already made. I think they saw that.

However, sometimes this well-ordered self-presentation conflicted with external temporal orderings, especially with regards to the slowness and 'red tape' practices of the Venezuelan bureaucracy and the deadlines demanded by the Canadian immigration system. Sometimes it was necessary to take time off from work to obtain documents, which could conflict with time pressures at work as well as the need for discretion regarding migration plans. In addition to these occasional obligations, there were obligations that required applicants invest time on a more general and long-term basis, such as, for example, saving up the required amount of money and learning French. The amount of points that Québec Immigration authorities accord candidates who speak French meant that learning the language was a high priority. This necessitated taking classes and studying at home, often on top of full-time employment and the exigencies of family life. Language skills were evaluated in the immigration interview, and failing this would require more time. Two of the interviewees had experienced this and had to go back to intensive study for another 8 months before they were interviewed again, and passed. Saving up money was also a priority, which typically translated into more and longer workdays and cutting expenses. One interviewee described the period as one in which she was only "working, working, working" to save up. In some ways, the pre-migration period could be described as liminal (Turner 1967); an in-between, transitional and ambiguous period during which they felt, as Eva noted, "neither here nor there" with regards to both time, space and status. One interviewee described the period through an analogy of knitting, as "casting off the stitches of one life while contemplating the pattern of another". It was a period during which no new projects were initiated, as Michelle relates:

You don't travel anywhere, because you are saving. You cut all kinds of expenses because you know you're going to need the money later. You don't initiate any projects. You don't buy new curtains, because you are leaving. You don't sign up for that course, you don't paint that wall, because you are leaving. Your life freezes. You don't plan anything because you are always on standby.

STAGNANT TIME, FRENZIED TIME

Running through these everyday dilemmas was the overarching uncertainty with regards to the outcome, as well as the temporal uncertainty over the future. Often the most difficult aspect of this was not knowing how long the period would last. As Eduardo noted in the citation in beginning of the chapter, no indications were given as to where one was in the process until the day the visa suddenly arrived. Eduardo:

> The possibility is there that you won't be accepted. And since that possibility is there, the decisions you make are never 100%. It's true, the [Canadian] government says, don't sell your house, don't sell your car, don't quit your job, until you have received the visa. And when you get the visa, that is when you are leaving. It creates a situation where psychologically you feel uncertain. People ask you but you cannot say for sure whether or not you are leaving.

The uncertainty related to the tempo and pace was a great source of frustration. While the feeling of urgency and impatience with regards to the developments in Venezuela was growing, time seemed to stand still with regards to the Canadian process. Griffiths et al. (2013: 18) note that "[e]xpectations, experiences and conflicts of speed are relevant at every stage of migration and are often felt to be in conflict. For example, the pace of change, or speed of bureaucratic or legal processes are often considered problematic by those subject to them". The feeling of stasis was fuelled by both the perceived slowness of the Venezuelan bureaucracy and the perceived slowness of the Canadian immigration regime. Felix:

> The period is too long. One year should be sufficient. After one year, you want to go on with your life. And things may have changed; even if you made plans, you cannot foresee everything. You may lose your job, you may get married, or have a child. And then suddenly there is more paperwork, and you need more money than you had expected. In that period of two years, your whole life may have changed.

These sentiments should also be seen in relation to life cycles and the fact that most of the interviewees were in a period of life where careers are developed, families formed and homes established. Decisions related to migration must be seen in relation to life stages, Gardner (2009) writes, and for most of the interviewees migration had been imagined as a way to regain some sort of control over the setting in which their children would be raised, their careers advanced and so on. The upcoming, though uncertain, emigration played in on these processes in several ways, mostly by way of decelerating them. Migration is often understood to represent temporal interruptions, for example, with regards to starting families (Griffiths et al. 2013). However, sometimes the opposite could be true. For example, in the Québec point-based system, a child equaled 4 points, and I was told anecdotes of migrants who had precipitated an addition to the family in part for this reason, though I never had such anecdotes confirmed. In the case of Eva and Eduardo, however, the unexpected arrival of a grandchild added a whole year to the process. Eva:

> The process stopped because our granddaughter was born. It delayed it with a year, because we had to do her paperwork too.

Eva related the moment the interviewees were notified by the Embassy that they had obtained the permanent resident visa as causing a dramatic shift of speed. After long months of stagnant suspense time was suddenly frenzied, since the visa stipulated that the migrants must 'land' in Canada within six months. The arrival of the visa thus offset a series of concluding actions, such as handing in one's notice at work, putting one's house up for sale, selling off or shipping off one's belongings, informing the school, buying plane tickets and health insurances. Eva relates:

> It happens so fast. You have been waiting for that moment and then suddenly you have to act. There are so many decisions. The car, do I sell it or not? The apartment, do I sell it or rent it? One thing is planning that you are going, another thing is when you get your visa and you have to go.

For some, the feeling of rush lasted until the last moments before leaving, and even interfered with the expected unfolding of events. Michelle:

> I had thought that the last months would be very sad, but you are so stressed and you have so much to think about, that you just don't have time to be sad or nostalgic. (…) I remember the day we left Venezuela, when we were

at the airport. All this time I had imagined that there, at the airport, I would cry and cry and cry because we were leaving. But I felt nothing. Nothing. In my head, I was going through the lists; had we forgotten anything?

'Winning Time'

Contemporary temporalities of international migration are largely driven by neoliberal forces, Robertson (2015: 46) writes. I have already mentioned the Canadian migration regime's drive to carve out an economic migration stream made up of 'already ready' migrants. The development that shaped today's market-driven immigration stream was in its early phase at the time of my interviewees' migrations, but it has accelerated since. Yet, the information directed at potential migrants at the time of the interviewees' migrations was already promoting the value of flexibility, goal-orientation and autonomy that is so central in neoliberally oriented politics. The migrants in this study faced certain expectations that they begin to adapt to Canadian work life while not yet knowing whether they would be admitted. The immigration authorities presented this as a strategy that benefits migrants, and supporting material was made available, such as the personalized action plan on the immigration authorities' website that proclaimed to help migrants "determine needs, define objectives and develop effective strategies to obtain them". A shift was already taking place here, related to the immigration regime's attempt at manipulating time motivated by ideas of 'winning time' in order to produce a 'fast result'; a shift that involved a temporal reframing of processes associated with integration and resettlement. Integration is conventionally understood as comprising certain processes that commence as migrants arrive in their new society, for example, immigrants becoming familiar with various parts of society, learning the language, searching for work and establishing social and professional networks.

Most researchers recognize that these processes do not necessarily unfold in a linear fashion; however, they are nevertheless approached as spatially and temporally anchored in the resettlement in the new society. I suggest that present immigration policies seek to impose a new temporal ordering in which candidates are expected to begin, or even complete, certain processes associated with integration and resettlement before they arrive. The ideal situation, from a neoliberal political point of view, would be that immigrants arrive 'already ready' to become economically productive. For example, applicants are encouraged to establish contact with potential employers during the pre-migration period so they learn how the labor market works and, ideally, already have a work contract lined up for them when they arrive. Similarly, a policy shift has taken place from trying to ensure efficient language training for newcomers to admitting only migrants who can document that they already have good language skills. As already mentioned, on the immigration authorities' websites comprehensive guides and online tools are available to aid and facilitate prospective immigrants in the planning and preparation of their new life—guides that carry the message that immigrants are expected to realize the better part of integration themselves. In sum, these policies work to dislocate the conventional unfolding of certain integration processes both spatially and temporally by making them part of pre-migration planning and preparation. At the surface, they appear to have made the application process faster; however, the new rules concerning, for example, language learning entails that prospective migrants now must begin to invest time in order to successfully comply with the immigration regime's requirements long before they can even apply.

CONCLUSION

The chapter has focused on discrepancies and ambivalence relative to the temporal frames imposed on migrants as they were experienced and narrated by the migrants themselves. By focusing on migrants' narratives of temporal dilemmas, pressures and ambivalences during what I have called the pre-migration period, this chapter has sought to capture some of the complex relationships between different temporal forces and orderings that structure, influence and intersect with migrants' experiences and decisions. Experiences and trajectories are configured relative to temporal frames of both source and destination countries. In the case of the migrants in this study, these included the temporal orderings and strategies of the Canadian migration regime, the political-historical moment in Venezuela, with its diverging social interpretations of migration, and time as individually experienced. I suggest that working with migrants' narratives can yield new and deeper insights into the lived experience of temporal discrepancies. Through their stories, we can apprehend how the complex interplay between different kinds of temporalities translates into concrete experiences in real, everyday lives. Their narratives bring forth the contradictive emotions, practical dilemmas and external pressures, and they present temporal forces as continuously negotiated with regards to personal aspirations, situations and anticipated and desired trajectories. With regards to the question of temporal forces, the chapter has also sought go beyond a static presentation of Canadian immigration policies by situating these in an ongoing development oriented towards a goal of admitting migrants only when they are 'ready'. I suggest that present policies dislocate certain processes of migration with regards to time and space, for example, by pressing applicants to begin to adapt to Canadian work life while not yet knowing whether they will be admitted.

Analytical notions such as timescape and time track are useful, since they underscore connections and complexity, as well as rendering the dynamic and qualitative dimensions of time more explicit. For example, several narratives expressed ideas of time as something they had invested, or that 'lost' time could somehow be recuperated through migration. Time, in this sense, was not presented as simply mechanically moving forward; on the contrary, in a temporal sense migration represented a going back in order to go forth.

References

Adam, Barbara. 1998. *Timescapes of Modernity: The Environment and Invisible Hazards.* London: Routledge.

———. 2000. The Temporal Gaze: The Challenge for Social Theory in the Context of GM Food. *The British Journal of Sociology* 51 (1): 125–142.

———. 2004. *Time. Polity Key Concepts Series.* Cambridge: Polity Press.

Barber, Pauline Gardiner. 2008. The Ideal Immigrant? Gendered Class Subjects in Philippine–Canada Migration. *Third World Quarterly* 29 (7): 1265–1285.

CIC. 2012. Transforming the Immigration System. Published May 25, 2012. http://www.cic.gc.ca/english/department/media/notices/notice-transform.asp.

Cohen, Robin. 2006. *Migration and Its Enemies. Global Capital, Migrant Labor and the Nation State.* Aldershot: Ashgate Publishing.

Cwerner, Saulo B. 2001. The Times of Migration. *Journal of Ethnic and Migration Studies* 21 (1): 7–36.

Ellner, S. 2008. *Rethinking Venezuelan Politics: Class, Conflict and the Chavez Phenomenon.* Boulder, CO: Lynne Rienner.

Emirbayer, Mustafa, and Ann Mische. 1998. What Is Agency? *American Journal of Sociology* 103 (4): 962–1023.

Faraday, Fay. 2012. *Made in Canada. How the Law Constructs Migrant Workers' Insecurity.* Toronto: Metcalfe Foundation.

Freitas, Any, Antonina Levatino, and Antoine Pécoud. 2012. Introduction: New Perspectives on Skilled Migration. *Diversities* 14 (1): 1–7.

Gardner, Katy. 2009. Lives in Motion: The Life-Course, Movement and Migration in Bangladesh. *Journal of South Asian Development* 4 (2): 229–251.

Glick-Schiller, Nina. 2012. Migration and Development Without Methodological Nationalism: Towards Global Perspectives on Migration. In *Migration in the 21st Century: Ethnography and Political Economy*, ed. Pauline Gardiner Barber and Winnie Lem. Abingdon: Routledge.

Griffiths, Melanie, Ali Rogers, and Bridget Anderson. 2013. *Migration, Time and Temporalities: Review and Prospect.* COMPAS Research Resources Paper, March 2013.

Halfacree, Keith. 2004. A Utopian Imagination in Migration's Terra Incognita? Acknowledging the Non-Economic Worlds of Migration Decision-Making. *Population, Space and Place* 10 (3): 239–326.

Hawkins, Freda. 1972. *Canada and Immigration.* Montreal: McGill University Press.

Kelley, Ninette, and Michael Trebilcock. 2010. *The Making of the Mosaic: A History of Canadian Immigration Policy.* Toronto: University of Toronto Press.

Knowles, Valerie. 1997. *Strangers at Our Gates: Canadian Immigration and Immigration Policy, 1540–1997.* Toronto: Dundurn Press.

Kuptsch, Christiane, and Eng Fung Pang, eds. 2006. *Competing for Global Talent.* Geneva: Institute for Labor Studies, ILO.

Paez, Tomas. 2015. *La voz de la diaspora venezolana.* Madrid: Los libros de la Catarata.

Pellegrino, Adela. 2001. Éxodo, movilidad y circulación: nuevas modalidades de la migración calificada. *Notas de población* 73: 129–162.

Rapport, Nigel. 2004. *I Am Dynamite: An Alternative Anthropology of Power.* London: Routledge.

Robertson, Shanthi. 2014. Time and Temporary Migration: The Case of Temporary Graduate Workers and Working Holiday Makers in Australia. *Journal of Ethnic and Migration Studies* 40 (12): 1915–1933.

———. 2015. The Temporalities of International Migration: Implications for Ethnographic Research. In *Social Transformation and Migration: National and Local Experiences in South Korea, Turkey, Mexico and Australia*, ed. Stephen Castles, Derya Ozkul, and Magdalena Arias Cubas. Basingstoke: Palgrave Macmillan.

Root, Jesse, Erika Gates-Gasse, John Shields, and Harald Bauder. 2014. *Discounting Immigrant Families: Neoliberalism and the Framing of Canadian Immigration Policy Change.* RCIS Working Paper No 7.

Sætermo, Turid Fånes. 2016. *Negotiating Belonging as 'Ideal Migrants'. An Ethnographic Study of Skilled Migration from Venezuela to Canada.* PhD dissertation, NTNU, Trondheim.

Simmons, Alan B. 2010. *Immigration and Canada: Global and Transnational Perspectives*. Toronto: Canadian Scholars' Press.

Turner, Victor. 1967. *The Forest of Symbols*. Ithaca, NY: Cornell University Press.

Vigh, Henrik. 2009. Wayward Migration: On Imagined Futures and Technological Voids. *Ethnos* 74 (1): 91–109.

CHAPTER 9

The Entanglements of Neoliberal Temporalities and Class Politics in Philippine Migration to Canada

Pauline Gardiner Barber

The path characteristically described by modern industry, which takes the form of a decennial cycle (interrupted by smaller oscillations) of periods of average activity, production at high pressure, crisis, and stagnation, depends on the constant formation, the greater or less absorption and the re-formation of the industrial reserve army or surplus population. In their turn, the varying phases of the industrial cycle recruit the surplus population, and become one of the most energetic agencies for its reproduction. (Marx 1977: 785)

MARXISM AND MIGRATION

Capitalism has long relied on the exploitation of surplus populations, whose complex social reproduction activities need to be analyzed as unfolding across regional, national and global economies (Smith 2014: 28).[1]

[1] I am grateful to SSHRC for funding this research and to Patrick Neveling, Luisa Steur, Shiva Nourpanah and Catherine Bryan for helpful comments on earlier versions of this chapter.

P. G. Barber (✉)
Department of Sociology and Social Anthropology,
Dalhousie University, Halifax, NS, Canada

© The Author(s) 2018
P. G. Barber, W. Lem (eds.), *Migration, Temporality,
and Capitalism*, https://doi.org/10.1007/978-3-319-72781-3_9

161

Migration is part and parcel of the making of a surplus population, and those mobile populations in search of work facilitate the constraining of wages for others by expanding employers' options. Induced migration, by deliberate policy or desperation, exacerbates existing class disparities. As Eric Wolf (1982) observed in his historical study of the expansive reach of capitalism, many of the populations studied by anthropologists have been compelled into migration as much as they have been generated by migration.

Marxism would thus seem indispensable to the anthropology of migration. Nevertheless, anthropologists have not excelled in research on how capital mobilizes social labor and 'mystifies', in a Marxian sense, while at the same time normalizing class exploitation for migrants (see Barber and Lem 2012). As Marxism gains increased saliency in interdisciplinary studies linking migration to developments in global capitalism (Cohen 2006; Glick Schiller and Faist 2010; Gertel and Sippel 2014), it confronts anthropology's longstanding preoccupation with culture difference and migrants' identity and ethnicity (see Brettell 2003; Brettell and Hollifield 2008). Likewise, the literature on transnationalism neglects, with notable exceptions (see Binford 2013; Glick Schiller 2012; Lem and Barber 2013), how migrants' social relations of production and reproduction make and are made within capitalism's global fields of power.

Drawing on ethnographic research on the Philippines as a major export country of multi-skilled migrants to Canada, this chapter shows how "the varying phases of the industrial cycle" (Marx 1977: 785) are structured by state policies best characterized as neoliberal. Based on an analysis of the entanglements of the Philippines' and the Canadian labor markets, I argue that Marxist analytics are instructive for understanding the relation between migrant sending and receiving nations and the discrepant temporalities of how and why individuals engage with global labor markets. This is especially so because anthropologists have embraced the idea that neoliberalism entails the universal devolution of state power. For example, Baca (2004) shows how even in the US it is impossible to identify a historical rupture towards neoliberalism; and, more focused on the present, Kalb argues that neoliberalism was and is "structurally driven by global capitalism, and not quite as a 'coherent and monolithic project'" as anthropologists have imagined (Kalb 2012: 325). Because neoliberalism is not a radical rupture but rather a manifestation of global capitalism that involves coincidence and contingency in the structuring and intersection of policies (Neveling 2014), it is important to consider the permanence of flexibility and accumulation and how their untimely coincidence, manifest in coexisting and contradictory patterns of accumulation, impacts the relationship between individuals and states. In the following I show how changing state-backed out-migration has been crucial to maintaining inequality in the Philippines while that nation's supply of labor also feeds Canada's ideologically contrived policies of labor exploitation. Such policies and their ideological underpinnings saw their most recent illustration through 2008–14, which may be understood as a high-neoliberal moment in the application of the restructured 'just-in-time' labor-on-demand immigration policy. It was during this moment of Canada's policy flexibilization that the Philippines became Canada's top immigration source country for both permanent and temporary migrants.

The neoliberal state's agenda thus created structured contingencies (Kalb 2012) where Canadian and Philippine workers suddenly found themselves competing in labor market segments that had recently been relegated to migrants. Once we turn our attention to the everyday lives of migrant workers we encounter more such temporal contingencies, synchronic ones (relating to present conditions) but also diachronic (historically developed) contingencies emerging from untimely coincidences of diverse modes of capitalist exploitation. The following considers this 'multi-culturalism' of exploitative practices along four main lines of enquiry: (1) the untimeliness of waiting for visas in Manila; (2) Canada's economistic immigration policy which I argue fetishizes immediacy, and just-in-time flexibility in labor market adjustments; (3) the class and community attachments of Canadian workers whose livelihoods are threatened with disruption by policy reform; and (4) how immigration reform exposes tension between large-scale capital and smaller-scale 'family' firms with respect to labor market strategies.

The chapter proposes then an analysis of the differing yet transnationally entangled neoliberal approaches in the policies of a sending country (the Philippines) and a receiving country (Canada). Neoliberalism is analyzed as a political economy project that reworks historical and political landscapes through a mixture of "coercion and consent" (Harvey 2003: 152) and exacerbates class polarities in both countries. The discourse of urgency around Canada's radical policy restructuring under the Harper conservative government from 2008 to 2014 contrasts with the long-term commitment to labor export in the Philippines. However, in both countries the unfolding of neoliberal just-in-time labor market priorities emphasizes the present over the past; migrants are deployed and received as units of labor and as bearers of capital. Likewise, neoliberal policies and politics deliberately exacerbate processes of social inequality engendered by state-planned migration established over the history of Philippine to Canada migration. Within Canada, seasonal and low-skilled workers experienced additional pressures to become mobile and remove themselves from the long-established seasonal rhythms of local livelihoods.

STRUCTURED CONTINGENCY AND NEOLIBERALISM'S UNTIMELY COINCIDENCES

If the task of anthropology is to show how transnational migration changes under rapidly escalating national and global alliances of capitalism's "structured contingencies" (Kalb 2012), it is then relevant to consider how neoliberalism in the Philippines differs from neoliberalism in Canada, but also to consider how these differences complement one another—both in regard to the timing of national policy changes and their impact on different classes. An additional task is to investigate the politics of waiting: the social consequences of living through the uncertainties caused by the untimely coincidence of changes in how capitalism structures movement (Neveling 2014). This necessitates study of the transnational articulations of state projects with regimes of mobility (Glick Schiller and Salazar 2013), with capitalist accumulation in particular historical moments, and with their uneven impact on classes and individual migrants. Historically, the geographical alliances associated with colonization and capitalist production systems were profoundly disruptive and reconfigured gendered divisions of labor (see Neveling 2015). These ruptures underlie the complex dialectics that define global migration and its geographic distortions of value production in the Marxian sense of extracting surplus value from labor.[2] As a geographically stretched class-making project migration allows value extraction for third parties through all stages of the migration process; recruitment, travel and housing, the migrant's labor, remittance and consumption practices. State brokerage under neoliberalism plays a critical role in facilitating value extraction.

Philippine global migration spans centuries (Gonzalez 1998). Landlessness and/or land expropriation and its revaluation for capitalist profits have long sustained the ongoing expulsion of people from rural livelihoods. Filipinos were linked into global labor markets under Spanish rule and participated in the global reach of capitalism throughout the

---

[2] See Capital, Part Six, on wages (Marx 1977).

nineteenth century (Aguilar 2002). The US colonial period from 1896 to 1946 introduced an English-language based educational system that continues to this day, allowing Filipinos access to countries such as Canada, where English is one of the two preferred languages. Out-migration escalated during the 1970s as political instabilities during the Marcos administration led to a 671 percent increase in migrants lining up for overseas work (Gonzalez 1998).

Philippine migration became feminized by the mid-1980s, when women's migration surpassed that of men. Crucially, in the Philippines as elsewhere the forces compelling rural people to migrate for employment lead to the feminization and racialization of global migration (Piper 2011). The expansion of women's entry into labor markets also demands that their social reproduction labor be replaced with that of lesser paid migrant women (Bryan this volume). Until today, land expropriation for new capital intensive projects displaces rural populations and pushes many into seeking employment abroad as a crucial contribution to household livelihoods (Eviota 1995; Aguilar 2014; Asis 2015). Over time, migration remittances have contributed to educating several new generations of potential migrants whose educational projects have been carefully selected, often in dialogue with relatives living abroad, with a view to anticipated middle-class occupations in popular migration countries such as Canada (see Barber and Bryan 2012). In this way, migration and remittances have become factored, in temporally disjunctive ways into the long-term social reproduction strategies of Filipino migrants, women and men. Philippine migration to Canada can thus be seen as the mobilization of gendered labor whose exits and entries into specific segmented wage labor markets are calculated on terms and in timelines beyond their control (Wolf 1982).

TRANSNATIONAL ENTANGLEMENTS

At the beginning of the nineteenth century record numbers of immigrants entered Canada, primarily from the US and the UK. After 1910, the numbers arriving from other European countries increased through to the early 1970s. A post-war immigration boom in 1946, lasting until the late 1950s, provided labor for urban manufacturing and services, but developments across the country were uneven, reflecting as much as producing regional economic disparities that continue to this day (see Innis 1995). The public debate in the early 1900s centred upon whether labor supply was more important than country of origin (Boyd and Vickers 2000).

From the 1960s, immigration came to be seen as a process necessary for the long-term prosperity of a vast country facing demographic challenges; hence tolerance for immigrants was fostered through state-promoted multi-culturalism (Fleras 2015).

In the Philippines, during the latter period, the state transformed understandings of migration as a necessary temporary economic measure into migration as something akin to performing "national service" (Tyner 2003). Migrants abroad were also encouraged to become entrepreneurs and feed back their expertise as development agents in the communities they left behind (see Baggio 2010). The Philippines' historical political economy has produced extreme wealth disparities, poverty rates and downward mobility so that even the most highly skilled workers might become surplus labor as state policies change (Rodriguez 2010). Now, how do the diverse Canadian and Philippine trajectories align?

Development policies in countries of origin and labor market policies in destination countries rarely work in favor of migrants if they are not members of the transnational capitalist class who can take advantage of various immigration schemes for wealthy migrants (see Ley 2010). Since 2006, as a result of greater efficiencies at state marketing of labor surplus, at least 1 million Filipinos have travelled abroad seeking work in over 190 countries. Unlike, for example, other top destinations such as the Gulf States Saudi Arabia and the United Arab Emirates, where employment contracts are temporary and workers remain migrants, Filipinos entering Canada seeking permanent residence have come to occupy an increasingly prominent role in Canada's immigration system as policy reforms through the same period (2008 onwards) sought more effective and *timely* labor market deployments across a broader range of visa programs.

Since the mid-1970s, before the latest round of policy restructuring opened up multiple immigration pathways, the Philippines was the top source country for live-in care workers, 90 percent of them women. While this program commenced with a temporary status, eventually and conditionally permanency was possible. Until 2014, care workers entered under an anomalous temporary contract that could be converted into eventual citizenship once certain conditions were met (Stasiulis and Bakan 2005). Responding to decades of criticism about exploitation and abuse, the live-in requirement was removed in 2014 but so also was the universal provision for transition to citizenship. Workers must now apply for permanent residency under an annual quota system. Many of these workers entered Canada as deskilled care workers, despite having been selected by their families to receive university education in such fields as teaching and nursing, specifically geared towards Canadian immigration priorities (Barber 2004). Beginning in 2008, Canada rapidly expanded its temporary worker program across a wider range of occupations well beyond care work. So even though by 2010 more temporary than permanent visas were issued, many temporary migrant workers with in-demand occupational skill sets, for example, in the service sector and hospitality sector, sought to switch from temporary to permanent status. A number of Canadian provincial immigration programs allow for such conversion (see Bryan and Sætermo's chapters in this volume).[3]

As a result of the visa pathway diversity, a revised archetypical Filipino migrant has appeared: no longer the compliant, well-educated child-friendly female nanny, but now a youthful, resilient, hardworking, eager to please fast-food server, female or male. This stereotype prevails in both countries. In Canada it appears in periodic media accounts of Filipino service workers in remote locations who are presented as incongruous but popular with locals. In the Philippines, the stereotype is rehearsed in communities by recruiters and state officials in compulsory pre-departure training sessions. Canada is the fourth most popular destination for migrant Filipinos (CFO 2014).[4] Through the presence of Canada's size-able Filipino diaspora, Canada had, until 2014, a relatively positive reputation in the Philippines as a destination country, with narratives circulating in both countries about immigrant-friendly multi-culturalism. As will be described below, recent events accompanying immigration reform have unsettled this mystifying, sentimental view of the classed aspects of neoliberal migration.

In liberal democracies, immigration politics become notoriously volatile in periods of economic uncertainty (Hampshire 2013). Despite Canada's reputation as a model multi-cultural society, disputes periodically surface between pro- and anti-immigrant factions with respect to the underlying premises of immigrant selection (Banting and Kymlicka 2010; Li 2003) and, prior to the expansion of temporary work across multiple sectors, the differential citizenship rights of temporary workers in care work (Pratt 2012;

---

[3] In 2015, Canada admitted 50,835 Filipinos as permanent residents http://open.canada.ca/data/en/dataset/f7e5498e-0ad8-4417-85c9-9b8aff9b9. Also in 2015, 11,685 migrants entered on temporary foreign work visas http://open.canada.ca/data/en/dataset/360024f2-17e9-4558-bfc1-3616485d65b9.

[4] The three overseas destinations above Canada are the US, Saudi Arabia and UAE.

Stasiulis and Bakan 2005) and agriculture (Preibisch 2010; Binford 2013). Concentration of immigrants in Vancouver, Toronto and Montreal has provoked discussion about the political character of so-called ethnic communities, or "enclaves" (Hiebert 2009) and about the need to disperse immigrants across provinces into smaller centres eager to boost declining economies (Bascaramurty 2017; Dobrowolsky and Ramos 2014). These debates provide the backdrop but in no way explain the radical restructuring of Canada's immigration policy after 2008 to privilege economic over demographic priorities within a crudely framed neoliberal agenda (Dobrowolsky 2013).

With Canada's increased reliance on foreign workers in sectors other than care there has been a parallel overhaul of national labor policies in recent years. Changes include tighter eligibility requirements for laid-off seasonal workers seeking employment benefits and have been most controversial in regions where whole communities have long relied on supplemental income from the state during the winter. These measures place new pressure on the unemployed to become mobile and assume positions occupied by temporary foreign workers, primarily Filipino. As the presence of temporary workers increased so too have public debates, fanned in part by right wing commentators musing over the legitimacy of employers' labor permits for temporary workers (for example, Wente 2013). Xenophobic exchanges have accompanied some media critiques of immigration policy (Canadian Press 2012). However, the larger agenda appears to be one of class interest expressed ideologically through a cost-cutting agenda that attempts to force Canada's locally unemployed to enter precisely those low-wage jobs where migrants have become the preferred workers (Sinoski 2014). I turn now to Manila with an ethnographic overview of the classed aspects of migration's temporality that remains invisible in Canadian politics.

WAITING AND DESKILLING IN MANILA

One hub in the transnational application of the Philippines migration regime lies at the intersection of Ortigas Avenue and EDSA, short for Epifanio de los Santos Avenue, a circumferential freeway linking major financial districts on a north-south axis. Under the freeway, on the opposite corner, is the gritty building housing POEA (Philippine Overseas Employment Agency), a bustling center that all Filipinos with overseas employment contracts must visit. Opposite POEA and well-known across the Philippines stands the EDSA shrine, a tall statue of Mary on a small

Catholic church built in 1989 to commemorate the two peaceful demonstrations of the People Power Revolutions that lead to the deposing of two presidents; Dictator Ferdinand Marcos (1965 to 1986) and Joseph Estrada (1998 to 2001).

In the office of an immigration consultant in a building right at this junction of urban traffic, migration pathways, institutions and landmarks of Philippine historical struggles against exploitation, I observed an intensive French language class with a group of 12 migrants-in-waiting early in 2014. The six women and six men were destined for employment in rural Québec. They elected to pay for language instruction in preparation for arrival in Francophone Québec. The Québécois instructor was preparing the students to become functional in conversational French. The recruits, all university graduates in management and related fields, had successfully transitioned through a drawn-out, costly series of regulatory processes necessary for entry to Canada. The average length of waiting for their documents was two years. They were all employed as managers in food services and were eligible to be classified as skilled workers under Canada's National Occupational Code. Nonetheless, deskilling occurred in their Canadian employment contracts; they were all hired for unskilled jobs as food counter attendants. Their intention was to enter Canada on temporary contracts and then seek a means to qualify for permanent status. Such movement, their recruiter said, was possible should they be reclassified into a managerial position by the employer. Visas in hand, they were in the final stages of migration, waiting for their employer to send tickets for their flights to Canada. These migrants, like many others interested in migrating to Canada, had researched the possibilities for permanency available in various provincial programs, and guided by their recruiter they had settled on Québec as their then best, albeit time-sensitive, option.

But there was a catch. Although migrants themselves are responsible for moving through the qualifying stages, travel documents are scheduled at the employer's discretion. This and every other step in the migration process involves temporal dimensions and communication lags well beyond migrants' control. Once they have gained the attention of a recruitment agency, they must undergo standardized screening, a process that involves preparing a DVD CV for close scrutiny by potential employers. Waiting for confirmation of interest from an employer is the final stage in the temporal vector of *migration time*. Migrants' access to information about their applications also involves waiting for the attention of busy agency staff. Queries can be made in person at the agency, by phone or on-line. Responses may take hours, days, weeks or months, depending upon the perceived urgency of the question, variabilities in document processing and the agency's best estimates of employers' plans.

Given that language politics have fueled anti-immigrant sentiments in rural Québec, the French classes in Manila were designed for migrants to learn everyday idioms appropriate to food service. Fittingly, they rehearsed (with me joining them) the correct grammar and accent for various conversations about time, work and skill: "Where do you work? How long have you worked there? What is your position in the company?" While French class helped pass the interminable waiting and to ease speculative worries about life in Canada, all continued with their full-time jobs because they could not afford, given the increasingly uncertain visa procedures, to go into the customary "stand-by mode" (Batan 2010) of departure preparations and farewells anticipated by migrants and their kin. Yet when the tickets arrive, time can be short, a matter of weeks.

The Québec employer's plan was to have workers travel in small groups to accommodate a projected, gradual increase in demand for fast food as seasonal workers were called back to factory jobs in the spring. Not unlike the model used for Canada's seasonal agricultural workers, this strategy follows a just-in-time logic matching labor supply to market demand on a much shorter temporal scale (McLaughlin 2010; Preibisch 2010). As in other instances of capitalist exploitation, new technologies for communication and document transferal enable the compression of time and space, and the more instantaneous treatment of workers as flexible units of labor and, therefore, a greater source of surplus value for accumulation projects (Harvey 1989). In contrast with the privileging of market urgency for employers, migrants subjected to just-in-time live under a protracted temporality, simultaneously backward- and forward-looking. All migrants in stand-by mode reflect on the prospect of the upcoming journeys with a mix of excitement and apprehension. However, they must also be prepared to switch gears rapidly and prepare for the looming realities of deployment: long hours, harsh labor discipline and the long, bleak Canadian winter. *Patience* along with faith and hope, thus take on heightened saliency for migrants-in-waiting, regardless of the stage they are at in their migration process. Migration requires a huge commitment, simultaneously projected across space and time during the waiting for the next obstacle in the neoliberal migration apparatus (Feldman 2011).

MIGRATION TIME

The above shows that neoliberal migration regimes and their transnational entanglements produce untimely coincidences. Migration temporality as such, however, remains under-theorized in the anthropology of migration. Auero's (2012) study of the politics of waiting in Argentina argues that the urban poor who navigate state bureaucracies learn to be "patients of the state"; (that is, temporal rhythms in bureaucratic procedure reproduce political subordination. Similarly, here I introduce the concept of *migration time* to emphasize the subordinating preparations for labor deskilling that occur within the temporal rhythms of migration; rhythms planned for by migrants and often disrupted by state policy and politics. Preparations can span decades and command the resources of several generations. Time must be *spent* accessing the capital not only to stage the migration itself, but also, long before that, to invest in education specifically targeted to a particular migration pathway. Migration as a class-improvement project is socially reproduced through remittances, typically from close kin; parents, spouses, siblings and parents' siblings (aunts and uncles), in that order. All such activities have a future-oriented temporality, often involving hardship for one generation rationalized as for the best interests of the next.[5]

Migration time being employer-driven and state-controlled is capricious. For example, the Québec employer of migrants attending French class suddenly decided to delay the worker's arrival because of Canada's late spring that year. Reasoning for this related to the realities of resource dependency in that region of Québec: laid-off workers have less disposable income hence the need for additional workers was somewhat tied to the seasonality of the particular local labor market serviced by the employer. The delay meant that some of the migrant's visas were at risk of expiring. The entire application process would then need to be repeated, recapitalized; more waiting time and plans suspended sometimes with serious financial consequences. A further aspect of capriciousness in migration time arose with the restructuring of Canadian immigration. As discussed above, a further series of policy reforms was introduced in 2014. Visas for lower skilled occupations in the food service sector became more closely

---

[5] See Pido (2017) for a discussion about how the political economy of migration has led to the increased involvement of migrants in new forms of property speculation productive for finance capital. To develop this subject is beyond the scope of this chapter but worth noting here regarding migration's projection into future-oriented capitalist temporalities.

calibrated to unemployment levels in particular labor markets, meaning many workers deployed to Canada faced non-renewal of their contracts. There was also a significant increase in the fees for permits to hire foreign workers, presumably to pressure employers to hire unemployed locals— in fact, the very seasonal workers the Filipino migrants-in-waiting hoped to serve. In January 2015, a new Express Entry on-line application system was implemented to further privilege in-demand skills. These reforms demonstrate the present-focused temporality embedded in just-in-time immigration policy. The entanglement of two neoliberal national policy regimes means, however, that for the migrants their carefully selected migration pathway, crafted over time at considerable expense, can be disrupted through the contingencies of restructuring; from a migrant's perspective, the coincidence is particularly cruel and untimely (Neveling 2014). Again, the intersection of Ortigas Avenue and EDSA is a space where such temporal disjunctions and classed realities becomes manifest.

CLASS STRUGGLE AND THE PRODUCTION OF STRUCTURED CONTINGENCY: EDSA AND POEA

In 1986 hundreds of thousands of Filipinos blocked the EDSA and confronted the military in the final hours leading up to the overthrow of President Marcos. While the EDSA shrine commemorates bravery—heroism even—and the collective commitment to a better future, its proximity to POEA redefines the site and has complicated its political meaning. EDSA, as a destination for those departing the Philippines, has become the site for the pre-deployment anxiety of the nation's migrants as new national heroes. The multi-faceted connotation of the site is perverse but instructive. Under the Marcos regime and subsequent administrations, labor export policies served the dual purpose of quelling social unrest arising from high unemployment, underemployment and poverty while also providing a boost to the foreign currency reserves necessary for the state to maintain its considerable debt obligations to the IMF and World Bank (Gonzalez 1998). With the firming up of a commitment to state labor brokerage on behalf of capital (Rodriguez 2010), there has been a concerted state effort to valorize the contributions of Philippine migrants to the national economy.

This ambition solidified under the Ramos presidency (1992–1998), when political struggles over the state's reliance on labor export met with such strong resistance that Ramos' re-election was threatened. One major issue was the escalation in women's care migration and their mistreatment abroad, with many observers pointing to two trials of women migrants in 1995 widely considered to have been wrongfully accused (Gonzalez 1998). First was the trial for murder and subsequent execution in Singapore of Flor Contemplación, ostensibly the outcome of a quarrel between friends. Later that year, in the UAE 16 year-old Sara Balabagan was found guilty of killing her male employer, who she claimed had tried to rape her. After massive protests in the Philippines and with extensive international support, Balabagan was publically flogged and repatriated to the Philippines after serving a one-year jail term. The Ramos administration met widespread public outrage with new legislation ordering stricter state monitoring over all stages of migration including repatriation and re-entry. Following the turbulence in domestic migration politics in 1995 there has been a shift from a laissez faire approach to a more deliberate system of migration oversight. New targets were also set to increase the total "export" of overseas workers to 1 million per year. Valorizing the migrant-hero was intended to disrupt the migrant-as-victim discourse, but it also smoothed the way for an even more deliberate labor brokerage role by the neoliberal state (Guevarra 2010).

Beyond revolutionary politics, EDSA the symbolical connotation of the migrant-hero is a construct whose aura can be stretched to embrace the 10.5 million Filipinos estimated to be living and/or working abroad (CFO 2014). In 2016 this diaspora was responsible for an all-time high record of $26.9 US billion remittances representing a 5 percent increase over 2015 and accounting for 9.8 percent of the gross domestic product (de Vera 2017).

The coincidence of images of heroic revolution and of the political economy of migration highlights the opposition between the revolutionary possibility of collective action and the individualized experience of neoliberalized migration and/or emigration for those who leave permanently. True, migration is often but not always conceptualized as a family project. Remittances support livelihood endeavors; for example, small convenience stores (*sari sari*) attached to the family home, or the purchase of a *pedicab*, a motorized tricycle with space for several passengers for local trips. As noted, remittances also pay educational fees for siblings and their children, many of whom go on to become overseas migrants themselves. Migrants' class aspirations are also registered in increased spending on middle-class consumer goods to distribute within social networks, and in some fewer cases the purchase of investment rental properties.

These realities have a complicated temporality relative to the past and the more 'hopeful future' to which migrants aspire. As labor market opportunities present themselves, migrants remain locked in a capital-centric agenda, vulnerable to the whim of employers and temporalities prioritized in unpredictable state policy. Migrants also become sources of greater extraction of surplus value than their local Canadian counterparts: despite the fact that Filipinos are often better educated, they are also more subjugated and vulnerable to exploitation at work and from family obligations. Put simply, they are perceived as more reliable because there is more at stake for them, which is readily acknowledged by employers and, at the same time, backed by the Philippines' national neoliberal policies.

JUST-IN-TIME IMMIGRATION

Canada is one of a few countries that qualify as an "immigration society", with more than one-fifth of Canada's inhabitants born out of the country (Fleras 2015: 78). When the Immigration Act of 1967 introduced a point system based on age, education, language, skills and economic characteristics, Canada's source countries diversified beyond the US, UK and Europe. Within 20 years, 27 percent of immigrants came from Asia (Boyd and Vickers 2000). From 1967 to 1976 policies also emphasized family reunification, a further factor contributing to diversification and to the increase in Filipino women entering as deskilled care workers attracted by the possibility of eventual citizenship for themselves and various family members at the conclusion of their contracts (Pratt 2012). The combined effect of these various visa streams continues through 2017 to maintain the Philippines as Canada's top immigrant source country. After Stephen Harper's reconstituted Conservative Party came to power in 2006, immigration policy reform was increasingly orchestrated behind closed doors, subject to ministerial discretion with no parliamentary debate. Canadians only learned about immigration policy changes through politicians' Twitter accounts and media releases (see McDonald 2014).

A key moment in full-blown neoliberalization was the Harper government's introduction in 2010 of an unprecedented omnibus budget bill. The bill proposed sweeping reforms across a broad range of social and economic policies, including immigration. Immigration reform shifted policy priorities towards exclusively economic goals, that is, away from demographic concerns (Banting and Kymlicka 2010), and the increased presence of foreign workers provided a means to discipline Canadian workers.

Untimely Suspensions: Waiting ... Again

As neoliberal policy reform unfolded and drastic sequential policy changes were announced in Canada, tens of thousands of Filipinos, migrants-in-waiting, had their plans crushed. The shift to a temporary immigration strategy was not only radical for Canada, but it was also disruptive for Filipinos suspended in *migration time* in Manila. Behind the scenes the restructuring involved major geographical and technological reorganization to enable greater speed and flexibility in where, how, when and who would be issued Canadian entry visas. One official euphemistically described the shift as "modernization". The aim was to "manage migration" with greater efficiency. Today, the majority of applicant files have been redirected to cyberspace; only those whose files are flagged for fact checking receive face-to-face attention (Satzewich 2015). As of 2015, skilled workers apply on-line through "Express Entry", which replaced the previous system of "first-in first-out" in the immigration queue. Embassy divisions of labor were also reassigned within the Southeast Asian region, with some offices closing. File monitoring is now geographically dispersed, confounding any sense of the neat ordering of applications emplaced within borders. This major backstage reorganization was one facet of the rolling out of "just-in-time" to prioritize temporal flexibility and labor exigency (Barber and Bryan 2017).

Of critical importance in the restructuring process were the suspensions of two major visa programs, both key pathways for Filipinos entering Canada. First, was the declaration of a moratorium on skilled worker visas announced in 2012 and held in place until May 2013, ostensibly to address a backlog. Over 280,000 visa applications were in the processing queue at that time. Many applications in progress for six years or more were cancelled. Migrant advocates reported that despite the Embassy's stated intent to work forward by processing applications from an undisclosed set date, there were ambiguities and inconsistencies surrounding the treatment of files and the timelines. When the moratorium ended, a relatively short list of "occupations in demand" was released, each with a quota. Individuals could refile a visa application, but the new system made the prospect of success less predictable, especially given the new emphasis on expeditious processing and quotas. The intent to reduce wait times had differential consequences for potential employers and aspiring migrants. Neoliberalism's temporal fixation purportedly addresses labor market priorities, but labor markets are volatile; demand can falter.

The second unexpected suspension, this time of visas for temporary foreign workers in food services, occurred in 2014. Announced in a press release, it responded to a series of incidents about alleged employer abuse of the program. Over the previous 12 months there had been just a few media reports of such incidents. Until the moratorium the official response to reported incidents was a news release promising closer review of labor market details. Cases reported in the period up to the program suspension were not confined to lower skilled occupations. For example, in 2012 the hiring of Chinese miners by a Chinese-owned firm in British Columbia was challenged by local unions, complaining that state policy at that time allowed employers to pay lower wages to foreign workers. The company argued there were technological and linguistic reasons for hiring Chinese nationals. The political response was to change the policy and remove the wage differential; from then on temporary foreign workers were to be paid the same wage as Canadian workers (Canadian Press 2012). In a second example, within days of the story going public in 2013, the Royal Bank of Canada was forced to cancel plans to use foreign workers from India to replace Canadian workers it had laid off (Tomlinson 2013).

These tensions were largely over "just-in-time" and rekindled the latent debate over the scale and function of immigration. However, by pursuing the link between neoliberal market discipline and immigration and labor policies, the negative repercussions for local workers, whether employed or job-seeking, become evident. Local employers who might otherwise embrace neoliberal agendas became unhappy with suspension of their access to foreign workers. Local workers were portrayed as feeling threatened by invidious comparisons between their work ethic and that of their "foreign" workmates. Any truth to such comparison can be traced to the brute fact that the majority of foreign workers have "invested" more in the time, money and education leading them to deskilled work abroad. Migrant workers typically focus on debt repayment and multiple other family obligations, and they are viewed by employers and often present themselves as more compliant than their Canadian counterparts. For example, the migrants-in-waiting from the French class in Manila reiterated in various ways their desire to please their employer with hard work and their hope that s/he would "like them". Such heartfelt comments echo the theme of the loyal Filipino migrant and citizen, ideologies that are endlessly rehearsed in the Philippine press, within migrant training sessions, and by state discourses about migrants as "national ambassadors" (Guevarra 2010). Elsewhere, I describe such events as "performances of subordination" (Barber 2013) that are required of migrants-in-waiting. In this regard also, Filipinos bear comparison with Auero's (2012) social service recipients, where subordination follows from economic necessity.

Prior to the 2014 suspension and with heightened media speculation about employers abusing the system, some migrant workers in food services were subjected to xenophobic social commentary. Temporary workers bore silent witness as the heated debates over their national presence played out in the media. Two media reports emerged, each instigated by a disgruntled ex-employee from a fast food employer in two separate provinces. They claimed the employers favored foreign workers. This was significant because under the regulations, foreign worker contracts require evidence of a labor market shortage. The two cases were treated by the media as symptomatic of widespread abuse, casting suspicion on the tens of thousands of foreign workers deployed across the country without any such controversy. Questions then surfaced about the volume of foreign workers and potential for displacement of local workers. As noted, in the normal course of events, the Canadian Press infrequently presents stories about Filipino workers following two general scripts. One variant is the Sacrificial Mother raising Canadian children, hopeful for a successful reunion with her own family after serving time as a live-in caregiver where she is prone to abuse. The later version is cheerful Filipinos serving coffee in some remote community as an incongruous yet adaptable presence. By the end of April 2014, such stereotypes were shattered.

During the suspension, media reports about immigration became even more reductive. Discussion about program flaws unfolded over time before different audiences and received varied reactions from many voices, including on social media. Some protagonists were confused about immigration policy and labor market structures, hardly surprising given the abruptness of program suspension. The Philippines' Consul-General held a press conference to defend the success of the temporary worker program from his nation's perspective. He appealed to Canada's federal government to "give some thought to the fate of workers currently in the country who would normally be looking for their next restaurant job but are now blocked from that sector" (Curry 2014). The debate raged for weeks until a new policy framework was released. New measures included restricting temporary workers to low unemployment areas, increased employer processing fees, and caps on migrants hired and hours worked (Government of Canada 2014).

CLASS POLITICS: CANADA

That 2014 moratorium was announced one day after release of a privately funded conservative think tank report questioning the very existence of Canada's labor shortage (Gross 2014). Timelines are important. C. D. Howe Institute, the agency that produced the report is known for promoting neoliberalism, a free market, limited government and individualized values (see Thunert 2003). Prior to the suspension, the immigration minister, Jason Kenney, reinforced the official narrative, defending the program and proposing tighter monitoring of employers' contracts. This conundrum requires explanation. Why would a right wing argument prefigure the suspension of employer access to skilled yet devalued labor? Especially given the popularity of the program and the fact that despite media clamor, only a handful of program violations were officially investigated. Such radical intervention into the newly configured entanglements of Canadian and Philippine neoliberalism caused tensions for Canadian and Filipino workers by suggesting they were in competition for the same jobs.

Employment and Social Development Canada, a 2014 rebranding of the government Department of Human Resources and Skills Development, not only manages foreign worker labor market approvals but also (un)employment insurance, for which new eligibility requirements had been introduced in 2013. Claimants were more closely monitored and the geographical range for job searching was expanded. With widespread reliance on state employment insurance by workers and employers alike in communities with long histories of seasonal employment in resource sectors (fishing, forestry, mining), severing access to insurance produces labor migration, temporary or permanent, and constitutes economic dispossession. Many workers from economically depressed regions are already engaged in circular migration to destinations such as Alberta's Fort McMurray (Dorow and O'Shaughnessy 2013). Moreover, national representatives of the federation of small businesses continue to insist foreign workers are imperative to their economic survival. Contradicting the right wing Institute's argument, Atlantic fish processors, for example, pressed hard for policy exemptions claiming an acute local labor shortage (Taweel 2014). More generally, the argument that temporary workers displace local workers becomes fictitious in light of claims about the scarcity of willing local workers.

The events above represent a narrative about class and a struggle over state oversight of accumulation strategies. Elite class factions, the primary audience for the Howe Institute's report, sought ideological power and material gain from Canadian labor rendered as surplus.[6] The discrediting of the foreign worker program without prior warning thus constitutes an historical "moment" when certain segments of Canadian labor were subjected to state disciplining around their refusal to uproot or to commute longer for work. From Marx's time forward, market volatility constitutes an arena for the manipulation of class interest where mystifications about economy abound, especially with regard to labor compensation and surpluses.

CONCLUSION

I have revealed how Canada's neoliberal state enhanced conditions for capital to obtain value from temporary immigrant labor while at the same time rationalizing the reproduction of a surplus population amongst precarious constituencies in both countries. This is just the most recent instance of a process of radical restructuring of Canada's immigration system that has produced various structured contingencies bringing into conflict different groups of immigrants, including temporary workers and locals. Such conflicts are predicated on a seemingly impersonal entrenched neoliberal ideology that pits good, hardworking citizens against fraudsters and a growing swath of the 'undeserving poor' (in Canada and 'offshore').

Such ambition in the Canadian bourgeoisie is, however, facilitated by the trajectories of emigration policies and family ambitions in the Philippines. This transnational setting of entangled neoliberal state policies is commonly overlooked in anthropology, which is why the case detailed above is so illuminating. Economically reductive political discourse in both countries frames how migration is packaged and sold to the public, and this creates vulnerability for all working class actors involved. Dispossession, not only of access to means of production but also of means of reproduction acquired in the process of migration, such as the right to family reunion, serves to discipline both national labor groups and establish ever more exploitative conditions. Ideological justifications normalize the geographically dispersed alliances of class and power that configure and facilitate the "formation and re-formation" of surplus populations identified by Marx as essential to the reproduction of capital. This occurs across multiple sectors of capitalist accumulation. Urban populations pitted against rural constituencies and elites in both contexts advance politi-

---

[6] See Bell (2012) on the complexities of differentiated surplus labor populations in northern Canada.

cal agendas to their advantage. Class privilege is disguised—not least through migration histories, which have created indebtedness for migrants in waiting and threatens working class people in Canada in times of crisis. This produces fear, compliance and sometimes complicity.

Indeed, the Canadian examples of pro- and anti-immigration campaigns show how in fact the hegemony of neoliberalism has come to be accepted, taken for granted in the Gramscian sense of common sense (Crehan 2016). Conflict as much as migration time and deskilling then emerge in the analysis presented here not as contradictory and irrational patterns but as coincidences that situate global capitalism in a particular "structurally contingent" configuration. This, in fact, is not unfamiliar in history. Eric Wolf (1982) describes how nineteenth and twentieth century large-scale migration met the demands of new processes of accumulation in that period. Wolf's analysis follows Marx's insights on labor markets reproducing the "fiction that this buying and selling (of labor) is a symmetrical exchange between partners" (1982: 354). In fact, it represents class asymmetry. Historically, these processes relentlessly created surplus populations moving across and between continents, as seen in contemporary migration (Cohen 2006).

The struggle as reviewed here describes the curious temporal paradox upon which neoliberalism depends, seen in the denouncing of Canadian working class immigration history. Canadian history fits Wolf's analysis of global capitalism's entanglements perfectly. Canada was founded through immigration; regional political economies were dependent upon a willing and creative labor proletariat, sprinkled with some bearers of capital in smaller and larger quantities, sufficient to take advantage of the presence of concentrated groups of new labor. Here we see how neoliberalism encourages historical amnesia by fetishizing the present and conjuring false enemies in political discourse, casting doubt upon the credibility of claims by small business employers. Those same accusations render suspect the mere presence of temporary foreign workers who are portrayed as job thieves. Meanwhile, in the Philippines potential migrants must contend with Canada's policy fluctuations, a situation which recruiters suggest has led some migrants to seek employment in other global contexts such as New Zealand, where temporary migrants can also entertain the prospect of permanent residency. Also apparent in the Philippines, as I attempted to show in the discussion of the shift in purpose occurring at EDSA, the key site of twentieth century people-power revolutionary commemoration: neoliberalism's present-to-future focused orientation serves to erase the past—for the past is a threatening space of class struggle and leftist emancipatory politics.

REFERENCES

Aguilar, Filomeno. 2002. *At Home in the World?: Filipinos in Global Migrations.* Quezon City: Philippine Social Science Council.

———. 2014. *Migration Revolution: Philippine Nationhood and Class Relations in a Globalized Age.* Quezon City: Ateneo de Manila University Press.

Asis, Maruja. 2015. 'All in the Family': Remittances, Gender and Public Policies in the Philippines. In *Women, Gender, Remittances and Development in the Global South,* ed. Ton van Naerssen, Lothar Smith, et al., 141–154. Farnham: Ashgate Press.

Auero, Javier. 2012. *Patients of the State: The Politics of Waiting in Argentina.* Durham: Duke University Press.

Baca, George. 2004. Legends of Fordism: Between Myth, History and Foregone Conclusions. *Social Analysis* 48 (3): 169–178.

Baggio, Fabio, ed. 2010. *Brick by Brick: Building Cooperation Between the Philippines and Migrants' Associations in Italy and Spain.* Manila: Scalabrini Migration Center.

Banting, Keith, and Will Kymlicka. 2010. Canadian Multiculturalism: Global Anxieties and Local Debates. *British Journal of Canadian Studies* 23 (1): 73–72.

Barber, Pauline Gardiner. 2004. Contradictions of Class and Consumption When the Commodity Is Labor. *Anthropologica* 46 (2): 213–218.

———. 2013. "Grateful" Subjects: Class and Capital at the Border in Philippine—Canada Migration. *Dialectical Anthropology* 37 (3–4): 383–400.

Barber, Pauline Gardiner, and Catherine Bryan. 2012. Value Plus Plus: Housewifization and History in Philippine Care Migration. In *Migration in the 21st Century: Political Economy and Ethnography,* ed. Pauline Gardiner Barber and Winnie Lem, 215–235. New York: Routledge.

———. 2017. International Organization for Migration in the Field: 'Walking the Talk' of Global Migration Management in Manila. *Journal of Ethnic and Migration Studies.* https://doi.org/10.1080/1369183X.2017.1354068.

Barber, Pauline Gardiner, and Winnie Lem, eds. 2012. *Migration in the 21st Century: Political Economy and Ethnography.* New York: Routledge.

Bascaramurty, Dakshana. 2017. *Canada Aims for Immigration Boost to Buttress Economy,* 1–4. Toronto: Globe and Mail.

Batan, Clarence. 2010. *ISTAMBAY A Sociological Analysis of Youth Inactivity in the Philippines.* PhD dissertation, Dalhousie University.

Bell, Lindsay. 2012. In Search of Hope: Mobility and Citizenships on the Canadian Frontier. In *Migration in the 21st Century: Political Economy and Ethnography,* ed. Pauline Gardiner Barber and Winnie Lem, 132–152. New York: Routledge.

Binford, Leigh. 2013. *Tomorrow We're All Going to the Harvest: Temporary Foreign Worker Programs and Neoliberal Political Economy.* Austin: University of Texas Press.

Boyd, Monica, and Michael Vickers. 2000. 100 Years of Immigration in Canada. *Canadian Social Trends* 58: 2–12.

Brettell, Caroline. 2003. *Anthropology and Migration: Essays on Transnationalism, Ethnicity, and Identity.* Walnut Creek, CA: Altamira Press.

Brettell, Caroline, and James Hollifield. 2008. *Migration Theory: Talking Across Disciplines.* New York: Routledge.

Canadian Press. 2012. Controversy Over Chinese Miners in B.C. Prompts Review. *The Canadian Press,* Posted November 8, 2012. http://www.cbc.ca/news/canada/british-columbia/story/2012/10/22/bc-coal-miner-permits-demand.html. Accessed March 23, 2013.

CFO. 2014. *Stock Estimate of Overseas Filipinos as of December 2012.* Manila: Commission on Filipinos Overseas. http://www.cfo.gov.ph/index.php?option=com_content&view=article&id=1309:statistics&catid=110:frequently-asked-questions&Itemid=858. Accessed December 29, 2014.

Cohen, Robin. 2006. *Migration and Its Enemies: Global Capital, Migrant Labor and the Nation-State.* Aldershot: Ashgate.

Crehan, Kate. 2016. *Gramsci's Common Sense: Inequality and Its Narratives.* Durham and London: Duke University Press.

Curry, Bill. 2014. Top Filipino Diplomat Defends Ottawa's Foreign-Worker Program. *Globe and Mail,* April 29. http://www.theglobeandmail.com/news/politics/top-filiino-diplomat-defends-ottawas-foreign-worker-program/article18320224/. Accessed April 29, 2014.

De Vera, Ben. 2017. OFW Remittances Hit Record High in 2016. *Philippine Daily Inquirer.* http://business.inquirer.net/224635/ofw-remittances-hi-record-high-2016. Accessed August 17, 2017.

Dobrowolsky, Alexandra. 2013. Nuancing Neoliberalism: Lessons Learned from a Failed Immigration Experiment. *Journal of International Migration and Integration* 14 (2): 197–218.

Dobrowolsky, Alexandra, and Howard Ramos. 2014. *Expanding the Vision: Why Nova Scotia Should Look Beyond Econocentric Immigration Policy.* Halifax: Canadian Centre for Policy Alternatives, NS.

Dorow, Sara, and Sara O'Shaughnessy. 2013. Fort McMurray, Wood Buffalo, and the Oil/Tar Sands: Revisiting the Sociology of "Community". *Canadian Journal of Sociology* 38 (2): 121–140.

Eviota, Elizabeth. 1995. *Women of a Lesser Cost: Female Labor, Foreign Exchange and Philippine Development.* London: Pluto Press.

Feldman, Gregory. 2011. *The Migration Apparatus: Security, Labor and Policymaking in the European Union.* Stanford: Stanford University Press.

Fleras, Augie. 2015. *Immigration Canada: Evolving Realities and Emerging Challenges in a Postnational World.* Vancouver: UBC Press.

Gertel, Jorg, and Sarah Ruth Sippel, eds. 2014. *Seasonal Workers in Mediterranean Agriculture: The Social Costs of Eating Fresh.* London: Routledge.

Glick Schiller, Nina. 2012. Migration and Development Without Methodological Nationalism: Towards Global Perspectives on Migration. In *Migration in the 21st Century: Political Economy and Ethnography*, ed. Pauline Gardiner Barber and Winnie Lem, 38–63. New York: Routledge.

Glick Schiller, Nina, and Thomas Faist, eds. 2010. *Migration, Development and Transnationalization: A Critical Stance*. New York: Berghahn Books.

Glick Schiller, Nina, and Noel Salazar. 2013. Regimes of Mobility Across the Globe. *Journal of Ethnic and Migration Studies* 39 (2): 183–200.

Gonzalez, Joaquin. 1998. *Philippine Labor Migration: Critical Dimensions of Public Policy*. Manila: De La Salle University Press, Inc. and Institute of Southeast Asian Studies.

Government of Canada. 2014. *Overhauling the Temporary Foreign Worker Program: Putting Canadians First, WP-191-06-14E*. Ottawa: Government of Canada.

Gross, Dominique. 2014. *Temporary Foreign Workers in Canada: Are They Really Filling Labor Shortages? Commentary No. 407*. Toronto: C.D. Howe Institute.

Guevarra, Anna. 2010. *Marketing Dreams, Manufacturing Heroes: The Transnational Labor Brokers of Filipino Workers*. New Brunswick: Rutgers University Press.

Hampshire, James. 2013. *The Politics of Immigration: Contradictions of the Liberal State*. Cambridge: Polity.

Harvey, David. 1989. *The Conditions of Postmodernity: An Enquiry into the Origins of Cultural Change*. Oxford: Blackwell.

———. 2003. *The New Imperialism*. Oxford: Oxford University Press.

Hiebert, Daniel. 2009. *Exploring Minority Enclave Areas in Montréal, Toronto, and Vancouver*. Ottawa: Citizenship and Immigration Canada, Research and Evaluation Branch.

Innis, Harold. 1995. *Staples, Markets and Cultural Change*. Montreal: McGill-Queens University Press.

Kalb, Don. 2012. Thinking About Neoliberalism as if the Crisis Was Actually Happening. *Social Anthropology/Anthropologie Sociale* 20 (3): 318–330.

Lem, Winnie, and Pauline Gardiner Barber, eds. 2013. *Class, Contention and a World in Motion*. New York: Berghahn Books.

Ley, David. 2010. *Millionaire Migrants: Trans-Pacific Life Lines*. Malden, MA: Wiley Blackwell.

Li, Peter. 2003. *Destination Canada: Immigration Debates and Issues*. Don Mills, ON: Oxford University Press Canada.

Marx, Karl. 1977. *Capital: A Critique of Political Economy, Volume One*. New York: Vintage Books.

McDonald, Marci. 2014. True Blue. *The Walrus* 11 (4): 41.

McLaughlin, Janet. 2010. Classifying the "Ideal Migrant Worker": Mexican and Jamaican Transnational Farmworkers in Canada. *Focaal* 57 (Summer): 79–94.

Neveling, Patrick. 2014. Structural Contingencies and Untimely Coincidences in the Making of Neoliberal India: The Kandla Free Trade Zone, 1965–91. *Contributions to Indian Sociology* 48 (1): 17–43.

———. 2015. Export Processing Zones and Global Class Formation. In *Anthropologies of Class: Power, Practice and Inequality*, ed. James Carrier and Don Kalb, 164–182. Cambridge: Cambridge University Press.

Pido, Eric. 2017. *Migrant Returns: Manila, Development, and Transnational Connectivity.* Durhan and London: Duke University Press.

Piper, Nicola. 2011. Towards a Gendered Political Economy of Migration. In *Migration in the Global Political Economy*, ed. Nicola Phillips, 61–82. Boulder: Lynne Rienner Publishers.

Pratt, Geraldine. 2012. *Families Apart: Migrant Mothers and the Conflicts of Labor and Love.* Minneapolis: University of Minnesota Press.

Preibisch, Kerry. 2010. Pick-Your-Own Labor: Migrant Workers and Flexibility in Canadian Agriculture. *International Migration Review* 44 (2): 404–441.

Rodriguez, Robyn. 2010. *Migrants for Export: How the Philippine State Brokers Labor to the World.* Minneapolis: University of Minnesota Press.

Satzewich, Vic. 2015. *Points of Entry: How Canada's Immigration Officers Decide Who Gets In.* Vancouver: UBC Press.

Sinoski, Kelly. 2014. Canada's Temporary Foreign Worker Program Fills a Need, Protects Other Jobs, Business Leader Says. *Vancouver Sun*, April 21.

Smith, Gavin. 2014. *Intellectuals and (Counter-) Politics: Essays in Historical Realism.* New York: Berghahn.

Stasiulis, Daiva, and Abigail Bakan. 2005. *Negotiating Citizenship: Migrant Women in Canada and the Global System.* Toronto: University of Toronto Press.

Taweel, Heather. 2014. Seafood Processors, Fishermen Unite in Opposing Temporary Foreign Workers Changes. *The Charlottetown Guardian.* http://www.theguardian.pe.ca/News/Local/2014-07-15/article-38011008/. Accessed July 16, 2014.

Thunert, Martin. 2003. Conservative Think Tanks in the United States and Canada. In *Conservative Parties and Right-Wing Politics in North America: Reaping the Benefits of an Ideological Victory?* ed. Rainer-Olaf Schultze, Roland Sturn, and Dagmar Eberle, 229–254. Opladen: Leske und Budrich.

Tomlinson, K. 2013. RBC Replaces Canadian Staff with Foreign Workers. *CBC News*, April 6. http://www.cbc.ca/news/Canada/british-columbia/rbc-replaces-canadian-staff-with-foreignworkers-1.1315008. Accessed December 12, 2013.

Tyner, James. 2003. *Made in the Philippines.* New York and London: Routledge.

Wente, Margaret. 2013. Who's Stealing Our Jobs? Computers. Toronto: *Globe and Mail*, April 13.

Wolf, Eric. 1982. *Europe and the People Without History.* Berkeley: University of California Press.

CHAPTER 10

The Dialectics of Uneven Spatial-Temporal Development: Migrants and Reproduction in Late Capitalism

Winnie Lem

As capitalist transformations persist to shape socio-economies, scholars who engage with the analytical paradigms of historical materialism continue to problematize the heterogeneous spatial and temporal formations that characterize trajectories of its development.[1] Recently this problematization has focused on the notion of unevenness in reinvigorated discussions of uneven and combined development (UCD).[2] In Development Studies and International Relations, for example, scholars have been thinking through the usefulness of UCD in efforts to move beyond the impasse in the development theory of the 1990s that followed on the heels of the post-structuralist turn in the social sciences (Makki 2015; Rosenberg 2010, 2013). In geography, Marion Werner (2012), Neil Smith (2010) and Neil Davidson (2016) have problematized the contours of

[1] See, for example, Aneivas and Kamron (Eds.) (2016), Harvey (2006), Smith (2010), Smith (2016).
[2] See Trotsky (1977 [1930]) and Lenin (1899) as well as Rosenberg (2010).

W. Lem (✉)
International Development Studies, Trent University,
Peterborough, ON, Canada

© The Author(s) 2018
P. G. Barber, W. Lem (eds.), *Migration, Temporality,
and Capitalism*, https://doi.org/10.1007/978-3-319-72781-3_10

185

unevenness in relation to formations of capitalism over space as new and varied forms of value creation proliferated over time and assert themselves in new places under distinct regimes of accumulation. Anthropologists have also entered into such discussions. Gavin Smith (2016), Jaume Franquesa (2016) as well as Lesley Gill and Sharryn Kasmir (2016) have attempted to grapple with the analytic optic of unevenness to theorize the heterogeneities of capitalist change across space and time. Gill and Kasmir (2016), for example, propose an approach to the study of unevenness that is refracted through the dimensions of history, spatial/scalar differentiations, state and the formation and development of labor. They draw attention to the fact that these interventions are in many ways encapsulated by, but not reducible to, the problematization of scale. The problematization of scale, too, has been undertaken by geographers[3] and anthropologists[4] who are engaged in thinking through how the mutually constituted local, regional, national and indeed global relations are entry points for an analysis of interconnected processes that span the planet.

The interventions made by such scholars of unevenness and scale considerably advance our knowledge of the forces, impact and conflicts that characterize capitalist transformation. Yet in much of this body of work there is a tendency to grant analytical primacy to space. When time is considered, it is conceived largely linearly and in terms of chronology and history.[5] This is particularly (and not surprisingly) the case in the work of key geographers most notably in David Harvey (2006, 2005). This tendency, for example, is also evident in Davidson (2016: 2), who asks:

> ...whether uneven and combined development can indeed be extended, not backwards through time, but sideways through space: in other words, whether the process has been generated in *every* society which has experienced capitalist modernity, rather than being confined to backward or underdeveloped area.

In the scholarship that addresses scale, moreover, when time is considered, an emphasis is placed on changing hierarchies of power that accompany shifts in regimes of accumulation that occur in segments of time.[6] Without denying the importance of histories and chronologies and

---

[3] See Brenner (1999) and Swyngedouw (2010).
[4] See Çağlar and Glick Schiller (2018) and Nonini and Susser (eds) (forthcoming).
[5] A notable exception to this is Makki (2015).
[6] See also Lem (forthcoming).

the necessity of understanding the changing hierarchies of power, in this chapter my aim is to explore how granting analytical eminence to time may enhance our understandings of how the lives of the people we study articulate with the imperatives of capitalist transformation over both space and time. My exploration is premised upon conceiving the relationship between the scales of space and time as a dialectic. In this chapter my purpose is to problematize the ways in which this dialectic ramifies in the lives of women, who in confronting the vagaries of the unevenness of capitalist transformation are socially reproduced as migrants.

Building on my research on transnational migration and the livelihoods of Chinese migrants France,[7] I focus on women who have relocated to Paris from the northeastern provinces of China, to address how spatial dislocations and temporal unevenness are implicated in the lives of migrants. To do this, I will draw on insights from Lefebvre's (1992) methodology of "rhythmanalysis" as well as Bloch's (1977) conceptualization of the "simultaneity of the non-simultaneous". My engagement with their works is intended to outline how their theoretical and methodological insights enable an understanding of the relationship between spatio-temporalities of migration and capitalist change that moves beyond an emphasis on time as chronological, linear and simply historical. I shall explore how an engagement with their insights expands current notions of scale beyond conventional conceptualization of the spatio-political. I do this by thinking through what conceptual possibilities are opened up by situating the analytical lens at the scale of migrant women's bodies. I stress that my conceptualization is not a bio-politics[8] but a historical materialism of bio-physicality. Here I address how women's bodies and lives are entangled within mutually constituted local, regional, national and globe-spanning processes of capitalist change that are interconnected but manifested unevenly across the scales of time and space. The chapter begins with a discussion of this methodology for reckoning with such unevenness, then proceeds to outline how the process of uneven development and regimes shifts in post-Mao, reform-era China are significant in the formation of migration and the making of women into migrants. The temporal ramifications of such unevenness are then traced though rhythmanalysis for migrant women who pursue livelihoods in the affective economies of urban industrial France.

[7] Ethnographic research upon which chapter is based has been generously supported by the Social Sciences and Humanities Research Council of Canada, the Wenner Gren Foundation or Anthropological Research and Trent University.
[8] Cf. Foucault (1997).

Rhythmanalysis and the Simultaneity of the Non-Simultaneous

In much of the work that focuses on the notion of unevenness in the development of capitalism over space, the work of Henri Lefebvre has been key. His insights on the production of space as a social relationship have been essential in illuminating the uneven geographic development of capitalism over time as well as the shifting scales of governance and power regimes over place. However, as Ryan Moore (2013) has pointed out, his work on the production of space is frequently abstracted from his complete body of work. This body of work was also much concerned with critiquing everyday life, exploring cultural practices and problematizing time. He was particularly concerned with exploring the dialectical relationship that prevails between space and time and its implications in everyday life as capitalism progressed to transform the lives of people in and outside work.

These concerns are encapsulated in his 1992 work that proposes a methodology of "rhythmanalysis". Lefebvre notes: "Everywhere there is interaction between a place, a time and an expenditure of energy, there is a rhythm." (2004: 15)

In building this methodological framework, he advanced a notion of temporality, which drew a distinction between the time scales that are subsumed by the rationalities of capitalism and those that are not. To Lefebvre, linear time is a feature of capitalism and is particularly rooted in industrial capitalism. Under industrial capitalism time comes to be reckoned linearly as it is segmented into a succession of quantified, interchangeable moments. These moments measure the exchange value of labor.[9] Cyclical time scales, on the other hand, are rooted in the biophysical world as the temporal round of birth and death, is rooted in nature and in the physiological rhythms of the human body. These elements form the framework of a methodology that he used to analyze the everyday of the real and concrete features of the everyday lives of people. So, everyday life is inflected by the elements of repetition, cyclical process and birth, growth, peak then decline as well as interferences of linear processes (Lefebvre 2004: 9–15). Lefebvre argued that post-war capitalism would colonize all times and spaces of human existence, and he was

---

[9] See, also, E.P. Thompson (1967), who argued that this temporal "work-discipline" is linked to the rise of capitalism, as increasingly precise units of clock time became the basis of quantifiable value in a manner that was imposed on the workforce (Moore 2013).

thus particularly concerned with how cyclical time comes to be subordinated to linear time. In this process of colonization, rhythmic temporality is subjected to being fractured, disrupted and flattened out as capitalism becomes more embedded in spaces of civil society and human existence. This concern extended beyond labor and work to include leisure, family, private life, sexuality and the body as well as the unconscious and the imagination (Mayer 2008; Goonewardena et al. 2008).

Drawing on Lefebvre, then, I focus on how the characteristics of late capitalism and the insistent demands of its cycles of production and accumulation both disrupt and subordinate the rhythms of human life to the imperatives generating a profit. I suggest that this disruption and subordination is manifested through the tempo, paces and cadences of two biophysical rhythms: the epigenetic rhythm and the circadian rhythm. The epigenetic rhythm is the *biological* clock of human life. The biological clock of human life is connected to age and the ways in which periods of life are socially defined. The circadian rhythm is the *body* clock of human life and refers to the 24-hour cycle of physical, mental and behavioral changes that respond largely to light and darkness. While both epigenetic and circadian rhythms refer to the biophysical characteristics of bodies, they are linked to social rhythms or social time. There are many ways in which social time is defined and theorized (Nowatny 1992), but most follow the Durkheimian view, which suggests that social time refers to a division of the rhythms of social life according to social activities. While often this conceptualization requires thinking through of time as socially constructed, it often refers to the symbolic and cultural realm. Here I wish to bring this into alignment with the material and physical realm by suggesting that social activities, particularly those activities dedicated to the reproduction of families, tend to follow circadian and epigenetic rhythms. Social time is the time in which the different activities of sociability—including social reproduction of distinctive social institutions such as the family—take place. This then raises the specter of another temporal disruption—the disruption of social time. For spatially dislocated women, as I later discuss, an additional rhythmic disruption prevails: the demands of commodified care work under late capitalism disrupts time scales social reproduction of kin in transnationalized migrant families.

Lefebvre also recognized the intrinsic temporal unevenness of this process of imposing a capitalist temporal discipline, for while cyclical time scales tend to be *subordinated to* linear time, cyclic time, so he observed, does exist *in conjunction with* linear time. In this respect, his notion of the conjunction of multiple temporalities resonates with Ernst Bloch's (1977) conception of the "simultaneity of the non-simultaneous" (see also Olwig Fog, this volume). As recent authors have emphasized, unevenness in the development of capitalism across space combines social relations that are subsumed by capitalism with those that are connected but not entirely subsumed (Smith 2016; Makki 2015). The interventions of scholars who draw on the work of Bloch and Lefebvre also offers insights into how such non-synchronicity[10] shapes terrains of conflict and struggle as populations contend with the forces that render people surplus to socioeconomies.[11] Such contentions and forces are evident in the everyday lives of the migrant women and men whose confrontations with the unevenness of capitalist development in China have resulted in their transformation into members of a population who move in and out of forms of commodified work in a series of differentiated spaces.

FORMATIONS OF CHINESE CAPITALISM AND THE SPATIO-TEMPORALITIES OF UNEVENNESS

In China, the spatio-temporal modulations of unevenness in the economy emerged from the efforts made by post-Mao, reform era governments to remake 'state socialism' into a regime of 'state capitalism' or 'market social-ism' through multiple strategies of liberalisation (Horesh and Lim 2016). The inconsistencies of this development trajectory are not only indexed by the incompatible valences of the notions of 'market' and 'socialism' but also by the geo-spatial divisions as well as social dislocations that have resulted from the restructuring a command and control agricultural and industrial economy into one based increasingly on laissez faire. This unevenness and socio-spatial inequality are encapsulated in the distinction made by Ching Kwan Lee (2007) between 'sun belt' of high industrial development and growth that emerged in China's southeast in the 1980's and the emergence

---

[10] See Lefebvre, H. 1992 with Catherine Regulier-Lefebvre Éléments de rythmanalyse: Introduction à la connaissance des rythmes, preface by René Lorau, Paris: Ed. Syllepse, Collection "Explorations et découvertes". English translation: Rhythmanalysis: Space, time and everyday life, Stuart Elden, Gerald Moore trans. Continuum, New York, 2004 and Bloch (1977) New German Critique 11 22–38.

[11] Smith notes with reference to Marx's (1973: 630) law of population that labor's capacity to attain its value can only be achieved when it is saleable labor under capitalism. That is to say when labor power is sold, it adds value to capital. So, when it is not sold it does not add value to capital. Unsalable labor then appears to be of no use and therefore is surplus (2014: 187). Also see Smith (2011).

in the 1990s of a 'rust belt' of industrial and economic decline in the north-east. This spatial division mirrored a temporal differences in the scope and scale of the development of an extensive commodified economy based on growth and capital accumulation. The reformatting of Chinese economy and society then proceeded in different phases. It also shaped the dynamics of what is often discussed in the migration literature in terms of sequential flows or newer and older waves of migration from the different regions in China, as socio-economic inequalities re-emerged under state capitalism. (Guerassimoff 2006, 2012).

Dong Mei and Xiao Li[12] whom I shall discuss later are migrants who are part of the new wave that arrived in Paris in the early 2000s. Originating from China's northeastern 'rust belt', Dong Mei works as a nanny for the Huang family. The Huangs were part of a first wave of migration in the post-Mao era that arrived in Paris during the 1980s and 1990s. They migrated from the 'sun belt' southeast provinces of China. Like many migrants of the first wave, the Huangs come from a small village in Yongia county near Wenzhou city in Zhejiang province located in southern coastal China.

The Huangs sustained an intergenerational household by farming until the early 1980s, when reforms that aimed to restructure an economy based on surplus redistribution to one based on surplus accumulation were implemented. Initiated in the late 1970s, the reforms to the agrarian economy involved such measures as contracting collective resources to individuals in ways that came increasingly close to de facto ownership; the replacement of communes with mixed (private and public) forms of economic organization; the revival of private marketing and the commodification of labor power; reduced state control over the production and sale of agricultural products; and the promotion of production and exchange in a commodity economy.[13] The dismantling of rural collectives and the development of private forms of cultivation and the transfer of collective resources to individuals meant that the Huangs, who operated a relatively small holding, could no longer pursue a sustainable agricultural livelihood. Moreover, as the reforms progressed a series of legislative changes were made in the late twentieth and early twenty-first century that allowed the

---

[12] All names that appear in this article are fictive.

[13] There are many detailed discussions of the nature of these reforms and effects of the reform program on agrarian livelihoods. See, for example, Zhang (2003) as well as Judd (1994), Oi (1999) and Murphy (2002).

appropriation of agricultural land for urbanization while also enabling land transfers for infrastructure, real estate and industrial development.[14] China's economic growth has been driven recently by heavy investment in infrastructural and real estate development. Such investments require land, and millions of hectares of arable land have been lost through appropriation and transfer because of 'land enclosure rushes', which took the form of speculation, industrial development and rehousing.[15]

The forces of reform and legislative change that enabled different forms of speculation to prevail in the Chinese economy are consistent with Marx's notions of how the historical processes of primitive accumulation (1976 [1867]: 874–875) separate producers from the means of production through "extra economic means".[16] Though at the time that the Huangs first migrated, the family had not fallen victim to such rushes, the specter of land appropriation loomed large as the expanding urban industrial complex was at their doorstep. Their holding was situated close to the edge of Wenzhou city and the Huangs felt that it was simply a matter of time before their meagre lands would be swallowed up by the expanding industries or appropriated for real estate development. This feeling emerged also from having witnessed neighbors who were expelled from their land which was transformed into a site for the development of factories. They also knew others whose lands were appropriated for the development of a new luxury housing development.[17] The possibility of losing livelihood and land under these circumstances added impetus to the search for alternative ways of making a living by adopting a strategy of migrating.

---

[14] For example, by 1995, 5 million hectares of arable land was transferred to infrastructure and real estate in China. In Fujian Province, 35 million hectares were transferred to industry (Banerjee-Guha 2011).

[15] According to Deepak (2011) there were three such rushes. The first was during the mid-1980s, when cities expanded, town and township enterprises mushroomed and peasants started to build new houses. The second 'land enclosure rush' occurred between 1992 and 1993 in the form of land speculation; huge tracts of arable land were seized for constructing commercial houses. The third land enclosures took place between 2002 and 2004, when the government invited and sold land to developers at a very low price. There was also a fourth, which was to be driven by government's resolve to convert rural population into non-rural by building 'mini cities' in the rural areas (see also Guldin 2001).

[16] See Marx (1976 [1867]: 874–875); also see Webber (2008) as well as Harvey (2003), who has discussed this process as "accumulation by dispossession".

[17] For a discussion of the details of interlocked mechanisms involved in the appropriation of rural land in the process of urbanization, see Webber (2008).

Such reforms and the liberalizations of the economy have contributed to the creation of masses of "surplus laborers" throughout China (Murphy 2002) and the migration of millions of people from rural localities to both urban centres. Like those millions who have been "freed" from land or anticipate these forms of future dispossession, adult members of the Huang household joined the ranks of the mobile proletariat and who migrated initially to such places as Wenzhou City where they could gain work by as members of the low-skilled labor for the development of a labor-intensive profit-making urban economy.

In the initial decades of market reform, such profit making economies were located in China's southeastern coastal provinces, where special economic zones were created. Such zones became the focus of development strategy and planning that implemented significant economic liberalizations within a system of developing private-public forms of industry and growing foreign investment (Naughton et al. 2008). This focus on industry as a development strategy converged with planning endeavors that have consistently favored the development of an industrial urban economy since the Great Leap Forward of 1958–1961 (Zhang 2003). This "urban bias" (Lipton 1977) in development strategy and it implementation is manifested not only in a significant spatial divide between the economies of the coast and interior but also an increasing inequality in the terms of trade between agriculture and industry, where agricultural commodities are relatively underpriced and industrial commodities overpriced relative to their respective "labor values".[18] Such a bias has not only fueled a rural-urban socio-economic divide but these divisions have been intensified by the effects of the *hukou* system of household registration. *Hukou* confers rights in residence and eligibility for certain jobs as well as subsidized welfare benefits that are tied to place of birth. First implemented in rural areas in 1955, it became a part of state policy in 1958 to ensure that the peasantry would stay tied to the land in a period of land reform followed by agrarian collectivization. Under this registration system, each household was allocated an occupational category, either agricultural or non-

---

[18]For example, in 1993, 50 kilograms of rice was worth only a bottle of pesticide. Furthermore, while prices for certain agricultural crops are fixed by planning mechanisms, industrial commodities such as chemical pesticide, chemical fertilizers and other industrial commodities were sold at market (Zhang 2003: 32).

agricultural, and a place of residence or *hukou*.[19] Interregional migration and the movements of people during the Maoist period,[20] then, were strictly regulated through the hukou system.

The hukou system continues to restrict interregional movements of people and their entitlements. Those who are registered in an urban place of birth are assured of stable social welfare services such as medical treatment, housing and transportation that are unavailable to city inhabitants, who are registered in a place of birth in the countryside. In recent years, the Chinese Communist Party has made gestures towards relaxing the controls, especially as migration is encouraged in official policies. Migration is seen as a means for the promotion of the economic development of the agricultural economy in a context in which official policies favor urban industrial development (Xiang 2003). Because of this urban bias in development planning and the restrictions of hukou, rural poverty has increased in southeastern China. Moreover, wages, rather than assets such as land, are the source of higher relative incomes, and work in industry yields higher incomes than incomes gained through farm work.[21] Thus, in a context in which official attention and resouces are diverted toward the development of urban industrial economies in order to foster rapid accumulation, the proletarianization of the peasantry is considered to be a long-term phenomenon, as rural to urban migration is regarded as the least expensive and most efficient way of developing the rural regions (Zhang 2003: 47).

The prefecture of Wenzhou is one such site of accumulation. Often touted as the place where China's first economic 'miracle' was experienced,[22] its economy grew rapidly through the development of private industry, based on small-scale family run enterprises. These enterprises produce shoes, eyeglasses, locks, transformers, switches, sex toys, lighters, razors

---

[19] Under the *hukou* system migrant flows in China are grouped into three categories: migration with residency rights (*hukou* migration), migration without *hukou* residency rights, and migrants who are engaged in short-term movements such as visiting, circulating and commuting. Changes in *hukou* must be approved by the official authorities who have historically granted them when they were not at odds with the state's developmental objectives and policies (for more details see Zhang 2003; Judd 1994).

[20] Interregional migration was common in the Maoist era, while international migration was forbidden. For a discussion of migration in different eras, see Lary (1999).

[21] Zhang (2003: 33) lists differences in income between urban and rural areas between 1978 and 2000. With the exception of 1984, urban incomes were at least double that of rural incomes.

[22] For discussion of the "Wenzhou Model of development", see Liu (1992), Parris (1993) and Bramall (1991).

and suits for the national and international market. Wenzhou, then, is a principle destination for much migrant surplus labor, which is absorbed into the burgeoning industries and expansive service sector that support the growing economies.[23] Yet many migrants also often find themselves rendered into a 'second surplus' and superfluous to such industrial economies as worker turnover and therefore job termination is high, and the demand for labor is often out of sync with labor supplies. So, under these conditions the second surplus labor force moves from city to city or hovers on the edge of such urban economies. In Wenzhou, members of this force are seen living under bridges, along river banks and on road in ramshackle homes. As Frank Pieke (1998) notes, the 'miracle' of economic growth in Wenzhou has been accompanied by significant social and economic polarization. So, it has also produced members of what is called in China the 'floating population', who swell the ranks of a mobile population.[24]

Wenzhou is also one of the first places in reform era China where significant numbers of people undertook migration across international borders. In the 1980s and 1990s, migrants from Wenzhou began to arrive in considerable numbers in Paris. They joined the ranks of the Wenzhounese population in Paris who had established themselves in the early and mid-twentieth century largely as labor migrants. This older population of migrants was recruited to fill labor gaps in French industry during World Wars and then settled in France. By navigating through social and economic networks established by these older migrants, Wenzhounese who arrived in the later twentieth century were able to gain work in industries and find employment in the businesses run by relatives, friends and fellow countrymen and women. Also, by mobilizing financial resources through these networks through rotating credit societies—called *tontines*—many Wenzhounese who were employed as wage workers eventually established

---

[23] It has been estimated that 100 million Chinese farmers have left their native villages to search for work in urban centres (Zhang 2003: 162).

[24] The 'floating population' refers to people who have not migrated officially. According to the Chinese conception, the chief characteristic of the floating population is that they "float and move", which implies they are not and cannot become a permanently settled group. In China, those considered members of the floating population have crossed over some administrative boundary but have not altered their permanent registration or *hukou*. Hukou migration or official migration is endowed with state resources and is referred to as "planned migration" by the government. "Floaters" are a "self-flowing population' whose movements occurs outside state plans and whose movements are described by planners as "anarchic" and "chaotic" (see Zhang 2001; Solinger 1999: 15; Chan 1999: 49; Murphy 2002).

themselves as petty capitalists though different forms of self-employment and entrepreneurship.[25]

In the late 1990s another group of migrants, one having no previous migration history to Europe, emerged in Paris. This flow emanated from northeastern provinces in China, where much of the state-run heavy industry served as the backbone of the economy during the Maoist era. In the 1990s, this region was targeted for aggressive restructuring in order to create a context favorable to forms of hyper-accumulation required for the admission of China to the World Trade Organization. Reforms called for the large-scale closures of state-run industries and extensive privatizations of the industrial sector as well as dismantling of the system of job security and benefits for state employees called the "iron rice bowl system".[26] Such privatizations were also applied to services such as health care, education and daycare. These closures and the increasing commodification of the economy therefore created the "rust belt" of the northeast, and intensification of such reforms altered and intensified the pattern of social, economic and spatial unevenness. A social and economic division between the north and the south emerged alongside the rural-urban divide, and the division between coast and interior. As capital became concentrated in urban industrial coastal economies and privatisations intensified, class polarization also intensified as people loss their means of making a living.

Employees in state-run enterprises in China's were made redundant once firms were closed or sold off to private interests. Deprived of their means of making a livelihood and ejected from the socio-economy, many former state employees now migrate between key spaces of capital accumulation in urban industrial centres in China in search of a means of

---

[25] Tontines are an investment vehicle that is a mixture of group annuity, group life insurance and lottery in which investors each pay a sum into the tontine. The funds are invested and each investor receives dividends. Usually the scheme involves an arrangement that is made upon the death of an investor so that when an investor dies his or her share is divided amongst all the other investors. This process continues until only one investor survives, who receives all of the remaining funds. Amongst the Chinese in Paris what is called a 'tontine' resembles more a rotating credit society, one in which investors each advance small loans to the borrower, who repays each investor with interest according to a predetermined schedule. The death of investors seems not to figure in the arrangements in a prominent way. For a detailed discussion of the ways in which tontines are organized amongst Chinese immigrants in Paris, see Pairault (1990).

[26] The iron rice bowl system was developed in the Maoist period in China and guaranteed job security to employees in state-run enterprises as well as benefited military and civil servants.

making a living. Such ejections and the processes of rendering labor surplus have been particularly acute over the course of the late twentieth and particularly the early twenty-first century as global financial crises have created the conditions of the saturation of industrial labor markets under the conditions of recession and forced industrial closures.[27] Such expulsions from the socio-economy are also exacerbated for mobile people in China through the exclusions rendered by the hukou system.

In the face of the depredations wrought by the processes of restructuring, segments of this surplus population from China's northeast have become transformed into a transnational mobile proletariat. A significant portion of this population consists of women from the provinces of Lianing, Jilin and Heilongjinag who have migrated to Paris, which is a site where a financial and service complex is burgeoning under post-Fordist forms of accumulation (Sassen 2002). Cognizant of the limits of securing and sustaining a livelihood through transregional migration, such women have relocated transnationally channeled through diasporic networks toward places where they are reabsorbed into the local social economies as workers in the service economies. Made redundant in restructured state industries, many of these women migrants now commit themselves to different forms of work that attend to the needs and desires of people whose own labors are directly inserted in the processes through which capital is reproduced. They undertake the work of care and as migrants who put together a livelihood by navigating the social and political ruptures posed by spatial dislocation. Such dislocations, territorial dispersals and relocations also impose ruptures in time both upon the realms of social life and the biophysics of bodies. These ruptures are evident in lives Dong Mei and Xiao Li.

DISCREPANT TEMPORALITIES AND THE EVERYDAY LIFE OF MIGRANT WOMEN

Dong Mei and Xiao Li arrived in Paris from Heilongjiang province in 2010. Both are married and left behind families of young children to be cared for by ageing parents. They form part of an important flow from China's rust belt region that consists of largely of middle-aged women (see also Levy and Thorneley 2012). In the epigenetic rhythm or biological clock of human

---

[27] In 2011, roughly 8 percent of the urban population came to be unemployed; much of this was the result of the restructuring of industries after accession to the WTO in 2001. See Banerjee-Guha (2011) and Tian (2008).

life, the middle decades for women tends to be a period when considerable labors are devoted to caring for young children and ageing parents. Yet, Dong Mei and many women who worked in state industries and firms found that their ability to provide care and support for their families was interrupted by sudden unemployment as state enterprises were closed. For Dong Mei, fears for her inability to provide for the well-being of her family were magnified by the decline of state subsidies for education and health care, combined with the increased privatisation of hospitals and schools. She cites the rise of fees for health care and schooling in the face of a long future of unemployment as reasons for migrating to Europe and leaving her children in the care of her mother in China. When Dong Mei was employed in state firm in China, the work of care in sustaining families and the work undertaken in sustaining livelihoods was socially spatially and temporally congruent. As a transnational migrant, Dong Mei must pursue work in spatially differentiated locations and so is unable to attend to the social reproduction of her children and her parents. Such spatial incongruities in the work of reproduction are marked by ruptures to the temporal rhythm of work for women in their middle years. Spatial dispersion provoked by livelihood crises then also provokes crises of sustaining the epigenetic rhythms of their lives as well as the normal social round of family life.

Indeed, many migrant mothers like Dong Mei lamented their inability to devote this time of life to raising their children. Dong Mei now works in Paris raising the children of other people. She is a live-in nanny who cares for three pre-school-aged children in the Huang family. Like many migrant women from northeastern China, she works for southern Chinese families from Wenzhou. Lily Huang and her husband, Kim, arrived in Paris in the late 1980s and were quickly incorporated into the Parisian economy working in the kitchen and serving in a restaurant owned by a relative. Now Lily and Kim own and operate a small Chinese caterer. The longer history of Wenzhounese migration and regional differences in place of departure fuels cleavages in a labor market that is hyper-segmented in terms of class, gender and ethnicity. In this hyper-segmented labor market where migrants from the northeast were derided by more established migrant from southern China, petty tyrannies intensify the structures of exploitation hidden within homes (Lieber 2008).[28] Such tyrannies are built into the temporal

---

[28]Women from China's northeast are referred to as *dong bei* women by people from the southern China to signal the regional distinctions that prevail between different cohorts of migrants in Paris. According to many informants, this is done to denigrate them as people and to devalue their work.

conditions of domestic care and nanny work. The daily routine of Dong Mei work is extended around the 24-hour daily cycle and across the 6-day weekly cycle. She is meant to get up early in the morning to prepare breakfast for the both parents as well as children while also using part of her day to maintain the cleanliness of the home, shop and prepare meals for the children during the day. Moreover, Dong Mei reports that her employers leverage their familiarity with the French context and language to exploit the vulnerabilities of her undocumented status to unilaterally define the conditions of her work. So, her duties as a live-in caregiver extend well into the night and she is on call to tend to the needs of the children who wake frequently, especially when they were ill. Such night work often means days of fatigue, for she seldom has uninterrupted period of sleep before having to wake early for the next round of daily duties.

The demands of productivity in the capitalist economy impose themselves differently on the bodies of nannies and their employers. Night work for nannies, such as Dong Mei, enables their employers to sustain normal rhythms of slumber and wakefulness. By contrast, night work for nannies means disruption to the circadian rhythm or the body clock. Nights for nannies are marked by sleeplessness and days are marked by fatigue. The circadian rhythm or the body clock of nannies is disrupted and subordinated to the time demands of service work that is embedded in the temporalities of capitalist productivity. As Jonathan Crary (2013) notes, late capitalism requires the despoliation of sleep in the interest of maximizing the individual's potential as a producer in the interest of generating profit. The despoliation of sleep and the temporal tensions that prevail in the everyday lives of nannies is also a feature in the everyday lives of the army of nocturnal workers that sustain the economies of capitalism in Paris. Such nocturnal workers consist of migrants who in a segmented labor market are assigned to the demeaning forms of work as street cleaners, office cleaners, garbage collectors and shift workers in factories. However, one of the most arguably demeaning but unequivocally dangerous ways of making a living in nocturnal economies is sex work.

Xiao Li makes a living as a sex worker. She was fired from her job as a nanny to a southern Chinese family "for being difficult", after having refused to take care of the child of her employer's sister for a weekend without extra pay. Xiao Li describes how word spread very quickly through the social networks of the Wenzhounese about her being an uncooperative person, and she was thus unable to find another position as a nanny. She turned to prostitution as a short-term solution to making a living.

Meanwhile, her personal economic situation became more fragile. She had borrowed money from a friend who works as a nanny for her rent and groceries and was not able to remit funds to her two children who were living with grandparents and attending school in her home town in Heilongjiang province. Her husband meanwhile had migrated to southern China and was working in a toy factory located in Wenzhou before the factory closed in a wave of closures that resulted from the financial crises in 2008. Xiao Li had considered relocating to find work in southern China; however, she decided it was imperative she optimize livelihood strategies by migrating abroad. The difficulties posed by the hukou system combined with the knowledge that there were limited opportunities for inexperienced mature women to find work in factories acted as an impetus for her to relocate internationally. With rising household debt owed to people that were obtained through personal networks combined with the increasing demands to support her children and ageing parents, Xiao Li found it difficult to turn her back on work that was more lucrative than nannying. Manifesting the hyper-segmentation of the labor market and its divisions by gender, age and ethnicity, Xiao Li services a clientele that consists largely of middle-aged working-class immigrant non-Chinese men. Young white European sex workers tend to service a bourgeois clientele, in the high-end hotels, clubs and brothels located in the more prosperous areas of the city. By contrast, middle-aged women from ethnic minority groups tend to service working class ethnic minority men.[29] As is the practice amongst many sex workers from China's northeast, Xiao Li refuses Chinese clients, to minimize any discussion and explanations of why she has taken up such work and the gossip that would target her and her work activities. So, Xiao Li remains a sex worker despite the shame and opprobrium associated with prostitution, and many Chinese women migrants see sex work as a temporary way of making a living, turning to it as a work of last resort.

Since much sex work is night work, for such women the normal diurnal and nocturnal cycles of work and rest are disrupted. Their labor is deployed in the intervals between the time when work ends and begins for their clients. In a market that is also spatially differentiated, the activities of

[29] See Levy (2005), who observes that his is a competitive economy, which increases Chinese migrants who have no other option in France besides prostitution. Arrivals from other parts of China reported to have entered prostitution as soon as they arrived, and there is also a tendency for professionalization, with the presence of younger Chinese women, often with legal status, who seek a wealthier clientele, and who, like prostitutes of other origins, work in wealthier areas of Paris.

women sex workers tend to be confined to the dark corners and shady hotel rooms in working class districts of Paris. Young white European sex workers, by contrast tend to service a bourgeois clientele in the high-end hotels, clubs and brothels located in the more prosperous areas of the city.

Along with nannies, sex workers also form part of the force of migrant workers who work and travel the streets in semi-darkness. Travelling at night for this force of workers is also travailing at night, according to Matthew Beaumont (2015), as they toil at the service of capital to support its rhythms of ceaseless production. They work when most people are sleeping to prepare for the next day's labor. They are also according Beaumont (2015) the city's internal exiles, whose everyday lives may be characterized as a terrain of conflict in which forms of cyclical time and the rhythmic, following Lefebvre, are pitted against the linear and quantitative temporality of capitalism. For migrant women who work as nannies, night workers and sex workers, such conflicts arise as the temporalities of capitalism require the disciplining of people and their bodies to the constancy and primacy of demands for continual productivity.

CONCLUSION

In this chapter, I have used the insights offered by scholars of unevenness and scale as a point of departure to suggest some possibilities for how social and economic heterogeneities are manifested through time as capitalist developments unfold through space. I have addressed the question of how the shifting histories of social, spatial and particularly temporal exclusions illuminates the present of the everyday lives of migrant women. In pursuing this goal, I have drawn on Lefebvre (n.d.), whose vision of everyday life suggests that the 'everyday' or the present consists of a terrain of conflict and struggle in which enduring forms of cyclical time and the rhythmic patterns are pitted against the linear and quantitative temporality of capitalism. Such conflicts are evident in the everyday lives of women, for whom spatial dislocations run concurrently with dislocations in the rhythms of their lives. Not only are diurnal and nocturnal cycles of work and repose disrupted and subverted, but life cycles are disturbed and often subordinated. The everyday lives of such women then are informed by the tensions and struggle of sustaining the simultaneity of the work of care as mothers and the work of commodified care across multiple spaces. Such struggles, so I have tried to describe here, take the form of attempts to sustain the tempo, paces and cadences of family life against the temporal demands of production and accumulation in different sites. It is a struggle against what Lefebvre (2004) calls the "colonization of private life" by capitalism. This colonization involves the imposition of a temporal order that subverts circadian and epigenetic rhythms and in which the rhythms of nature, human bodies and social life are subordinated and flattened out. I have also highlighted how a consideration of the spatio-temporalities of migration in its relationship to capitalist change may move beyond a singular emphasis on linearity or time as chronology and history.

While the temporal binaries that appear in both Bloch's and Lefebvre's work may be overdrawn, their interventions remind us nonetheless that the spatio-temporality of capitalist world development is complex and differentiated. Bloch's work on non-synchronicity reminds us that it is imperative we think through unevenness also in relation to the question of politics. Much concerned with the rise of fascism in Germany, Bloch's work is informed by how unevenness frames possibilities for a politics that is driven by dreams of the excluded for overcoming the deprivations that result from the heterogeneities of capitalist development.

As Makki (2015: 488) argues:

> Capital accumulation has in fact proven to be profoundly compatible with a wide variety of political forms and institutional arrangements whose net effect has been to multiply the sites of social antagonisms and the agents of social change in ways unanticipated by the liberal or Marxist traditions. Over and above the structural persistence of the peasantry in large parts of the world, the massive growth of the informal sector across the global south has generated a heterogeneous social universe of wage and non-wage relations within an expanding planet of slums.

With their sensibilities derived as ethnographers, Gill and Kasmir (2016) also ask us to explicitly consider the question of labor and its formations over time and space. Here I have tried to highlight the entanglements of those who must sell their labor power in order to make a livelihood in a series of wage and non-wage relations as they confront the vagaries of changing regimes of accumulation. What these reminders and the imperatives of such politics call for are analytical approaches that account for such heterogeneities. Here I have responded to such a call by suggesting how such heterogeneities and unevenness may be manifested in the biophysics of women's bodies as well as the socio-physics of their lives as migrants. I have drawn considerably on the experiences of Dong

Mei and Xiao Li, advancing an understanding of the relationship between time and migration that moves beyond the purely phenomenological. A discussion of their experiences may be read as an attempt to problematize the relationship between time and migration within the paradigm of a realist ethnography.[30] Such an analytical approach to studying migration and time focuses on people's experienced practices and structures of feeling within the broad reach of an historical materialism that links experiences to the uneven spatialities and temporalities of capitalist change.

REFERENCES

Banerjee-Guha, S. 2011. Status of Rural Migrant Workers in Chinese Cities. *Economic and Political Weekly*, 33–37.

Beaumont, M. 2015. *Nightwalking: A Nocturnal History of London*. London: Verso Books.

Bloch, Ernst. 1977 [1932]. Nonsynchronism and the Obligation to Its Dialectics. Trans.: Mark Ritter. *New German Critique* 11: 22–38.

Bramall, Chris. 1991. The Wenzhou 'Miracle'. In *The Wenzhou Debate*, ed. Peter Nolan and Dong Fureng. London: Zed Publishers.

Brenner, N. (1999). Beyond state-centrism? Space, territoriality, and geographical scale in globalization studies. Theory and society, 28(1), 39-78.

Çağlar, Ayşe, and Nina Glick Schiller. 2018. *Migrants and City-Making: Dispossession, Displacement, and Urban Regeneration*. Durham, NC: Duke University Press.

Chan, Kam Wing. 1999. Internal Migration in China: A Dualistic Approach. In *Internal and International Migration*, ed. Frank Pieke and Hein Mallee. London: Curzon.

Crary, J. 2013. *24/7: Late Capitalism and the Ends of Sleep*. London: Verso Books.

Davidson, Neil. 2016. Uneven and Combined Development: Modernity, Modernism, Revolution. In *Historical Sociology and World History: Uneven and Combined Development Over the Long Duree*, ed. Alexander Aneivas and Kamron Matin. London and New York: Rowan and Littlefield.

Deepak, B.R. 2011. China's Rural Land Grabs: Endangering Social Stability. *South Asia Analysis Group*. Paper 4412. http://www.southasiaanalysis.org.

Don, Nonini, and Ida Susser, eds. forthcoming. *The Politics of Scale*. London, New York: Routledge.

Foucault, Michel. 1997. The Birth of Bio Politics. In *Ethics, Subjectivity, and Truth*, ed. P. Rabinow and J.D. Faubion, 73–79. New York: New Press.

---

[30] For a discussion of realist ethnography, see Smith (1999).

Franquesa, J. 2016. Dignity and Indignation: Bridging Morality and Political Economy in Contemporary Spain. *Dialectical Anthropology* 40 (2): 69–86.

Gill, Lesley, and Sharryn Kasmir. 2016. History, Politics, Space Labor: On the Concept of Unevenness. *Dialectical Anthropology* 40: 87–10.

Goonewardena, Kanishka, et al. 2008. *Space, Difference, Everyday Life: Reading Henri Lefebvre*. New York: Routledge.

Guerassimoff, C. 2006. Gender and Migration Networks: New Approaches to Research on Chinese Migration to France and Europe. *Journal of Chinese Overseas* 20 (1): 134–145.

Guerassimoff, Carine. 2012. *La Chine et sa nouvelle diaspora. La mobilité au service de la puissance*. Paris: Ellipses.

Guldin, G.E. 2001. *What's a Peasant to Do? Village Becoming Town in Southern China*. Boulder, CO: Westview Press, Inc.

Harvey, David. 2003. *The New Imperialism*. London: Oxford University Press.

———. 2005. *A Brief History of Neo-Liberalism*. London: Oxford University Press.

———. 2006. *Spaces of Global Capitalism*. London: Verso.

Horesh, N., and K.F. Lim. 2016. China: An East Asian Alternative to Neoliberalism? *The Pacific Review* 30: 425–442.

Judd, Ellen. 1994. *Gender and Power in Rural North China*. Stanford: Stanford University Press.

Lary, Diane. 1999. The 'Static' Decades: Inter-Provincial Migration in Pre-Reform China. In *Internal and International Migration: Chinese Perspectives*, ed. Frank Pieke and Hein Mallee, 29–48. Richmond: Curzon.

Lee, C.K. 2007. *Against the Law: Labor Protests in China's Rustbelt and Sunbelt*. Berkeley: University of California Press.

Lefebvre, H. 1992. With Catherine Regulier-Lefebvre Éléments de rythmanalyse: Introduction à la connaissance des rythmes, Preface by René Lorau, Paris: Ed. Syllepse, Collection *Explorations et découvertes*. English Translation: Rhythmanalysis: Space, Time and Everyday Life. Stuart Elden and Gerald Moore, trans. New York: Continuum, 2004.

———. 2004. *Rhythmanalysis: Space, Time and Everyday Life*. London: A&C Black.

———. n.d. *Critique of Everyday Life*. Vol. II. London: Verso.

Lenin, Vladimir Illyich. 1899. *The Development of Capitalism in Russia*. Moscow: Progress Publishers.

Lem, W. forthcoming. Time, Space and Scale in the Work of Reproduction: Migrant Women in Service Economy of Paris. In *The Politics of Scale*, ed. Don Nonini and Ida Susser. London, New York: Routledge.

Levy, F. 2005. Les femmes du Nord, une migration au profil atypique. *Hommes & Migrations* 1254: 45–57.

Lévy, Florence, and Will Thornely. 2012. The Migration of Women from Northern China: A Gender-Oriented Choice? *China Perspectives* 4 (2012): 43.

Lieber, M. 2008. Clivages ethniques, domination économique et rapports sociaux de sexe. Le cas des Chinois de Paris. In *Sexe, race et classe: pour une épistémologie de la domination*, ed. E. Dorlin. Paris: PUF.

Lipton, Michael. 1977. *Why Poor People Stay Poor: Urban Bias and World Development*. Temple Smith, London: Harvard University Press (2nd ed., Avebury, 1988).

Liu, Yia-Ling. 1992. Reform from Below: The Private Economy and Local Politics in the Rural Industrialization of Wenzhou. *The China Quarterly* 130: 293–316.

Makki, F. 2015. Reframing Development Theory: The Significance of the Idea of Uneven and Combined Development. *Theory and Society* 44 (5): 471–497.

Marx, Karl. 1973. *Grundrisse*. London: Penguin.

Marx, Karl. 1976 [1867]. *Capital*. Vol. 1. New York: Penguin Books.

Mayer, Kurt. 2008. Rhythms. Streets. Cities. In *Space, Difference, Everyday Life: Reading Henri Lefebvre*, ed. K. Goonewardena et al., 147–160. New York: Routledge.

Moore, Ryan. 2013. The Beat of the City: Lefebvre and Rhythmanalysis. *Situations: Project of the Radical Imagination* 5: 1. https://ojs.gc.cuny.edu/index.php/situations/article/view/1293.

Murphy, Rachel. 2002. *How Migrant Labor Is Changing Rural China*. Cambridge: Cambridge University Press.

Naughton, Barry, et al. 2008. A Political Economy of China's Economic Transition in China's Great Transformation. In *China's Great Transformation*, ed. Loren Brandt and G. Thomas Rawski. Cambridge: Cambridge University Press.

Nolan, Peter, and Fureng Dong, eds. 1991. *The Wenzhou Debate*. London: Zed Publishers.

Nowatny, H. 1992. Time and Social Theory Towards a Social Theory of Time. *Time & Society* 1 (3): 421–454.

Oi, Jean C. 1999. Two Decades of Rural Reform in China: An Overview and Assessment. *China Quarterly* 159 (Special Issue: The People's Republic of China After 50 Years September): 616–628.

Pairault, Thierry. 1990. *L'intégration silencieuse: la petite entreprise Chinoise en France*. Paris: l'Harmattan.

Parris, Kirsten. 1993. Local Initiative and National Reform: The Wenzhou Model of Development. *The China Quarterly* 134: 342–263.

Pieke, Frank. 1998. Introduction. In *The Chinese in Europe*, ed. Gregor Benton and Frank Pieke. New York: S. Martins Press.

Rosenberg, J. 2010. Basic Problems in the Theory of Uneven and Combined Development. Part II: Unevenness and Political Multiplicity. *Cambridge Review of International Affairs* 23 (1): 165–189.

Rosenberg, Justin. 2013. The 'Philosophical Premises' of Combined and Uneven Development. *Review of International Studies* 39: 569–597.

Sassen, Saskia. 2002. Locating Cities on Global Circuits. *Environment and Urbanization* 14 (13): 13–29.

Smith, Gavin. 1999. *Confronting the Present: Towards a Politically Engaged Anthropology.* Oxford: Berg.

———. 2014. *Intellectuals and (Counter-) Politics: Essays in Historical Realism.* London: Berghahn.

Smith, Neil. 2010. *Uneven Development: Nature, Capital, and the Production of Space.* Athens, GA: University of Georgia Press.

———. 2011. Selective Hegemony and Beyond, Populations with 'No Productive Function': A Framework for Enquiry. *Identities: Global Studies in Culture and Power* 18 (1): 2–38.

———. 2016. Against Social Democratic Angst About Revolution: From Failed Citizens to Critical Praxis. *Dialectical Anthropology* 40: 221.

Solinger, Dorothy. 1999. *Contesting Citizenship in Urban China: Peasant Migrants, the State and the Logic of the Market.* Berkeley: University of California.

Swyngedouw, Erik. 2010. Globalisation or 'Glocalisation'? Networks, Territories and Rescaling. *Cambridge Review of International Affairs* 17 (1): 25–48.

Tian, L.I. 2008. The Chengzhongcun Land Market in China: Boon or Bane?—A Perspective on Property Rights. *International Journal of Urban and Regional Research* 32 (2): 282–304.

Thompson, E.P. 1967. Time, Work-Discipline, and Industrial Capitalism. *Past and Present* 38 (1967): 56–97.

Trotsky, Leon. 1977 [1930]. *The History of the Russian Revolution.* London: Pluto Press.

Webber, M. 2008. Primitive Accumulation in Modern China. *Dialectical Anthropology* 32 (4): 299–320.

Werner, M. 2012. Beyond Upgrading: Gendered Labor and the Restructuring of Firms in the Dominican Republic. *Economic Geography* 88 (4): 403–422.

Xiang, Biao. 2003. Emigration from China: A Sender's Perspective. *International Migration* 41 (3): 21–48.

Zhang, L. 2001. *Strangers in the City: Reconfigurations of Space, Power, and Social Networks Within China's Floating Population.* Palo Alto, CA: Stanford University Press.

Zhang, Mei. 2003. *China's Poor Regions: Rural Urban Migration, Poverty, Economic Reform and Urbanization London.* Curzon: Routledge.

Index[1]

---

[1] Note: Page numbers followed by 'n' refer to notes.

© The Author(s) 2018
P. G. Barber, W. Lem (eds.), *Migration, Temporality, and Capitalism*, https://doi.org/10.1007/978-3-319-72781-3